M000249148

The God Who Believes

The God Who Believes

Faith, Doubt, and the Vicarious Humanity of Christ

Christian D. Kettler

Cascade Books
A division of *Wipf & Stock Publishers*
199 West 8th Avenue, Suite 3 • Eugene OR 97401

For Ray S. Anderson
teacher, pastor, friend

The God Who Believes
Faith, Doubt, and the Vicarious Humanity of Christ

Copyright © 2005 Christian D. Kettler. All rights reserved. Except for brief quotations in critical articles or reviews, no part of this book may be reproduced in any manner without prior written permission from the publisher. Write: Permissions, Wipf and Stock Publishers, 199 W. 8th Ave., Suite 3, Eugene, OR 97401.

Cascade Books
A Division of Wipf and Stock Publishers
199 West 8th Avenue, Suite 3
Eugene, Oregon 97401

ISBN: 1-59752-188-4

Printed in the United States

Contents

Abbreviations

ANF	*Ante-Nicene Fathers*
CD	Karl Barth, *Church Dogmatics,* edited by Geoffrey W. Bromiley and T. F. Torrance, Edinburgh: T. & T. Clark, 1936–1969
FC	*Fathers of the Church,* edited by R. J. Deferrari. Washington, D.C.: The Catholic University of America Press
Calvin, *Institutes*	John Calvin, *Institutes of the Christian Religion,* edited by John T. McNeill, translated by Ford Lewis Battles. Philadelphia: Westminster, 1960
LCC	*Library of Christian Classics*
NPNF	Nicene and Post-Nicene Fathers, Series 1 and 2
SJT	*Scottish Journal of Theology*
TDNT	*Theological Dictionary of the New Testament,* edited by Gerhard Kittel and Gerhard Friedrich, translated by Geoffrey W. Bromiley. Grand Rapids: Eerdmans, 1964–1974

Preface

Faith was easy in those early days. I am a child of "the Jesus Movement," a crazy, exhilarating, immature, profound time in the early 1970s when many of the "hippie" culture or just non-churched teenagers embraced Jesus Christ. Often more a reflection of the narcissism of the age than a deeply rooted Christianity, its influence was nonetheless significant for many of us. Seven hundred kids meeting in a Presbyterian church fellowship hall (the congregation never grew enough to build a sanctuary) sat on the barren floor for several hours every Saturday night, listening to long sermons and "praising the Lord." It was exciting to be in the midst of it. Enthusiasm for Bible study, "witnessing," and even ministry to the poor was kindled by the continual influx of those who "came forward" on Saturday night and became Christians. Faith was not opposed to sight; it was easy to see.

The years go by, of course. Life, growing up, success, failure, disappointment all intervene. Questions arise inevitably; about the Bible, the presence of evil, and even the presence of God in a crazy-quilt world. Doubt is inevitable.

Christian apologetics became attractive, and then out of desperation, necessary for me during my college days. I rightly wanted to possess a faith that was not simply a reflection of the old Sunday School answer to the question, What is faith? Faith, it is said, means believing in something you know ain't true! No, I rebelled against a Christian credulity and like many sought for certainty and assurance in a logical system of thought as a way to resolve my emotional insecurity. In looking back, perhaps what I left behind was Christ himself. The infinite patience of my beloved pastor, Bob Myers, continually called us back to the unconditional gospel of God's grace in Christ. For alienated teenagers, alienated by both middle class materialism and counter-culture idealism, this had been a powerful message. Yet a certain kind of apologetics had an enticing draw. An assurance of Jesus' divinity and truth was to be the end result of my quest, but he had ceased to be the substance. I was not really aware that my problem was emotional as well as intellectual. Perhaps I was still desperate for unconditional acceptance, yet seeking a security in my own logic and certainty. The deep needs of the emotions in a young adult were not fed. We may prove Christ to be divine and still be wracked with the doubts that affect the totality of our being including our emotions.

The reading of Karl Barth in college began to chip away at much of my rationalism. The Swiss theologian was exhilarating in scope, passion, audacity, and faith. If God is God, then who are we to demand that he meet up to our criteria? The lyrical, doxological passion of Barth's theology became soothing for my soul. I came to study at Fuller Theological Seminary primarily because his translator, Geoffrey Bromiley, was a professor there. At Fuller, the profound implications of Barth's theology for the integration of theology and ministry were further being explored by Ray Anderson. Anderson became the source for my exposure to his doctoral mentor, and a former student of Barth's, Thomas F. Torrance of the University of Edinburgh. Through a remarkable opportunity to serve as Dr. Torrance's teaching assistant while he was a visiting lecturer at Fuller, my attention was grabbed by his Christology, particularly what he called, "the vicarious humanity of Christ." Torrance's proposal was plain: As common as it has been to consider Christ's *death* to be vicarious, carried out in our place and for us, what if we were to consider that the entirety of his *humanity* was lived vicariously for us and in our place? This spoke powerfully to the inadequacy I felt before God, but probably more strongly, before others.

Several visits with Torrance's brother, James, whose pioneering work investigated the implications of the vicarious humanity of Christ for worship, further intrigued and excited me. The Eucharist is not simply our response to God's love, but our participation in the perfect and faithful response of Jesus Christ, our High Priest (Heb. 8:1). Christ was "the perfect Eucharistic Being," in the words of the Orthodox theologian Alexander Schmemann.[1] Christ was eucharistic in that in his genuine humanity he *gave thanks* to the Father (Luke 10:21; Matt 11:25), perfectly responding in faith and obedience to the Father. The Son was thankful to the Father as he "rejoiced in the Holy Spirit," (Luke 10:21); the very trinitarian life of God. His thanksgiving tugged mightily at my emotional needs. My doctoral studies eventually bore fruit in my book, *The Vicarious Humanity of Christ and the Reality of Salvation,* and then further studies on the implications of the vicarious humanity of Christ for the ministry of the Church, and the issues of emotional weakness and providence, evil and suffering.[2]

In recent years my concern has been to take the groundbreaking paradigm of Barth, the Torrances, and Ray Anderson, and especially in terms of the vicarious humanity of Christ, ask: What happens when Christ the Word of God penetrates deeply into our wounded flesh, wounded physically, emotionally, and spiritually? Could not a genuine Christian theology exist that seriously explores the implications of "the Word made flesh" (John 1:14) for the existential cries like despair, guilt and shame, emotional weakness, loneliness, and anxiety, without becoming existentialist? And what are the implications of the vicarious humanity of Christ for the great theological doctrines, such as the doctrine of God? Can this be of help in meeting those cries of the heart?

Such an incarnational theology can welcome the insights of literature in a day in which literary critics seem to abandon literature as a womb for ideas in place of social and political critical reductionism. The reader will

---

[1] Alexander Schmemann, *For the Life of the World: Sacraments and Orthodoxy* (Crestwood, N.Y.: St. Vladimir's Seminary Press, 2002), 38.

[2] Christian D. Kettler, *The Vicarious Humanity of Christ and the Reality of Salvation* (Lanham, Md.: University Press of America, 1991); "The Atonement as the Life of God in the Ministry of the Church" in Christian D. Kettler and Todd H. Speidell, eds., *Incarnational Ministry: The Presence of Christ in Church, Society, and Family: Essays in Honor of Ray S. Anderson* (Colorado Springs: Helmers and Howard, 1990), 58–78; "'For I Do Not Do the Good I Want . . . and I'm Tired of Trying': Weakness and the Vicarious Humanity of Christ" in Todd H. Speidell, ed., *On Being Christian . . . and Human: Essays in Celebration of Ray S. Anderson* (Eugene, Or.: Wipf and Stock, 2002), 51–69; and "He Takes Back the Ticket . . . for Us: Providence, Evil, Suffering, and the Vicarious Humanity of Christ," *Journal of Christian Theological Research* 8 (2003), 35–55.

[3] Wendell Berry, *Jayber Crow* (Washington, D.C.: Counterpoint, 2000).

readily note my indebtedness particularly to Wendell Berry's contemporary classic novel, *Jayber Crow.*[3] Berry is not afraid to follow Dostoevsky and all great writers in seriously wrestling with ideas in the context of human experience. *Jayber* and other such literature create a matrix for an incarnational theology to be further enfleshed and tested out in genuine human cries. As Anderson reveals so pointedly, "Unrealized hope cannot be healed by words that do not touch the pain and emptiness we all feel to some degree."[4]

Here is what this book is about: the relationship of the humanity of Christ to our doubt and how that humanity includes a genuine faith that should be the basis for our faith. We are not left, as James Torrance cautions us, to be thrown back upon ourselves.[5] Can we say that *Jesus believes,* not just as an example of a believer, but *believes for me and in my place, vicariously,* so that I can be helped in my unbelief (Mark 9:24)? Can we say, "*Jesus* believes . . . help me with my unbelief"? Does Jesus believe even when it is difficult, if not impossible, for me to believe?

When we do take the faith of Jesus seriously, it is often only in terms of imitating his faith. There is certainly a strong biblical tradition for the *imitatio Christi*: "A disciple is not above the teacher, nor a slave above the master," Jesus teaches, "it is enough for the disciple to be like the teacher, and the slave like the master" (Matt 10:24). Paul boldly instructs his churches, "Be imitators of me, as I am of Christ" (1 Cor 11:1). In the history of Christian spirituality much is made of imitating Christ by such influential figures as Francis of Assisi and Thomas à Kempis.

However, the imitation of Christ is not the whole story of the Christian life. Paul speaks decisively of the Christian life as an *imitatio* of Christ in Phil 2:5-11: In the midst dissensions in Philippi (4:2; 2:2), Paul calls upon the church to "Let the same mind be in you that was in Christ Jesus," a mind of emptying oneself for the sake of others (2:5-11). But what appears to be a call simply to ask "What would Jesus do?" is based more on his rich understanding of the Christian life as being "in Christ" (Eph 1:1; Phil 2:21; 2 Cor 5:17). Paul prefaces his exhortation to be of the same mind by saying, "If there is any encouragement in Christ, any

[4] Ray S. Anderson and Dennis Guernsey, *On Being Family: A Social Theology of the Family* (Grand Rapids: Eerdmans, 1985), 128.

[5] James B. Torrance, *Worship, Community, and the Triune God of Grace* (Downers Grove, Ill.: InterVarsity Press, 1996), 44.

consolation from love, any sharing *(koinovia)* in the Spirit . . ." Sharing in the Spirit is the reality of participating in the continuing life of Christ. Imitation of Christ is imperative, yet apart from our sharing in the Spirit, our participation in Christ, imitation can end in so much frustration, what James Torrance means by being thrown back upon ourselves. Participation before imitation speaks of the fellowship and communion (cf. the Eucharist) with Christ through the Spirit that is organic to being Christian. *Koinovia* is a relational term, reflecting the communion between the Father and the Son through the Spirit. The Trinity is closely at hand here. Partaking of the cup and the bread of the Lord's Supper is often called "communion" because it is a continuing fellowship with the Lord, a participation in his life. We are called to imitate Christ because we participate in his life. This life, we suggest, includes his life of faith, indeed, the entirety of his humanity is lived vicariously for us and in our place.

We will proceed in this way: Chapter one explores the challenge of doubt as both intellectual and emotional issues in terms of implications for faith and the knowledge of *God,* vocation and the knowledge of *oneself,* evil and suffering and the knowledge of *the world,* and pluralism and postmodernism as the knowledge of *the culture.* Doubt as a problem is all pervasive, we will argue, and therefore needs a response that addresses the totality of our humanity. We conclude chapter one with an addendum, presenting the biblical basis for the vicarious humanity of Christ as found in the Gospels, and its implications for the above-mentioned challenges. Chapter two faces the controversy of the value of doubt. Chapters three and four then explore the implications of the vicarious humanity of Christ for *how* Christians know God as well as *who* the God is whom Christians know. What are the implications of the vicarious humanity of Christ for theological epistemology and the doctrine of God? What will this mean for how we deal with doubt? Chapter five takes the doctrine of God one step further in terms of the question of the providence of God in a world of evil and suffering. We end in chapter six with a look at the doubting self today: What does Christ's faith mean to one whose faith falters today and in the future?

An earlier form of chapter five was published in the *Journal of Christian Theological Research* 3, 2003, under the title, "He Takes Back the Ticket . . . for Us: Providence, Evil, Suffering, and the Vicarious Humanity of Christ."

Several good and judicious friends have contributed to sharpen the form and engage the ideas of this book. I would like to thank Dale Allison, Ray Anderson, Judy Boudreaux, Christie Breault, Warren Farha, Bill Glennen, Charles Hughes, Gordon Houser, Jennifer Jantz, Robin Langhart, Deborah Seely, Rusty Smoker, Todd Speidell, Claire Vanderpool, and Mark Wells for their help.

My thanks to the helpful and professional people at Cascade Books: K. C. Hanson, Heather Carraher, and Jim Tedrick.

My thanks to Dr. John Yoder and Friends University for the research grant provided during the summer of 2005 in order to finish the work.

My assistant Megan McDonald was invaluable in helping to prepare the indexes.

Faith may not be easier these days, but maybe more interesting.

1
Doubt and the Vicarious Faith of Christ

"Seven days," said Faramir, "But think not ill of me, if I say to you: they have brought me both a joy and a pain that I never thought to know. Joy to see you; but pain, because now the fear and doubt of this evil time are grown dark indeed. Éowyn, I would not have this world end now, or lose so soon what I have found."

Faramir to Éowyn, J. R. R. Tolkien,
The Return of the King; The Lord of the Rings part three[1]

God have mercy on the man
who doubts what he's sure of.

Bruce Springsteen, "Brilliant Disguise"

---

[1] J. R. R. Tolkien, *The Return of the King; The Lord of the Rings part three* (Boston: Houghton Mifflin Company, 1993), 240.

The Dilemmas of Doubt

The pain would be unbearable if the joy were not indescribable. Doubt is a problem of living with two realities: unbelief and belief, or pain and joy. Doubt is a problem, but it is not just an intellectual problem. It is an agony of the soul, of our very being. Pain is bad enough, yet it is truly pain because of the joy in life, the indescribable joy.

"Upon my bed at night I sought him whom my soul loves" cries the woman in the Song of Solomon. "I sought him, but found him not; I called him, but he gave no answer" (3:1).[2] The joy of love gives birth to the pain of longing, C.S. Lewis's understanding of joy as longing.[3] The young Lewis treasured joy as a sense of the longing evoked when summer gives way to autumn, or a longing for other worlds, worlds of imagination such as in the Norse legends, science fiction and fantasy tales, preparing one for the reality of heaven, a world without pain and death. The lover may be longing for the missing loved one. What lover has not doubted at times the love of the beloved?

Doubt is not just a question of God's existence. Doubt tears at the fabric of our being when we live between pain and joy. There is no problem of pain without joy. The young poet's first encounter with nature in Jane Kenyon's poem, "In the Grove: The Poet at Ten," juxtaposes joy and pain: "Nothing could rouse her then/ from that joy so violent/ it was hard to distinguish from pain."[4] Joy is usually conceived to be benign and effervescent. Genuine joy is made of sterner stuff. Genuine joy has even a

---

[2] Cf. Origen, *Sermons on the Song of Songs* I, 7, in Olivier Clément, *The Roots of Christian Mysticism: Texts from the Patristic Era with Commentary,* trans. Theodore Berkeley and Jeremy Hummerstone (Hyde Park, N.Y.: New City, 1993), 189: "Then she [the Bride in the Song of Songs] looks longingly for the Bridegroom who has shown himself and then disappeared. This happens often throughout the Song of Songs and can be understood by anyone who has experienced it himself . . . This happens often until I hold him truly and arise, leaning on my beloved."

[3] C.S. Lewis, *Surprised by Joy: The Shape of My Early Life* (New York: Harcourt, Brace and World, 1955). See also Chris Kettler, "Joy and Logic in a Glad Embrace: The Theology of Narnia," in *C.S. Lewis's The Chronicles of Narnia: A Study Guide and Workbook for Groups and Individuals,* ed. Frank Kastor (Wichita, Ks.: St. Mark's Press, 1998), 93–101; Corbin Scott Carnell, *Bright Shadow of Reality: C.S. Lewis and the Feeling Intellect* (Grand Rapids: Eerdmans, 1974).

[4] Jane Kenyon, *Otherwise: New and Selected Poems* (St. Paul, Minn.: Graywolf, 1996), 3.

"violence," like the kingdom of heaven "suffers violence," perhaps by the contrary passions it engenders (Matt 11:12). Genuine joy, the indescribable joy, therefore, can live with the unbearable pain. So also the disciples, in a wonderfully poignant way, "disbelieved for joy" when they were confronted by the risen Lord and nonetheless possessed doubts (Luke 24:41, RSV). The joy was too wonderful to be believed. The disciples shared the great longing of the ancient Jews for the coming of the Messiah. Like the lover daring the risk of love, the fear of disappointment was formidable.

The fear of disappointment may be fueled by our lack of appreciation for grace. Jane Kenyon, in her poem, "Happiness," challenges our common view that happiness is to be pursued, even demanded and coerced. No, happiness is that which "finds you asleep midafternoon as you so often are during the unmerciful hours of your despair."[5] Happiness is grace. Grace pursues us, finds us by surprise in the friends, loved ones, nature, and art that God gives us, not because we can demand or coerce it. These gifts are ordinary, not idealized or spectacular, but may come "to the monk in his cell," "to the woman sweeping the street with a birch broom, to the child whose mother has passed out from drink," and "to the clerk stacking cans of carrots in the night."

Yet such happiness is couched with "the unmerciful hours of your despair," "disbelieving for joy" in the midst of doubt. The late night customer in a convenience store demands cash from the register, and not being pleased with $86.75, permanently interrupts the clerk's happiness with a revolver. What kind of society do we live in that tolerates such a crime? Here is doubt about *the culture.* What kind of world is this? Here is doubt about *the world.* What does my life mean if it can be so cruelly and suddenly terminated? Here is doubt about *ourselves.* Why would a loving and all-powerful God allow such evil in the world? Here is the most wrenching doubt: doubt about *God.*

The Problem of the Jesus of History and Culture

We have been suggesting the hope of a christological approach to doubt. Yet such an answer might create more problems than it solves.

[5] Kenyon, *Otherwise,* 3.

No person is less known in the history of the world than Jesus Christ. No person is better known in the history of the world than Jesus Christ. How can these two statements both be true? But they are. World events, whether they involve political coups, elections, natural catastrophes, or epidemics, blithely go on their way regardless of whether or not Jesus Christ lives or lived. Popular culture is filled with music videos, films, and television, all content to ignore Jesus of Nazareth. Apart from the occasional historical television program, there seems to be a conspiracy of silence. Mel Gibson's film, *The Passion of the Christ,* was such a sensation in part because it was an anomaly: a film that sought to portray the Jesus of the Gospels honestly and sincerely. The vast majority of contemporary movies ignore religion or portray it as an oppressive, reactionary relic of an unenlightened former age. Jesus Christ, the Jesus of the four Gospels, is blatantly, yet quietly, ignored.

But is Christ also *too* well known in the contemporary world? Walker Percy's fictional character Sutter Vaught bemoans the fact of how well known Christ is. He has, moreover, become particularly offensive because of "the company he keeps," e.g., the narrow-minded, bigoted, anti-intellectual, and anti-cultural fundamentalist.

> Christ should leave us. He is too much with us and I don't like his friends. We have no hope of recovering Christ until Christ leaves us. There is after all something worse than being God-forsaken. It is when God overstays his welcome and takes up with the wrong people.[6]

Malachi Martin's picture of how we make Jesus in our own image is helpful, comical, tragic, and depressing: whether it is "Jesus Caesar," "Jesus Monk," "Jesus Pentecostalist," "Jesus Goodfellow, " or the epitome of Protestant individualism, "Jesus Take-My-Marbles-and-Etc."[7] This is too much Jesus! So much so that one becomes jaded and cynical about any genuine knowledge of the man from Nazareth. The recent attempts by some radical biblical scholars to uncover the "real" Jesus seem simply to reveal just more confusion about the man from Nazareth: Was Jesus "the

---

[6] Walker Percy, *The Last Gentleman* (New York: Ivy, 1986), 293.

[7] Malachi Martin, *Jesus Now* (New York: Dutton, 1973).

itinerant sage," "the Hellenistic cynic," "the apocalyptic prophet," "the inspired rabbi," or the "classic Jesus" of the creeds?[8] Is "Jesus" really just a cipher for whatever our greatest values are, as Feuerbach argues in his description of religion?[9]

The Promise of the Vicarious Humanity of Christ

Into this contemporary confusion, the Scottish theologian T. F. Torrance suggests an understanding of Jesus not separate from the four Gospels but including a perspective not often emphasized, which he calls "the vicarious humanity of Christ."[10] In an older theology, it was common to speak of the vicarious *death* of Christ, in the sense that Christ died in our place, was our substitute, on the cross. While not meaning to dilute the importance of the death of Christ, Torrance urges that the vicarious death

[8] "Who Was Jesus?," *Time* (August 15, 1988), 37–42; David Van Biena, "The Gospel Truth," *Time* (April 8, 1996), 52–59. See also the state of scholarly discussion of Jesus in *Theology Today* (entire issue on the historical Jesus) (April, 1995); John Dominic Crossan, *The Historical Jesus: The Life of a Mediterranean Jewish Peasant* (San Francisco: HarperSanFrancisco, 1991); Marcus Borg, *Meeting Jesus Again for the First Time* (San Francisco: HarperSanFrancisco, 1994); and the critique of the above in Dale C. Allison, *Jesus of Nazareth: Millenarian Prophet* (Minneapolis: Fortress Press, 1998); Robert J. Miller, ed., *The Apocalyptic Jesus: A Debate* (Santa Rosa, Ca.: Polebridge Press, 2001); and Marvin Meyer and Charles Hughes, eds., *Jesus Then & Now: Images of Jesus in History and Christology* (Harrisburg, Pa.: Trinity, 2001).

[9] Ludwig Feuerbach, *The Essence of Christianity*, trans. George Eliot (New York: Harper and Row, 1957), 12ff.

[10] The most important writings on the vicarious humanity of Christ are found in T. F. Torrance, *The Mediation of Christ*, rev. ed. (Colorado Springs: Helmers and Howard, 1992); "The Word of God and the Response of Man" in *God and Rationality* (Oxford: Oxford University Press, 1971), 133–164; James B. Torrance, "The Vicarious Humanity of Christ" in T. F. Torrance, ed., *The Incarnation: Ecumenical Studies in the Nicene-Constantinopolitan Creed* (Edinburgh: Handsel, 1981), 127–147; James B. Torrance, *Worship, Community and the Triune God of Grace*; and Thomas F. Torrance, James B. Torrance, and David W. Torrance, *A Passion for Christ: The Vision That Ignites Ministry* (Edinburgh: Handsel, 1999). Elmer M. Colyer provides a helpful survey of the vicarious humanity of Christ in Torrance's thought in *How to Read T. F. Torrance: Understanding His Trinitarian and Scientific Theology* (Downers Grove, Ill.: InterVarsity, 2001), 97–126. Alister E. McGrath ably reviews the whole of Torrance's thought in the context of his life in *T .F. Torrance: An Intellectual Biography* (Edinburgh: T. & T. Clark, 1999).

must be seen in terms of the wider context of both the entire humanity of Christ and our entire humanity. His humanity involves a vicarious act. The nature of Christ's vicarious work is not simply one moment on the cross, but his entire life, so that the entirety of our lives might be affected. The Word took on the entirety of humanity, body and soul, in order to save the entire human (Athanasius).[11]

"Vicarious" may be a strange and outmoded word, but I am unable to come up with a better alternative. Let me then carefully define what "vicarious" means in terms of the vicarious humanity of Christ. Unfortunately, it can often mean to some people "pseudo" or "false," as in a father getting a "vicarious" thrill from his son's accomplishments as an athlete. The son experiences the authentic thrill from his athletic accomplishment. The father's thrill is not based on any accomplishment of his own. In that way it is "false," not real. But Torrance's meaning of "vicarious" is not of that sort. The vicarious humanity of Christ does not mean that Christ's humanity is unreal. Quite the contrary! It does mean that the vicarious humanity of Christ speaks of the deep interaction between Christ's humanity and our humanity at the level of our *being*, the *ontological* level. So the atoning work of Christ is neither simply a means by which we are declared righteous by God, nor simply a demonstration of God's love. It is both, but much more, in the sense of God desiring to recreate our humanity at the deepest levels, addressing our needs and fears, our doubts from within our very being.

A *vicarious* sense of Christ's humanity signifies that Jesus Christ is both the *representative* of and *substitute* for my humanity.[12] He represents my humanity before God the Father, having taken my humanity upon himself, bringing it back to God from the depths of sin and death. He is the High Priest, representing the people before God (The Epistle to the Hebrews). But he is also the sacrifice himself. He is the substitute, doing in my place, in my stead, what I am unable to do: live a life of perfect faithfulness to, obedience to, and trust in God. "Vicarious" at its heart means doing something for another in their stead, doing something that they are unable to do. Dietrich Bonhoeffer calls this *Stellvertretung*, recently

[11] Athanasius, *On the Incarnation of the Word* 15, NPNF, second series, 44. See also T. F. Torrance, *The Trinitarian Faith: The Evangelical Theology of the Ancient Catholic Church* (Edinburgh: T. & T. Clark, 1988), 150.

[12] T. F. Torrance, *Space, Time, and Resurrection* (Grand Rapids: Eerdmans, 1976), 116.

translated as "vicarious representative action" and earlier as "deputyship."[13] Deputies in the old western movies were appointed by the sheriff to represent him and to do what he was unable to do by his lonesome: form a posse and apprehend the bad guy. So also, Bonhoeffer argues, we act as a deputy whenever we act on behalf of someone else, whether it is as a teacher for a student or a parent for a child. A young child is unable to tie his shoelaces. The parent has to intervene and do it for him. (The parent, however, should not tie the child's shoelaces for the rest of his life! This is the importance of the question, If Christ has believed for us, do we have to believe? We will have to address this throughout our discussion.) Notice the emphasis here on *need* and *inability.* We have already noted the question of our inability to believe in terms of doubt. Here is where the vicarious humanity of Christ yields rich theological and spiritual dividends.

Certainty has been the crucial issue for me. How can I know for certain that Christianity is true? How do I know that I am not a Christian simply because it is convenient or that it gives me friends, or worse yet, (for a college professor and an ordained minister) provides an income? Again, I keep coming back to the center of the faith: Who Jesus Christ is, Christology. How does our Christology affect our deepest crises: despair, guilt, shame, loneliness, anxiety, and doubt? In the Gospels, the risen Christ is the real manifestation of God that becomes the only check upon the disciples' doubt, so that Jesus can exhort them, "Do not doubt, but believe" (John 20:27) and Thomas can respond appropriately, "My Lord and my God!" (John 20:28).[14] "O strange wonder, unbelief hath given birth unto steadfast faith!"[15] If there is certainty it is not apart from Jesus Christ.

Hearing the Cry of the Heart

The existential lostness of humanity does not seem to reflect, however, the glory of Christ. The incapacity of humanity is made manifest by the

[13] Dietrich Bonhoeffer, *Ethics,* trans. Reinhard Krauss, Charles C. West, and Douglas W. Stott (Minneapolis: Fortress Press, 2005), 257–60.

[14] Barth, *CD,* III/2, 449.

[15] Sunday of Thomas, *The Pentecostarion* (Boston: Holy Transfiguration Monastery, 1990), 68.

cry of the heart, like a child crying for one's mother in utter need.[16] Pascal speaks of becoming "terrified" by "the blindness and wretchedness of man," "the whole silent universe," and "man without light."[17] Why should Christianity join the choruses of deceit that optimistically sing the praises of technophilic humanity? All of our pretensions of technological and scientific knowledge often mask the dire straits we live in. To such an extent they become comical. Walker Percy wryly expresses this:

> Why is it possible to learn more in ten minutes about the Crab Nebula in Taurus, which is 6,000 light-years away, than you presently know about yourself, even though you've been stuck with yourself all of your life?[18]

The myriad of human experience cries for solace. The glory of human reason, with all of its accomplishments, often seems to pale compared with what we truly value in life: a loved one's smile, a friend's embrace, a Kansas sunset, the sweetness and awe of worship, or the ecstasy of intellectual insight. Those values can be smothered and even crushed by cruel twists of fate and unrealized hopes in life. How often does Christian teaching really speak to these depths? "Who will teach a child born with a twisted body that life is a gift to be accepted and valued?" Ray Anderson asks.[19] Still, the wonder of life's goodness and the sheer contingency of the universe cry silently for some kind of explanation, proclamation, announcement (at least a press release!) of meaning.[20] Death, most of all, mocks our pretenses of immortality, revealing the transitory nature of our humanness. The very existence of God in such a vacuum is questioned.[21]

Cry for explanation

---

[16] Pseudo-Macarius, *Forty-Sixth Homily,* cited in Clément, *The Roots of Christian Mysticism,* 183.

[17] Blaise Pascal, *Pensées* (New York: Dutton, 1958). See also Daniel Taylor, *The Myth of Certainty: The Reflective Christian and the Risk of Commitment* (Grand Rapids: Zondervan, 1992), 10.

[18] Walker Percy, *Lost in the Cosmos: The Last Self-Help Book* (New York: Washington Square, 1983), 7.

[19] Ray S. Anderson, "Spirituality is a Domestic Skill," in Ray S. Anderson and Dennis B. Guernsey, *On Being Family: A Social Theology of the Family* (Grand Rapids: Eerdmans, 1985) 128.

[20] T. F. Torrance, *Reality and Scientific Theology* (Edinburgh: Scottish Academic Press, 1985), 58. See also Colyer, *How to Read T. F. Torrance,* 204.

[21] Alan E. Lewis, *Between Cross and Resurrection: A Theology of Holy Saturday* (Grand Rapids: Eerdmans, 2001), 92.

Not all feel this angst, however, particularly in the Church. For some, Christianity is a triumphalistic affair, a celebration of a muscular piety or a heady apologetic, and, most of all, a self-importance founded on the truth that one is *right*. So Wendell Berry's barber in his novel *Jayber Crow* remarks that only a few of the young preachers who came to the small town of Port William, Kentucky, "were troubled enough in their own hearts to have something to say."[22] Existential angst needs to be taken seriously, even by the committed Christian. Christians are taught by the New Testament, "Do nothing from selfish ambition or conceit, but in humility regard others as better than yourselves" (Phil 2:3), but humility is often hard to find. This humble attitude found in Jesus Christ (Phil 2:5) becomes a check against self-righteousness (Phil 3:7-9) and identifying our formulations of the truth with the truth itself.[23] Only then can we be free to admit the angst in our lives and in our world with the honesty they deserve. Often, Christian theology, however, has been more concerned with precise doctrinal formulations or mimicking the *Zeitgeist* than encountering the world in which the Word became flesh.

Hearing Christ, the Word of God

We need some christological clarity. Perhaps no one has said it as clearly as Dietrich Bonhoeffer: "Whoever sees Jesus Christ does indeed see God and the world in one. He can henceforward no longer see God without the world or the world without God."[24] A christocentric theology demands that we take existential issues in humanity seriously. Too often the concern of theology has been about the precise relationship between the deity and the humanity of Christ without delving deeply into the radical implications of the Word that became flesh for the world of despair, guilt, shame, weakness, loneliness, anxiety, and doubt.[25] Popular theology such as in the *Left Behind* novels still reflects the kind of theological mindset that

---

[22] Berry, *Jayber Crow*, 162.

[23] Taylor, *The Myth of Certainty*, 127.

[24] Bonhoeffer, *Ethics*, trans. Reinhard Krauss, Charles C. West, and Douglas W. Stott, 82.

[25] Mark A. McIntosh, *Christology from Within: Spirituality and Incarnation in Hans Urs von Balthasar* (Notre Dame: University of Notre Dame Press, 1996), 138.

obsesses over the time of the Great Tribulation at the end of the world and ignores our own personal "tribulations" of loneliness, despair, and doubt. Academic theology may be concerned with making the gospel relevant to a postmodern technological world of revolutionary dimensions and yet ignore the quiet revolutions of desperation occurring every day in distressed individual souls.

Is not there a danger, however, of making experience the criterion of theology? Christian experience is grounded on the self-revelation of God in Jesus Christ, an act of God's grace. In James Torrance's memorable words, "More important than our experience of Christ is the Christ of our experience."[26] Our experiences may be intense but without any necessary connection to God. Moreover, in our culture, we face the temptation of the narcissistic preoccupation with self-fulfillment and human potential (even a magazine entitled, *Self!*).[27] We seem to be very far from knowing God. Indeed, is not our only chance of knowing God found in God's initiative, to know God according to his nature by his act alone?[28] To do theology is simply to be a witness, as the witness answers the questions of a judge.[29] We may be begging to ask questions ourselves but for the Christian we must be content to listen to the questions of the Judge, Jesus Christ.[30] Our experience is an experience of Christ, so it should only bear witness of him.

The Word of God who is Jesus Christ still *meets* our experience because he took upon our "flesh." Therefore, its effect is seen in our concrete, real-life experiences.[31] This includes our concrete experiences, as difficult as they may be, among others, of despair, guilt, shame, weakness, loneliness, anxiety, and doubt. We must avoid the problem of reductionism in terms of viewing truth as only theological, psychological, sociological, etc.[32] What

---

[26] James Torrance, *Worship, Community, and the Triune God of Grace,* 34.
[27] Ibid., 106–7.
[28] T. F. Torrance, *The Trinitarian Faith*, 127–39, 207. See also Barth, *CD,* II/1, 44: "God is known through God and through God alone."
[29] Barth, *CD,* I/2, 817–18.
[30] T. F. Torrance, "Questioning in Christ" in *Theology in Reconstruction* (Grand Rapids: Eerdmans, 1965), pp. 117–27.
[31] Ray S. Anderson, *The Soul of Ministry* (Louisville, Ky.: Westminster/John Knox Press, 1997), 15. See also Michael Jinkins, "CrossRoads: A Christian Understanding of Vocation" in Speidell, ed., *On Being Christian . . . and Human,* 147–66.
[32] Gary W. Deddo, "Resisting Reductionism: Why We Need Theological Anthropology," in Speidell, ed., *On Being Christian . . . and Human,* 171.

we need to avoid is isolating doubt from the totality of our humanity.[33] Bonhoeffer's insight is helpful here as well. Because of the incarnation, the humanity God took upon himself was the totality of our humanity, not just our "spirituality." The whole action of God, Creator, Reconciler, and Redeemer, takes upon the whole person.[34] Doubt should neither be "artificially enlarged" so that it becomes an absolute with a life of its own and therefore with a right to exist on its own, nor should it be ignored in a triumphalistic faith. Doubt will be among those existential phenomena that become the crucibles of authentic faith.

Christology in the midst of our experience includes the place of the godforsaken, known infinitely deeply to the Son of God ("My God, my God, why have you forsaken me?" Matt 27:46) as well as to common humanity, from the broken hearted to victims of murder. One must not rush too quickly to the resurrection. The cross and the burial of Christ were spaces of death, spaces of God's absence (real, or at least felt). We must not pretend that they never happened to Jesus or to us.[35] The ministry of grace and love is not to deny the abandonment but *to take its place in its loneliness.* We are still lonely, but we are not lonely alone. We are still abandoned, but we are not abandoned alone. Someone (not something) has taken its place, become our *substitute.* This substitute is Jesus Christ himself, the godforsaken one. God's presence is with the godforsaken![36] But the substitute always reminds us of whose place he has taken. Jesus does that with the Samaritan woman (John 4). She wants to talk an abstract theology about where to worship. Jesus cuts to the chase and brings up her relationships, where she most deeply hurts. That hurt is holy, because the eternal Son of God will cry it himself to his Father. The experience of the godforsaken is an essential part of our experience of the Holy Trinity, for it reflects an inexpressible moment in the life of God, between the Father and the Son through the Spirit, in which (dare we say it?) God rejects God! God knows rejection among the multitude of other human experiences because he has taken upon himself our humanity including

[33] Max Picard, *The World of Silence,* trans. Stanley Godwin (Wichita, Ks.: Eighth Day, 2002), 78.

[34] Barth, *CD,* I/2, 873.

[35] Alan E. Lewis, *Between Cross and Resurrection,* 96.

[36] Ibid., 97.

the devastating and unspeakable in human experience. There is a "humanity of God"![37]

But where can the humanity of God be found today? What are the challenges in the world today to a christological approach to doubt? If there is a christological perspective on doubt, it will have to face the challenges to 1) faith: the problem of the knowledge of *God,* 2) vocation: the problem of the knowledge of *oneself,* 3) evil and suffering: the problem of the knowledge of *the world,* and 4) pluralism and postmodernism: the problem of the knowledge of *the culture.* Woven within these themes we will then present the basic witness in the Gospels concerning the vicarious humanity of Christ and its relevance for these issues.

Faith: The Problem of the Knowledge of God and the "Lost Traveler"

Doubt is more than an intellectual problem, but it is not less. Intellectual issues do create doubt. Jayber Crow, in Wendell Berry's novel of the same name, is a Christian college student preparing for ministry who experiences problems with the Bible.[38] His professors have an unshakable belief in the truth of the Bible; historically, theologically, ethically, and geographically. Jayber, however, wrestles with what he perceives to be the changes in the biblical narrative, particularly from Old to New Testament. How could Yahweh tell Israel to war upon their enemies and still be the same God of Jesus who said to love your enemies? This is just the beginning of a series of questions that culminate with a question about Jesus' prayer in Gethsemane. Jayber realizes that Jesus' most fervent prayer was refused: "Father, if thou be willing, remove this cup from me; nevertheless, not my will, but thine be done." Here is the meaning of the Lord's Prayer, "Thy will be done," that is, "It means that your will and God's will may not be the same. It means there's a good possibility that you won't get

[37] Karl Barth, *The Humanity of God,* trans. Thomas Wieser and John Newton Thomas (Atlanta: John Knox Press, 1960). The multi-leveled relationship between our experience, our apprehension, and the Triune God himself is discussed in T. F. Torrance, *The Christian Doctrine of God: One Being, Three Persons* (Edinburgh: T. & T. Clark, 1996), 83.
[38] Berry, *Jayber Crow,* 49–51.

what you pray for. It means that in spite of your prayers, you are going to suffer. It means you may be crucified."[39]

Jayber's immediate question is, How can he preach to people if prayer only in the end means "Thy will be done"? Why bother even to pray if Jesus' own prayer wasn't answered? The questions became almost "deafening" to Jayber.[40] The only voice he hears in Scripture becomes that of the questions. If he becomes a preacher, how could he find the *strength* to pray "Thy will be done" for the sake of others, if it is such a futile act?

Indeed, how can we find the strength to pray "Thy will be done" if we are realistic about the events of our lives? Does such a prayer only become a duty at best and a charade at worst?

Furthermore, Jayber asks, How could he even *know* the will of God in order to pray, "Thy will be done"?[41] Jayber discovers that faith is not the opposite of the knowledge of God but its essence.[42] But this simply exacerbates the problem. Knowledge of God is so elusive. If it is connected to faith, then that calls into question the practice of faith.

Jayber's professors are no help. They have no doubts.[43] They do not even ask his kind of questions. To tell Jayber to give up his questioning is useless. His questioning does not give him up. As we have seen, doubt is not just an intellectual problem; it affects our entire being. For Jayber, doubt and its relationship to faith and the knowledge of God cuts deeply into the abyss of his prayers, so that he is unable then to pray for himself or others.[44] Jayber leaves the college, what he thought was his "calling," and his sense of being: "I was a lost traveler, wandering in the woods," he laments, "needing to be on my way somewhere but not knowing where."

Jayber's professors are no help, but they do have their own answer: Jayber needs more faith. Doubt is simply the sign of weakness of faith. No. This is hardly any help when the lack of faith is the problem! The one exception among his professors is Dr. Ardmire who agrees with Jayber that he cannot preach if he does not have "any answers."[45] But he does not

[39] Berry, *Jayber Crow,* 51.
[40] Ibid., 50.
[41] Ibid., 52.
[42] Karl Barth, *Dogmatics in Outline,* trans. G.T. Thomson (New York: Philosophical Library, 1949), 22–27. See also Calvin, *Institutes,* 3.2.2.
[43] Berry, *Jayber Crow,* 52.
[44] Ibid.
[45] Ibid., 54.

deny that Jayber has been called, only called to something else than what he thought. This calling will have to be discovered by Jayber over a period of a lifetime, and maybe "longer." Here is a similarity to Kierkegaard's commendation of the ancient Greeks whose proficiency in doubting *and* faith was developed over a lifetime in contrast to modern doubters, who, thinking that they are following Descartes, believe that everything can be doubted and faith can be discarded.[46]

Not only is faith a matter of knowledge but it is also a matter of the will. So believes Clarence, the Presbyterian pastor who loses his faith in John Updike's novel *In the Beauty of the Lilies.*[47] He no longer has the strength (like Jayber's lack of strength to pray "Thy will be done") to believe the "sad pap," the cheerful optimism and idealism of Christianity in light of the reason and "simple humanity and decency" on the side of God's opponents such as Hume, Darwin, and Nietzsche.[48] The twentieth century is filled with scientific and cultural accomplishments, all done without appeal to God. His faith has "fled." The doubting that began with Descartes' methodological doubt in the seventeenth century, ushering in the modern age, leads to a godless world.[49]

The possibility of faith "fleeing" or "losing" one's faith may seem to make faith a precarious enterprise. But as the church father Hilary of Poitiers remarks, the very incomprehensible nature of God speaks of faith's virtue in its weakness.[50] Faith realizes its power in its "incompetence" to apprehend its Object. Recognizing faith as "incompetence" is "the proper service of faith." The way is then paved for faith to be considered as "an empty hand" that is received as the gift of God (Eph 2:8), not as simply the ability of the will to believe or the mind to comprehend.[51]

---

[46] Søren Kierkegaard, *Fear and Trembling/Repetition,* ed. and trans. Howard V. Hong and Edna H. Hong (Princeton: Princeton University Press, 1983), 5–7.

[47] John Updike, *In the Beauty of the Lilies* (New York: Fawcett Columbine, 1996), 18.

[48] Updike, *In the Beauty of the Lilies,* 20, 61.

[49] René Descartes, *Meditations on First Philosophy,* trans. Donald A. Cress (Indianapolis: Hackett, 1979); Michael Buckley, S.J., *At the Origins of Modern Atheism* (New Haven: Yale University Press, 1987), 97.

[50] Hilary of Poitiers, *On the Trinity,* II.11, NPNF, second series, 10: 55.

[51] Barth, *CD,* IV/1, 631; cf. 630–31: "Faith comes about where Jesus Christ prevails on man, and in Jesus Christ the self-demonstration of the justified man. Faith knows Him and apprehends Him . . . It is this positive aspect that makes the negative form of faith so necessary. For because it is faith in Jesus Christ, it can be true and living faith only as

Recognizing the "incompetence" of faith is not far from acknowledging the element of truth in nihilism.[52] We may very well have too rosy a view of our knowledge of the world, that all might really be *maya,* illusion, that our senses really do deceive us (Plato and Descartes) and that we simply see connections out of habit, not out of any genuine knowledge (Hume). Faith is acknowledging a Word from outside, a Word that we cannot speak. We should only sit in silence before the Word made flesh.[53] Is not the utter "incompetency" of faith the beginning of dealing with doubt?[54] In Jesus Christ there is a witness of God to our minds that does not leave us with only the lonely, individual, thinking mind of Descartes so formative for the modern consciousness.[55]

Sola fide (faith alone), the slogan of the Reformation (or faith's "incompetency"), should not be seen as exclusively in opposition to works, but as the texture of faith living in a world often without hope. Jayber Crow, as he pursues his new "calling," falls in love with a married woman, Mattie, never declaring his love for her to anyone, yet "married" to her in his mind and heart. The ethical questions this raises are obvious. The wisdom of such a love is an obvious problem for Jayber. He does not love without trepidation, well aware of his potential for self-deception.[56] He might easily be idealizing Mattie, not admitting that if they were together the trials and tribulations of any couple would be all too evident. Why

---

the humility of obedience; it has to be an empty hand, an empty vessel, a vacuum." See also 1 Cor 4:7; 15:10. "To the extent that he tries to rely on himself and man and the will and achievement of man, he will be forced to despair of himself and man. For he himself, the man on whom he can rely, is not here but there, in that One. He lives in His history. He must be sought and found in Him. Faith ceases to be faith, it becomes its opposite, unbelief, hating and despising God, rejection, the crucifying afresh of the One in whom He gave Himself for us, if it looks anywhere but to Him, if the believer tries to look at himself and to rely and trust on his own activity and accomplishment."

[52] Barth, *CD,* III/1, 345–46.

[53] See also Dietrich Bonhoeffer, *Christ the Center,* trans. Edwin H. Robertson (San Francisco: Harper and Row, 1978), 27: "Teaching about Christ begins in silence . . . The silence of the Church is silence before the Word ... 'In silence I worship the unutterable' (Cyril of Alexandria) . . . To speak of Christ means to keep silent; to keep silent about Christ means to speak."

[54] Barth, *CD,* III/1, 350.

[55] Ibid. See also Eberhard Jüngel, *God as the Mystery of the World,* trans. Darrell L. Guder (Grand Rapids: Eerdmans, 1983), 116–26.

[56] Berry, *Jayber Crow,* 247.

would he think he would love Mattie all her life? Why would he think Mattie loves him? Doubt, again, is not just an intellectual tempest, but the stuff of sleepless nights. And Jayber has much at stake. "It is a fearful thing to be married and yet live alone, and sleep alone (as I felt in my worst nights) like the dead in the ground." There are times he feels like he is in a desert, without joy or hope or feelings. "Then I lived by faith alone, faith without hope."

Jayber's only answer to these questions and this pain is that he does love the real, concrete Mattie. "I do love her all her life, and still, and always."[57] The *actuality* of love for Mattie speaks louder for Jayber than questions of its *possibility*.[58] So also it must be with our faith in and love for God. In this way Moses is confronted with the presence of Yahweh on Mount Sinai (Exodus 3). Questions of *possibility* could have run roughshod through Moses' mind. Who is this voice speaking out of the burning bush? Why should I trust it? Why not investigate other gods? No, Moses responds with the only appropriate response to the *actuality* of God: worship ("Remove the sandals from your feet, for the place on which you are standing is holy ground," Exod 3:5). Mattie is not "better" than any other woman. (Yahweh is not "better" than any other god.) Moses does not choose Yahweh after comparison shopping with other gods.

Yes, Mattie does have her own wonderful characteristics. Jayber speaks of her "dignity and good humor, and with a kind of loveliness that was her own."[59] "She had the lightness of a girl, a woman's gravity in her eyes."[60] "She was intact and clear within herself."[61] Nevertheless, Mattie is more than her characteristics. Mattie is just Mattie, standing before Jayber in all her wonder. Her wonder is in the revelation of who she truly is. "The most deciding event of my life took place," Jayber relates, when he observed Mattie with her Vacation Bible School children,[62] at "that moment she was as free with children as she had been a child herself—as free as a

---

[57] Berry, *Jayber Crow,* 248.

[58] See also T. F. Torrance, *Theological Science* (New York: Oxford University Press, 1968), 1: "Genuine critical questions as to the *possibility* of knowledge cannot be raised *in abstracto* but only in concrete, not *a priori* but only *a posteriori."*

[59] Berry, *Jayber Crow,* 343.

[60] Ibid., 283.

[61] Ibid., 241.

[62] Berry, *Jayber Crow,* 191.

child, but with a generosity and watchfulness that were anything but childish. She was just perfectly there with them in her pleasure." Jayber accepts Mattie's presence, accepts her as she is. "Whatever she gave you—a look, a question, an answer—was honest. She didn't tell you everything she knew or thought. She never made reference even by silence to anything she suffered. But in herself she was present."[63] "She would be wholly present within her presence."[64] Jayber experiences a transition, however, from viewing her in terms of his ideal expectations and then viewing her according to her own reality, including her commitment to her marriage. In doing so, "I loved her more, and more clearly, than I did before. I became able to imagine her as she was and not a subject of a dream. In my thoughts of her, she stood apart from me. I seemed to see her whole."[65]

The beloved of the lover (in one's reality, whether it is God or a human person) reveals oneself to us. This should not be coerced, so even "nature must be respected and courted, not imposed upon" in order to respect it.[66] God gives Moses the proper response ("remove your sandals"), the response of worship, so that Moses is not left with the alternative of imposing on God his own criteria for certainty and knowledge. This is the "one basic way of knowing" T. F. Torrance speaks of, allowing reality to speak to us, yet respecting the "different modes of rationality," such as between God and a human person.[67] Yes, theological knowledge is not a kind of gnosis, completely disconnected from the rest of knowledge. There is "one way of knowing": allowing reality to disclose itself to us, and thereby criticize our opinions. But there is also a distinction between knowledge of God and the knowledge of a frog on a biology class dissection table. God will demand different instruments of knowledge than simply the tools of empiricism. One cannot know God through a telescope.

Here is the knowledge of grace, something that we cannot and should not try to control but only respond appropriately to what is given. We should only respond with the "empty hands" of a faith that works through love (Gal 5:6). So Jayber continues, "That is my answer, but in fact love

[63] Ibid., 189.
[64] Ibid., 193.
[65] Ibid., 198.
[66] T. F. Torrance, *The Ground and Grammar of Theology* (Charlottesville: University Press of Virginia, 1980), 9.
[67] Ibid.

does not answer any argument. It answers all arguments, merely by turning away, leaving them to find what rest they can."[68] Doubt is real, but its reality can be relativized by faith working through love. However, will we have the strength to possess such a faith?

The burden remains on Jayber: Is it the real Mattie that he loves or just an ideal, a woman of his fantasy? Is this not the burden of every believer in God? Is it the living God we worship or simply the highest expression of our values? We value love, so "God" is love (Feuerbach). "God" is just our highest value. Does Jayber know the real Mattie? Can one ever really *know* another person, with all of one's complexities and history? But do we let people know us? Are we imprisoned both by the stereotypes *of* others and the masks we wear *for* others? How much more is this true with God? Do we try to imprison God with our stereotypes of him? God does not wear a mask, but names himself. That is the significance of God as Trinity.[69] "God is known through God and through God alone" declares Barth.[70] The distinct "mode of rationality" (Torrance) that God possesses demands that his creation is completely dependent on God's initiative for any knowledge of God. How much more is that true of our relationships with other people. We have to go beyond our expectations of persons, who we *want* them to be and to be open to *listen* to who they actually are. We need to be continually *surprised* by that person. The worst thing to say in a relationship, Ray Anderson observes, is to say, "I knew you were going to say that!" The body language is important as well. We might add, "I know what that expression means!" The minute that *surprise* is gone, the relationship is in trouble. How much more is this true with God? (Why is it that those portrayed in icons never smile? Could it be that our tendency would be to read into an expression what we want to see in the icon? The dispassionate face keeps us from that.)[71] We are not far from the importance of Christ, the Word of God, and the significance

[68] Berry, *Jayber Crow,* 248.

[69] Barth, *CD,* I/1, 306–8.

[70] Barth, *CD,* II/1, 44.

[71] See also Mahmoud Zibawi, *The Icon: Its Meaning and History* (Collegeville, Minn.: Liturgical, 1993): "The aesthetics of the icon prefers a frontal presentation of the personality. Opposite us, the face of the saint inhabits the silence of the pure prayer, which, beyond every distraction, gives him a unique reflection. The immense eyes contemplate the spectator. In their welcome, the regard is the locus of a living encounter"

of our listening in silence to the Word made flesh. However, do we really know how to listen? We need help here as well.

The way of love is the way of listening. What does it mean to listen, however? It must include a listening that is also a seeing: "We declare to you what was from the beginning, what we have *heard,* what we have *seen* with our eyes, what we have looked at and touched with our hands, concerning the word of life . . ." (1 John 1:1). This involves both proper hearing (words from the mouth) and proper seeing (expressions of the face). It must mean to get beyond our distorted, preconceived notions, whether it is of people or of God.[72] Responding can be appropriate or inappropriate.[73] Who among us really listens to God? Who among us really listens to one another? We are back to the imperative of Christology. Jesus calls upon God as Father and thus makes him known as peculiarly his own Father.[74] Jesus Christ is the only One who makes the appropriate response, the One who truly listens to the Father. Our responses to God (and others!) are often inappropriate, to say the least. Our selfish expectations of others can harm friendships and destroy community. Christ presents the true knowledge of God in that he brings reconciliation between God and humanity.[75] The only response Jayber can give to Mattie, given his situation, is thanksgiving. So also the essence of Jesus' prayers to the Father is thankgiving: "I thank you, Father, Lord of heaven and earth . . ."

---

(37). "Rarely are the saints depicted in profile; such a profile constitutes a rupture, it interrupts the mixing of the eyes" (38). See also Barth, *CD,* III/2, 250–51: "Being in encounter is . . . a being in which one man looks the other in the eye . . . When one man looks the other in the eye, it takes place automatically that he lets the other look him in the eye. . . . The participation which we grant one another by the very fact that we see and do not see one another, and let ourselves be seen and not unseen by one another, these are the first and indispensable steps in humanity, without which the later ones cannot be taken, and which cannot be replaced by the exercise of any human capacity or virtue, however highly rated this may rightly or wrongly be."

[72] Andrew Purves, "The Christology of Thomas F. Torrance" in *The Promise of Trinitarian Theology: Theologians in Dialogue with T. F. Torrance,* ed. Elmer M. Colyer (Lanham, Md.: Rowman and Littlefield, 2001), 71.

[73] Elmer M. Colyer, "A Scientific Theological Method" in Colyer, ed., *The Promise of Trinitarian Theology,* 211. See also Daniel W. Hardy, "Thomas F. Torrance" in *The Modern Theologians,* ed. David F. Ford, 1 (Oxford: Blackwell, 1989), 77.

[74] T. F. Torrance, *The Christian Doctrine of God,* 57.

[75] Colyer, *How to Read T. F. Torrance,* 93, 230. See also 230: "We cannot know the truth without becoming at-one with the truth."

(Matt 11:25). Moreover, the Son who thanks the Father is the one to whom all things have been handed and who is the only source of the revelation (Matt 11:27). This mutual relation of knowing implies a mutual relation of being.[76] The Son is God as well as the Father. The appropriate response has been given by God himself![77] "It is He who offers and it is He who is offered" sings the Orthodox liturgy.[78] Knowledge of God proceeds from the mutual relationship between the Father, the Son, and the Holy Spirit.[79] The Son reveals the Holy Trinity (Matt 11:25-27; 28:19-20), and therefore the significance of the distinct Persons of the Godhead must be recovered.[80] Far from being the "crazy uncle in the attic" that the Church is embarrassed by because of its perceived abstractions and logical problems, the Trinity is "God in his revelation" (Barth).[81] The personhood of God is revealed in the thanksgiving and praise the Son offers to the Father in the Spirit.[82] *Who* God is and *how* we know him have profound implications for how we deal with doubt (see our chapters three and four).

Vocation and the "Lost Traveler": The Problem of the Knowledge of Oneself

If doubt extends beyond the intellectual world into the entire being of humanity, this might include the very practical question of vocation. To what am I called? Does God call individuals to particular tasks? How would I know that God has called me? One does not have to be a Moses with a question about a burning bush speaking to me to ask the more mundane question: What am I to do with my life? Doubts arise here as well.

---

[76] T. F. Torrance, *The Mediation of Christ,* 54.

[77] T. F. Torrance, *The Christian Doctrine of God,* 106. See also Colyer, *How to Read T. F. Torrance,* 93.

[78] Schmemann, *For the Life of the World,* 35.

[79] T. F. Torrance, *The Christian Doctrine of God,* 132.

[80] Alan J. Torrance, *Persons in Communion: Trinitarian Description and Human Participation* (Edinburgh: T. & T. Clark, 1996), 324.

[81] Barth, *CD,* I/1, 295.

[82] T. F. Torrance, *The Christian Doctrine of God,* 165, 242. See also Eberhard Jüngel, *The Doctrine of the Trinity: God's Being is in Becoming,* trans. Horton Harris (Edinburgh: Scottish Academic, 1976).

Jayber Crow, the "lost traveler," as we have seen, believes that he has a call to "full-time Christian service," to be a preacher. In his circles, this is the only legitimate kind of call.[83] There is a certainty about this call; it is final and you know it, without any doubts. This kind of call is attractive to Jayber, not least because in his mind it involves a pleasant future as a well-liked pastor, a parsonage, stocked with plenty of food and, most of all, a wife. As a lonely orphan, this is highly desirable.[84] Ultimately uncertainty, the motivation of doubt, pushes Jayber towards an ill-conceived goal to become a preacher. To relieve doubt becomes the motivation to at least make a commitment, just to be on the safe side of God![85] This "self-deception" is exposed when Jayber begins to have his "doctrinal troubles."

Yet his conversation with Dr. Ardmire will set him on the road to a different kind of calling, a calling that will involve becoming a simple rural barber but with real opportunities for *relationships*—with the land, the people in the community, and ultimately with God.[86] The calling will come, but as Dr. Ardmire advises him, it will come in a way he does not expect, the way of grace.

Jayber has plenty of reasons to doubt his calling and his future and even his meaning in life. We do, too. Jayber is plagued by the fear of not hearing the call of God, but then initially takes things into his own hands.[87] Our fears go back to our inadequacies, our lack of faith that only exposes our need for help and not to take things into our own hands. Who will give us that help?

Evil, Suffering, and the "Lost Traveler": The Problem of the Knowledge of the World

Being a "lost traveler" is also acute during the journey of life when one inevitably confronts the reality of evil and suffering. The reason for doubting the existence of an all-powerful and good God in light of this is

83 Berry, *Jayber Crow,* 43.

84 Ibid., 45.

85 Ibid., 43.

86 Ibid., 66.

87 Ibid., 43.

obvious. Not much needs to be said at this point (see chapter five). Dostoevsky states this famously through his character Ivan's argument with his saintly brother Alyosha in his novel *The Brothers Karamazov.*[88] Ivan makes it clear that he is all too aware of the absurdity of believing in the providence of God in a world of needless suffering, especially the suffering of children. If God needs this suffering to contribute to the "eternal harmony" of the universe, Ivan declines the ticket to such a world. Doubt has another ripe field for harvest. The *providence* of God, God's care for the world, is called into question.

Do we dare keep the ticket ourselves today? How can we do this in all honesty? Our world is Ivan's. In Albert Goldbarth's poem, "Even, Equal," he describes the "two schoolgirls" found "under half-receded ice, the bruises frozen, into lustrous broaches at their frozen throats."

> Whoever did it is still out there, is free and maybe
> needing more. The word "injustice" doesn't include
> the choking gall that burns through me[89]

Who can believe in such a world if one really feels the pain of the anguished? *Who,* indeed, is the question. The difficulty of living with this question is all too obvious. Can God be the "Father" of such a world? "This is my Father's World" the old hymn sang. Can we still sing it?

Pluralism, Postmodernism, and the "Lost Traveler": The Problem of the Knowledge of the Culture

A "lost traveler," wandering in the maze of doubt, can be challenged by the questions of the knowledge of God, of oneself, and the world, as we have seen. In addition, the knowledge of the contemporary *culture* is equally troubling. *Pluralism* is the phenomenon of a society much more connected by communication than past years. The internet opens up all sorts of webpages featuring an almost countless number of religions, philosophies,

---

[88] Fyodor Dostoevsky, *The Brothers Karamazov,* trans. Richard Pevear and Larissa Volokhonsky (New York: Farrar, Strauss and Giroux, 1990), 246–64.

[89] Albert Goldbarth, "Even, Equal," in *Beyond* (Boston: Godine, 1998), 21.

and worldviews. Immigration in the West creates a further explosion of pluralism. A Buddhist temple exists in Wichita, Kansas. One cannot afford anymore to be ignorant about non-western religions or worldviews. How, then, dare I say that I or my religious tradition have the right idea of God?[90] Perhaps it does not matter whether or not one has an idea of God that is "right," it is argued. We all have different ideas of God that are mostly reflections of our culture and background, right? The seeds of doubt are firmly sown.

Another cultural manifestation in recent years has been the rise of *postmodernism.*[91] Born as a critique of the Enlightenment project of exalted reason, this movement is expressed in everything from philosophy (Nietzsche, Derrida, Foucault) to the rapid sensory explosion of MTV images. Whereas the Renaissance thinker Francis Bacon may proclaim "knowledge is power," the postmodern critique views such knowledge as the oppression of one group by another, with an unwarranted assumption that there is a universal reason that can be achieved (Kant). Such optimism is dismissed by postmodernists who see tolerance as the bottom-line value. Truth is not known by isolated individuals but is a reflection of a particular community. As such, each community must become tolerant of one another. Seemingly contradictory worldviews must learn to co-exist, side by side. To be troubled by doubt is irrelevant because there are no universal principles or objective truths to doubt. Doubt is an unqualified virtue if it is doubt about objective truth claims.

Both pluralism and postmodernism raise the legitimate question: Who is qualified to decide what is truth? Whom can you trust? Can you even trust yourself? Is doubt really the way of humility? The "lost traveler" might as well give up the journey, it seems.

---

[90] For the standard advocacy of accommodation to pluralism, see John Hick, *An Interpretation of Religion: Human Responses to the Transcendent* (New Haven: Yale University Press, 1989); *God Has Many Names* (Philadelphia: Westminster Press, 1982). See the perceptive response to Hick in Charles T. Hughes, "Pluralism, Inclusivism, and Christology," *Jesus Then and Now,* eds. Meyer and Hughes, 154–69. T. F. Torrance views the contemporary obsession with pluralism as a regression back into polytheism. See his attention to the uniqueness of Christ in *Preaching Christ Today: The Gospel and Scientific Thinking* (Grand Rapids: Eerdmans, 1994).

[91] Stanley J. Grenz, *A Primer on Postmodernism* (Grand Rapids: Eerdmans, 1996) is a good survey of the concerns with a Christian critique.

Concluding Biblical Postscript: The Vicarious Humanity of Christ in the Story of Jesus

"He Trusts in God": Faith, the Knowledge of God, and the Faith of Jesus

How biblical is the doctrine of the vicarious humanity of Christ? A look at the Gospels might be important at this point. The story of Jesus in the Gospels is an active, adventurous story, a story of faith in God. Here we find the foundations for the doctrine of the vicarious humanity of Christ, as well as some possible responses to our problems of faith, vocation, evil and suffering, and pluralism and postmodernism. First of all, Jesus commends faith to others. He recognizes great faith when he sees it. Gentiles such as the centurion (Matt 8:10; Luke 7:9) and the Canaanite woman (Matt 15:23-28) who demonstrate faith in Jesus' ability to heal and who cast out demons are said to have great faith. Jesus makes plain that faith can make you well; to the blind man (or men) receiving their sight, since there is faith that Jesus is able to do this (Matt 9:27; 20:29-34; Mark 10:46-52; Luke 18:35-43); or for Jairus' daughter and the woman with a hemorrhage (Matt 9:18-21; Mark 5:21-43; Luke 8:40-56). "Your faith has saved you," Jesus says to the woman who anoints him with ointment (Luke 7:50). But those with "little faith" are chastised by Jesus, contrasting their doubt with faith, such as he does with Peter when Peter is unable to walk on the water: "You of little faith, why did you doubt?" (Matt 14:31). Jesus exhorts Thomas: "Do not doubt but believe" (John 20:27; cf. Mark 16:14). Not only does Jesus commend faith to others, however, he also demonstrates faith himself; just as the messianic "righteous one" of Hab 2:4 is said to "live by faith" (cf. Rom 1:17).[92] Jesus has faith and not doubt in order to walk on the water unlike Peter (Matt 14:28-31).[93] The disciples wonder how he made the fig tree wither (Mark 11:12-14). Jesus responds by exhorting them to "Have faith in God," that even mountains can be removed "if you do not doubt in your heart," and ask in prayer (Mark 11:24). Jesus did not doubt but believed, and the fig tree was withered.[94] Jesus himself is viewed as having faith by those

[92] Ian G. Wallis, *The Faith of Jesus Christ in Early Christian Traditions* (New York: Cambridge University Press, 1995), 79–80.

[93] Ibid., 39.

[94] Ibid., 42.

who mock him as he hangs on the cross: "He trusts in God; let God deliver him now, if he wants to; for he said, 'I am God's Son'" (Matt 27:43).

The incident of the spirit cast out of a boy by Jesus because the disciples were unable to do so brings out the vicarious aspect of Jesus' faith (Matt 17:14-21; Mark 9:14-29; Luke 9:37-43).[95] Origen implies the faith of Jesus in this instance.[96] The thrust of Jesus' whole teaching, such as the parables, confesses faith in the compassion, righteousness, power of God, and the goodness of his creation.[97] The most "disturbing" instance of Jesus' faith may be because it comes from the cross: "Father, into your hands I commend my spirit" (Luke 23:46).[98] This is disturbing because it raises the question of how we can have faith if suffering is our lot as well. His life is a life of faith in the Father, an "amen" that is to become our "amen."[99] Jesus trusts in God but does not "entrust" himself to the crowds.

> When he was in Jerusalem during the Passover festival, many believed in his name because they saw the signs that he was doing. But Jesus on his part would not entrust himself to them, because he knew all people and needed no one to testify about anyone; for he himself knew what was in everyone. (John 2:23-25)

Jesus also "confesses human inadequacy; if people should pray for the coming of the kingdom it can be only because the kingdom doesn't come without a transcendent mover."[100]

---

[95] Ibid., 27.

[96] Origen, *Commentary on Matthew,* ANF, 10: 477–81. See also Wallis, *The Faith of Jesus Christ in Early Christian Traditions,* 183.

[97] Dale C. Allison in Miller, ed. *The Apocalyptic Jesus,* 150.

[98] Emilie Griffin, *Clinging* (Wichita, Ks.: Eighth Day, 2003), 3.

[99] Schmemann, *For the Life of the World,* 29: "It is Christ's gift to us, for only in Him can we say Amen to God and the Church is an Amen to Christ."

[100] Dale C. Allison in Miller, ed., *The Apocalyptic Jesus,* 150.

"I Thank You, Father . . .": Faith, the Knowledge of God, and the Prayers of Jesus

The faith of Jesus in the Gospels is the story of an intimate relationship to God the heavenly Father. Essential to the faith of Jesus are his prayers to the Father. "I thank you, Father, Lord of heaven and earth . . ." begins Jesus, "because you have hidden these things from the wise and the intelligent and have revealed them to infants" (Matt 11:25; cf. Luke 10:21-22; John 3:35; 17:2; 13:3; 7:29; 10:14-15; 17:25). The prayer of thanksgiving recognizes the inability of humanity (those not wise and intelligent), so crucial in dealing with doubt. The crucial knowledge involved here is the knowledge of the mutual relation of being between the Father and the Son and the Son as the only means of knowing the Father (Matt 11: 27). On this basis is the call to come to Jesus and take *his* yoke upon you (11:28-30). Here is the core of communion as *Eucharist* (thanksgiving); primarily, the thanksgiving the Son offers the Father and our participation in his thanksgiving.[101]

Jesus prays for others as a part of his vicarious mission. He prays all night before he selects the Twelve (Luke 6:12-13). Martha expects that whatever Jesus asks of God will be given, and so asks him to pray for the raising of Lazarus (John 11: 22). Jesus exhorts the disciples to ask the Father "in my name . . . and you will receive, that your joy may be full" (John 16:23-28). In his High Priestly Prayer Jesus prays for the disciples to be kept in the Father's name, "that they may be one, even as we are one" (John 17:1-26). He does not pray for them to be taken out of the world, but to be kept from the evil one, who will ask Jesus permission to sift the disciples like wheat (Luke 22:31). Jesus responds to Peter in

[101]See also *The Divine Liturgy of Our Father Among the Saints John Chrysostom* (Antiochian Orthodox Christian Archdiocese of North America, 1997), 125: "We give thanks unto thee, O Lord who lovest mankind, benefactor of our souls and bodies, for that thou hast vouchsafed this day to feed us with thy heavenly and immortal Mysteries . . ." and the "Great Prayer of Thanksgiving" in *The Service for the Lord's Day: The Worship of God: Supplemental Liturgical Resources 1* (Philadelphia: Westminster, 1984), 106–7: "We give you thanks, O God, through your beloved servant, Jesus Christ . . . It is he who fulfilled all your will . . . We ask you to send your Holy Spirit upon the offering of the holy church, gathering into one all who share these holy mysteries . . ." (Presbyterian Church [U.S.A.]).

particular that he will pray for Peter that his faith would not fail, so that he in turn would strengthen his brothers (Luke 22:32).[102] Ultimately, as Jayber Crow observes, Jesus' prayer for the cup to be taken from him is not granted, although his caveat, "not my will but thine be done" is (Matt 26:36-46; Mark 14:32-42; Luke 22:39-46).

"And When Jesus Had Been Baptized . . .": Solidarity, Identification, and Vocation

The story of the vicarious humanity of Christ begins with the humility of Bethlehem. The genealogical roots of Jesus as established by Luke connect Jesus with Adam who is also "the son of God" (Luke 3:38). God is now in solidarity with Adam, as well as with Israel. With the beginning of Jesus' public ministry his identification with the people is solidified by the remarkable act of Jesus desiring and being baptized (Mark 9–11; Matt 3:13-17; Luke 3:21-23). Baptism by John is obviously for sinners, a testimony of repentance. So when Jesus comes to be baptized, John, knowing much about Jesus, objects ("John would have prevented him" Matt 3:14). John rightly concludes that he needs to be baptized by Jesus; he needs the power of the deity of Christ, but he cannot understand why he should baptize Jesus. Is this not because of his failure (and ours) to see that the response of faith should not begin with the weakness and vacillation of our faith, but with the faith of Jesus, a faith that is part of his wider human response in every way, even including repentance?[103] Solidarity with us in baptism is not enough (Christ as only our representative). Solidarity is the means for Christ to be our substitute. His baptism then becomes the foundation for our baptism (Matt 20:23).[104] Jesus the Son of God must walk the path of sinful humanity, sharing in our stories, including our doubts and fears. This is the path of both representing our humanity and taking our place.

---

[102] Augustine, "On Rebuke and Grace" XII.35, cited by J. Patout Burns, S.J., ed., *Theological Anthropology* (Philadelphia: Fortress Press, 1981), 104.

[103] See also C. S. Lewis, "The Perfect Penitent," in *Mere Christianity* (New York: Macmillan, 1960), 56–61.

[104] T. F. Torrance, "The One Baptism Common to Christ and His Church," *Theology in Reconciliation: Essays Toward Evangelical and Catholic Unity in East and West* (Grand Rapids: Eerdmans, 1975), 82–105.

The baptism of Jesus is followed immediately with his temptations by the devil. These are temptations to avoid walking the path of sinners and rather to demonstrate before the right time his divine power. "If you are the Son of God . . ." command these stones to become bread, throw yourself down from the pinnacle of the temple and the angels will catch you, and worship the tempter in order to be given the kingdoms of the world (Matt 4:3-9). These are not temptations to break the Law of God, but temptations to break free of solidarity with sinful humanity.[105] Something must be important about this solidarity! Jesus' "vocation" is constantly being challenged.

Jesus does appear to break the law of God when he instructs the disciples to pluck the grain for food on the Sabbath (Matt 12:1-8; Mark 2:23-28; Luke 6:1-5). His theological reason is based both on the purpose of the Law being for the sake of humanity ("The sabbath was made for humankind, and not humankind for the Sabbath," [Mark 2:27] and Jesus, "the Son of Man" being "the Lord of the Sabbath" [Mark 2:28]). In solidarity with humanity he is able to make decisive interpretations of and actions based upon the implications of the law of God for humanity. The assumption is that we do not and cannot interpret the Law rightly. Jesus needs to read the Bible for us!

This solidarity with humanity includes the emotional depths of the human condition. When Jesus saw Mary weeping at the grave of Lazarus, being "greatly disturbed in spirit and deeply moved," he too wept (John 11:33-35). Mary's tears are not enough. Jesus must also weep. (Must Jesus doubt with us as well?)

"I Have Not Come to Abolish but to Fulfill": Jesus' Humanity as Fulfillment and Vocation

Jesus' vicarious humanity is a story about our humanity too and its need for completion, for fulfillment, to fill up what has been lacking. (Is our search for "vocation" a part of that quest?) "Do not think that I have come to abolish the law or the prophets," says Jesus. "I have come not to abolish but to fulfill" (Matt 5:17). While this may mean at first glance

---

105 Barth, *CD,* IV/1, 260–64.

that Jesus comes to fulfill Old Testament prophecy, might there not be a wider and deeper meaning in the fulfillment of the law of God by Jesus, "the one, true, obedient Israelite" (Barth)? He keeps the Law that we have been unable to keep. So the balance of the Sermon on the Mount's ethical teachings may be viewed as fulfilled in the life of Jesus:[106] Jesus teaches to turn the other check, which he will subsequently do (Matt 5:38-42; Luke 6: 29-30). He teaches to love your enemies (Matt 5:43-45; Luke 6: 27-28, 22-36). Paul adds that while we were "enemies" we were reconciled by the Son (Rom 5:10). Jesus lived a life himself of serving God not mammon (Matt 6:24; Luke 16:13). His exhortation not to judge (Matt 7:1-5; Luke 6:37-42) was lived out with his refusal to judge the woman caught in adultery (John 7:51–8:11). He warns that not every one who says to him "Lord, Lord" will enter the kingdom of heaven, "but only the one who does the will of my Father in heaven" (Matt 7:21-23; Luke 6:46; cf. Luke 13:25-27). However, Jesus is the one who does the will of the Father (Matt 26:42; Mark 14:36; Luke 22:42). The exhortation "Be perfect, therefore, as your heavenly Father is perfect" (Matt 5:48) may be an intolerable burden apart from Christ fulfilling it first, for us. As such, he is rewarded by God as the one poor in spirit, who mourns, who is meek, hungers and thirsts for righteousness, who is merciful, pure in heart, a peacemaker, and who is persecuted for righteousness' sake. He will possess the kingdom of heaven, be comforted, inherit the earth, be satisfied, obtain mercy, see God, and be called the Son of God (Matt 5:3-12; Luke 6:20-23). "Here at last is a man who loves the Lord with all his heart and soul and mind and strength and his neighbour as himself."[107] Who among us has been able to do this? Who is really able to deal with doubt about ourselves? It must be done *for us*.

"I Do as the Father Has Commanded Me . . .": The Obedience of Jesus as Vocation

The story of the faith of Jesus in the Father is never portrayed apart from his obedience to the will of the Father in contrast to the rest of humanity.

[106] See Eduard Thurneysen, *The Sermon on the Mount,* trans. William Childs Robinson, Sr., with James M. Robinson (Richmond: John Knox, 1964).
[107] Tom Smail, "Can One Man Die For the People?' in *Atonement Today,* ed. John Goldingay (London: SPCK, 1995), 87.

Here is Jesus' vocation, and our vocation. Jesus does what the Father commands so that "the world may know that I love the Father" (John 14:31). He heals the man at the pool because he only does what he sees the Father doing. "The Son can do nothing on his own," since he seeks to do "the will of him who sent me" (John 5:19, 30). Jesus is "the bread of life" because he does the will of the one who sent him, the Father (John 6:26-59). His will is food for the believer. The vicarious humanity of Christ in the sense of his obedience is not antithetical to faith in Christ. Jesus "sees" the Father (John 6:46). "The will of the Father" is "that all who see the Son and believe in him may have eternal life; and I will raise them up on the last day" (John 6:40). The believer "eats" of Jesus "the living bread . . . and the bread that I will give for the life of the world is my flesh" (John 6:51). The humanity (flesh) of Christ is integrally connected to the life of the believer. Jesus' "food," in turn, "is to do the will of him who sent me and to complete his work" (John 4:34). The works that Jesus does "in my Father's name" bear witness of him (John 10:25, 31, 37-38). Jesus' "zeal" for God's house "consumes" him so much that he creates the disturbance in the temple (John 2:13-22).

Only the one who obeys the Father will enter the kingdom of heaven (Matt 7:21). Jesus is the only one we know for sure who completely does the Father's will. Others vacillate according to how they build their foundations (Matt 13:1-9; Mark 4:1-9; Luke 8:4-8). With some the word becomes unfruitful because of the worries and enticements of the world (Matt 13:18-23; Mark 4:13-20; Luke 8:11-15). The one who does "the will of my Father in heaven" is Jesus' "brother, and sister, and mother" (Matt 12:46-50; Mark 3:31-35; Luke 8:19-21 cf. John 15:14). In all of this, in Barth's phrase, "His servitude is His lordship."[108] Jesus is the obedient servant who summons one to "follow" him (Matt 5:19) "who in accordance with the will of his heavenly Father does all that these demands indicate." He is present, not absent, not afar, from those who follow him: "Whoever serves me must follow me, and where I am, there will my servant be also" (John 12:26). Where the Son dwells is always in relationship with the Father (Matt 11:27).[109] His intercessions for his disciples are founded

---

[108] Barth, *CD*, II/2, 570. "It is good to be with Jesus and not elsewhere. This is good because it is there that God Himself is good for us."

[109] James Torrance, *Worship, Community, and the Triune God of Grace*, 31.

on his act of "sanctifying" himself to the Father: "And for their sakes I sanctify myself, so that they also may be sanctified in truth" (John 17:19 cf. Heb. 2:11).[110] Therefore they share in the same Father: "I am ascending to my Father and your Father, to my God and your God" (John 20:17).[111]

"Our Father": The God of Jesus and Us in a World of Evil and Suffering

Persons are stories. The story of God's "imaginative embrace" of humanity in the incarnation continues with the revelation of a relationship between the "persons" of the Father and the Son through the Spirit.[112] There is a "story" going on within God himself from all eternity that is made manifest by the incarnation! Jesus is unique in that he has seen the Father (John 6:46). But he invites the disciples to participate in that relationship by praying "Our Father . . ." (Matt 6:9). Because he is in solidarity with the disciples, they ask him, "Lord, teach us to pray . . ." (Luke 11:1). This extends to all of what it means to be a disciple of Jesus. "Jesus said to them, 'Very truly, I tell you, the Son can do nothing on his own, but only what he sees the Father doing; for whatever the Father does, the Son does likewise" (John 5:19). So the paralytic at the pool is healed, based on the dependence of the Son on the Father, not just the Son's sheer, overwhelming divine power. The dependence of the Son on the Father does not exclude the responses of the disciples. The disciples are exhorted to acknowledge Jesus and not deny him so that he will acknowledge and not deny them before "my Father" (Matt 10:26-33; Luke 12:2-9; cf. Mark 4:22; 8:38; Luke 8:17; 9:26). And even at the end of his earthly life and ministry the risen Jesus relates his ascension to "my Father and your Father, to my God and your God" (John 20:17). Jesus is able to believe in a heavenly Father who cares for us as well as the birds of the air (Matt 6: 26), who does not

---

[110] Ibid., 48.

[111] Ibid., 49.

[112] For a defense of language of persons for the Trinity, see Alan J. Torrance, *Persons in Communion.* C. S. Lewis speaks of the incarnation as the myth of God's "imaginative embrace" of humanity that has become fact in *God in the Dock: Essays in Theology and Ethics* (Grand Rapids: Eerdmans, 1970), 66–67.

forget the sparrows or the hairs on your heads (Luke 12:6, 7) when it is difficult for us to do so. (See our further discussion in chapter five.)

"The Blood of the Covenant Poured Out for Many": Jesus as Substitute for Pluralism and Postmodernism

Jesus does for us what we have been unable to do for ourselves. This is the story of his life. We may not feel qualified to decide what is true. Postmodernism has rightly warned us of our epistemological problem. We may not even trust our own judgment, let alone the judgment of others. Jesus is our substitute, beginning with knowledge of God. "I have made known to you everything that I have heard from my Father" (John 15:15). The knowledge of God that the disciples possess comes from Jesus. He knows God when they are unable to know God. He is their substitute. If there is a vicarious humanity of Christ there is also a vicarious *deity* of Christ. Christ represents and stands in for us before the Father. So he also represents and stands in for the Father: ". . . and no one knows the Father except the Son and anyone to whom the Son chooses to reveal him" (Matt 11:27). Christ puts himself in God's place since the relationship between the Father and the Son "falls within the very being of God."[113]

Such substitution goes beyond knowledge into action. Jesus washes the feet of the disciples as an imperative for them to wash each others' feet (John 13:12-16). This is an "example" for them, but only because Jesus takes the initiative and washes their feet first. There is no moral exhortation to wash feet without Jesus doing it *for* them and *to* them first of all. The foot-washing is an act of intercession, washing their feet when it was obvious that they could have washed them themselves.[114] When Jesus

[113] Colyer, *How to Read T. F. Torrance,* 75. See also T. F. Torrance, *The Trinitarian Faith,* 119; *The Christian Doctrine of God,* 46.

[114] Barth, *CD,* II/2, 475: "He gave Himself to this service of the rejected even to the final point of self-offering. This is what is signified in the feet-washing. On the basis and in the power of His service, the apostles are enabled to live as those for whom He intercedes, for whose uncleanness He repents, and to whom He gives His purity. It is in this office as the Reconciler of the world to God, as the King and the Prophet who also is the High Priest sacrificing Himself, that Jesus is the Head of the Church. And it is before this Head of the Church that Peter and Judas now stand side by side and on the same footing, at least in respect of their need. All His own, including Peter would be lost if the subjective

speaks of going to prepare a place for the disciples he is speaking of doing something they cannot do, as their substitute (John 14:3). He is "the way" because they do not know the way, as Thomas asked, "How can we know the way?" (John 14:5, 6).[115] Because Jesus asks, the Father will send the Paraclete (Helper, Advocate, Comforter, i.e., the Holy Spirit) to them (John 14:16-17). "Because I live, you also will live" (John 14:19). The disciples are exhorted to "abide in me . . . because apart from me you can do nothing" (John 15:4-5).

Jesus' death is for the many. The Last Supper presents his body and blood "poured out for many for the forgiveness of sins" (Matt 26:28). The disciples are to "eat" this body and "drink" this blood, to participate in something that has been done for them, on their behalf and in their place.

What has been done for the disciples? The life of Jesus demonstrates that he fulfills Isaiah's prophecy, "He took our infirmities and bore our diseases" (Matt 8:17). We are not able to heal ourselves. In addition, however, Jesus must suffer, be killed, and be raised on the third day (Matt 16:21 cf. Luke 24:26). Death and resurrection are both vicarious here. "It is better for you to have one man die for the people than to have the whole nation destroyed" (John 11:50). The grain of wheat must die in order to bear much fruit (John 12:24). This action is an expression of the "greater love" that lays down its life for its friends (John 15:13-16). As he predicts in Gethsemane, Jesus is going to experience the anguish of death

---

side of the relationship between Jesus and His own were not controlled by His death; if in defiance of their own nature they were not born again as new subjects by the substitutionary death of Jesus; if they were not given the freedom to live a new life in the world by the power of the life which He sacrificed for them. 'Without me ye can do nothing' (John 15:6)—this is as true for Peter and the rest as it is for Judas."

[115] Bishop Kallistos Ware is right in stressing that Christ's suffering does not exempt us from suffering. His suffering love is also not just an example, but has "a creative effect" upon us. Yet he rejects the language of substitution, meaning that Christ suffers "instead of me." He only accepts the language of representation; Christ suffers "on my behalf." *The Orthodox Way* (Crestwood, N.Y.: St. Vladimir's Seminary Press, 1979), 82. Unfortunately, this only limits substitution to suffering when the biblical testimony of the vicarious *humanity* of Christ (not just his suffering) is much wider and deeper, a point particularly relevant to dealing with existential issues like doubt. In regards to suffering, certainly Christ did suffer in a way that we never will, in our place ("It is finished.") (John 19:30). He was the one who became a curse for us (Gal 3:13), although we do continue to suffer with him (Col 1:24).

for the sake of others, "the anguishing terrors of a lost soul … the reality of eternal death."[116] Who is this one on the cross but "the Man" ("Behold, the Man!"), the representative and substitute for all who is mocked for all (Matt 27:27-31; 38-43; Mark 15:16-20, 27-32; Luke 23:35-38). This is the man who will utter from the cross, "My God, my God why have your forsaken me?" (Matt 27:46), yet also declare, "Father, into your hand I commend my spirit" (Luke 23:46). Here Jesus refuses to act divinely. Is this a failure of divine love or divine power?[117] Is Jesus just himself godforsaken, or is he godforsaken for all of humanity, a representative of and substitute for the hopelessness of our godforsakeness? The disciples, Jesus says, will share in his baptism and drink his cup with him (Matt 20:20-28; Mark 10:35-45; Luke 22:24-27 cf. Luke 12:50). He has become "the ransom for many" (Mark 10:45).[118]

Life "In My Name": The Fruit of the Vicarious Humanity of Christ in a Pluralistic, Postmodern Culture

The vicarious life of Jesus does not leave people untouched, whatever their response to him might be. It can have a positive or negative response. To share in Christ's vicarious humanity is not to be released from faith and discipleship. In fact, discipleship is intensified. Jesus predicts that his disciples will be handed over to be tortured, put to death, and hated "because of my name" (Matt 24:10 cf. v.22). The follower of Jesus will now act vicariously *for Jesus* ("because of my name"). The "sheep . . . blessed by my Father" will be rewarded because they acted *on behalf of Jesus, meeting Jesus himself* when they clothed the naked, fed the hungry, and visited the imprisoned (Matt 25:31-46). But a more insidious, "dark" vicarious humanity will also arise. The disciples will be "blessed … when people revile you and persecute you and utter all kinds of evil against you falsely on my account" (Matt 5:11). "For many will come in my name,

---

[116] William Law, cited by Ware, *The Orthodox Way,* 79.

[117] Alan E. Lewis, *Between Cross and Resurrection,* 55.

[118] Ibid., 447: "Christ's whole ministry, indeed, was an extended baptism, plunging deeper and deeper into the waters of our wickedness and weakness, which led through the wilderness temptation to climactic violence, trial and passion in Jerusalem."

saying, 'I am the Messiah!' and they will lead many astray" (Matt 24:5 cf. 24:24). The reality of the vicarious humanity will be in contrast with a dark manifestation, those who do evil, pretending to do so "in my name" or persecuting those "falsely on my account." Either kind of response demonstrates the profound effect God's vicarious life has on the life of humanity, even to the depths of its crises such as doubt. Those implications leave much to be explored.

2

Doubt: Virtue or Vice?

One of the amazing developments of thought in modern times is the glad acceptance of doubt. In the past, doubt was always something to be feared, a sign of unbelief. But in recent times, even that stalwart defender of traditional Christianity, Malcolm Muggeridge, can remark on a "Firing Line" television program with William F. Buckley that all the saints have doubted. In fact, Muggeridge contends, one cannot have faith without doubt. It is a kind of refiner's fire, sifting out the true metal from the dross. Doubt toughens one up, matures one's faith.

True enough. But doubt in the contemporary world has also been the source of great anguish for people of faith. The very existence of God is now called into question in our world.[1] The modern questions are well-

[1] See the discussion in Frederick Ferré, *Basic Modern Philosophy of Religion* (New York: Scribner, 1967), 119–54; John Hick, ed., *Classical and Contemporary Readings in the Philosophy of Religion,* third edition (Englewood Cliffs, N.J.: Prentice-Hall, 1990); John Hick, *Arguments for the Existence of God* (New York: Seabury, 1971); *The Existence of God* (New York: Collier, 1964); Michael Goulder and John Hick, *Why Believe in God?* (London: SCM, 1983); C. Stephen Evans, *Philosophy of Religion* (Downers Grove, Ill.: InterVarsity, 1985), 45–76; Barth, *CD,* II/1, 3–256; Torrance, *The Trinitarian Faith,* 47–75; *The Christian Doctrine of God; The Ground and Grammar of Theology,* 146–79; Colyer, *How to Read T. F. Torrance,* 129–39; Calvin, *Institutes,* 1.1–3; Otto Weber, *Foundations of Dogmatics,* Vol. 1, trans. Darrell L. Guder (Grand Rapids: Eerdmans, 1981), 218–27. The classic Christian critique of proofs for the existence of God is found

known: Is God simply a projection of my greatest values (Feuerbach), a wish fulfillment for a heavenly father (Freud), or a way to establish my control over others (Nietzsche)? Or is *he* simply a reflection of my male desire to "deify" my maleness in order to dominate women (feminism)? And if God does exist, with myriads of rivaling conceptions of God in the history of humanity, how *dare* I say that *I* have the right idea of God? Perhaps it doesn't even matter to have an idea of God that is "right," but simply to tolerate one another's beliefs (postmodernism). Is the experience of doubt helpful to the believer (a virtue) or a hindrance to faith (a vice)?

Two twentieth-century theologians offer strikingly different attitudes toward faith and doubt. Paul Tillich, on the one hand, reflects the modern discovery of the sublimity of doubt. For him there is a close connection between faith and courage.[2] As risk is important to courage, so also it is to faith. There is the risk of failure, if one's "ultimate concern" is falsely placed, e.g., on a nation. Faith is not incongruent with doubt because faith involves risk and is grounded in one's ultimate concern. In fact, doubt is a "necessary element" in faith. "It is a consequence of the risk of faith."[3] This is so because faith is not a belief that something is true. In that case, doubt would be incompatible with faith.

The kind of doubt involved with faith, for Tillich, is not the doubt that is needed for a scholar to ascertain facts. That is methodological doubt. Nor is it the doubt of a skeptic towards all religions. That is more of an

in Søren Kierkegaard, *Philosophical Fragments/Johannes Climacus,* ed. and trans. Howard V. Hong and Edna H. Hong (Princeton: Princeton University Press, 1985), 39–44. The implications of the Cross and the Trinity for the existence of God are discussed by Jüngel in *God as the Mystery of the World*, 223–24.

[2] Paul Tillich, *Dynamics of Faith* (New York: Harper and Row, 1957), 16. For the seminal discussion on faith as risk, see Kierkegaard, *Fear and Trembling*. See alsoKarl Barth, *The Epistle to the Romans,* trans. Edwyn C. Hoskyns (Oxford: Oxford University Press, 1933), 98: "Faith is the faithfulness of God, ever secreted in and beyond all human ideas and affirmations about Him, and beyond every positive religious achievement. There is no such thing as mature and assured possession of faith: regarded psychologically, it is always a leap into the darkness of the unknown, a flight into empty air." See also Rudolf Bultmann, *Jesus Christ and Mythology* (New York: Charles Scribner's Sons, 1958), 40–41; and the critique in Klaus Bockmuehl, *The Unreal God of Modern Theology,* trans. Geoffrey W. Bromiley (Colorado Springs: Helmers and Howard, 1988), 78–84. See also Avery Dulles, S.J., *The Assurance of Things Hoped For: A Theology of Christian Faith* (New York: Oxford University Press, 1994), 116, 119, 232–33.

[3] Tillich, *Dynamics of Faith,* p. 18.

"attitude than an assertion."[4] Rather, it is the doubt that accompanies every risk, what Tillich calls "existential doubt."[5] "It does not question whether a special proposition is true or false. It does not reject every concrete truth, but it is aware of the element of insecurity in every existential truth."[6] This is an essential part of faith. This is where faith differs from that which we perceive or reason immediately. Tillich's statement is telling:

> There is no faith without an intrinsic 'in spite of' and the courageous affirmation of oneself in the state of ultimate concern . . . If doubt appears, it should not be considered as the negation of faith, but as an element which was always and will always be present in the act of faith. Existential doubt and faith are poles of the same reality, the state of ultimate concern.[7]

So, a believer should not fear doubt. Rather, "serious doubt is confirmation of faith. It indicates the seriousness of the concern, its unconditional character."[8] This may involve doubting a creedal statement or even doubt about the Christian message concerning Jesus as the Christ. No matter. "The criterion according to which they should judge themselves is the seriousness and ultimacy of their concern about the content of both their faith and their doubt."[9]

In stark contrast to Tillich is the position of Karl Barth.[10] For Barth, not everything named "God" on the basis of free choice can possibly be God. There is a definite constraint to the knowledge of the true God, bound to God's Word given to the Church. Surrendering to whatever free choice calls "God" can only lead to the problems of doubt and anxiety. "God" can be very easily questioned from "without, a position where we begin to experience anxiety and doubt."[11]

---

[4] Ibid., 19.
[5] Ibid., 20.
[6] Ibid.
[7] Ibid., 21–22.
[8] Ibid., 22.
[9] Ibid.
[10] Barth, *CD*, II/1, 6–7.
[11] Ibid., 7.

> For if the knowledge of a 'God' is or even can be attacked from without, or if there is or even can be anxiety and doubt in the knowledge of him, then that 'God' is manifestly not God but a false god, a god who merely pretends to be God.[12]

Barth puts it very bluntly: "True knowledge of God is not and cannot be attacked; it is without anxiety and without doubt. But only that which is fulfilled under the constraint of God's Word is such a true knowledge of God."[13] There is still a battle against uncertainty and doubt for the believer. But it will always be a "victorious battle."

The Virtue of Doubt

From the Realism of Life

The nature of life, the realism of living, teaches us to value doubt. We are often annoyed by the know-it-all, especially when it comes to religious matters. If age can bring any virtue, it can (but not always) produce humility, acknowledging how little we know. I like the student who doesn't jump quickly with the answer to a question, showing a bit of thought behind one's comments. I can tell more about intelligence from a student's silent expression as one is wrestling with an idea (or maybe just trying to comprehend my ramblings) than the student who speaks without thinking, merely to announce one's presence. The great thinkers seem to be the most humble; the lesser lights seem to need to boast of their intellectual prowess. Likewise, laughter is often missing among those who in their arrogance have no doubts and therefore cannot but take themselves with the utmost seriousness.[14] Theologians, most of all, need to cultivate this life of laughter. How else can we presume that our little attempts at theology can come close to the majesty of God? This can become strategic in

---

[12] Ibid.

[13] Ibid.

[14] Geddes Macgregor, "Doubt and Belief," in *The Encyclopedia of Religion,* Vol. 4, ed. Mircea Eliade (New York: Macmillan, 1987), 429.

avoiding equating the truth of our systematizations of theology with the thoughts of God himself.[15]

Doubt may be seen as the purely human act of deciding, of making a distinction, to judge between two possibilities (as in the Greek word *diakrinō).*[16] Judgments have to be made if we are aware of how easily we can deceive ourselves. We have remarked how Jayber in *Jayber Crow* asks if he is simply deceiving himself in his belief that he knows the real Mattie. Is he simply idealizing her? A dose of healthy "doubt" is needed here, as certain as he is in his love for her. We tend to believe what we want to believe, whether it is the wife who refuses to admit her husband's adultery or even the historian's view that one knows the Jesus who lived two thousand years ago.[17] Doubt means using your judgment, the argument goes. Doubt should be a daily part of life, and therefore must be respected. The counsel of Jayber's professors just "to have more faith," in the sense of giving up his questioning, is not possible for Jayber. The questioning is a part of life, of who Jayber is. The questioning does not give Jayber up.[18] This is not in the sense of some kind of "possession," but admitting that this is a part of life that should not be ignored.

When one examines life, there are good reasons for doubt, as even that staunch opponent of doubt, Karl Barth, recognizes.[19] The gospel

[15] See also Bernard Ramm, "The Laughing Barth," in *After Fundamentalism: The Future of Evangelical Theology* (San Francisco: Harper and Row, 1983), 193–97. See also T. F. Torrance, *Karl Barth: Biblical and Evangelical Theologian* (Edinburgh: T. & T. Clark, 1990), 12–13: "Barth's humour played a fundamentally critical role in his thinking. He was able to laugh at himself, and therefore to criticise himself, and hence to direct even ruthless critique at others in such a way that he could appreciate their intention and respect their persons and their sincerity . . . But above all Barth's humour had critical significance for the nature and form of his own theological construction, because it meant that he was ever open to the question as to the adequacy of his own thought-forms to their proper object, and that he would never let himself become a prisoner of his own formulations." Barth is not above relating joy and laughter: Looking at Jesus Christ transforms a person "into a fundamentally joyful being. We may as well admit it; he has got something to laugh at, and he just cannot help laughing, even though he does not feel like it." *Deliverance to the Captives,* trans. Marguerite Wieser (New York: Harper and Row, 1961), 47.

[16] Donald McKim, "Doubt," in *International Standard Bible Encyclopedia, Revised,* ed. Geoffrey W. Bromiley, Vol. 1 (Grand Rapids: Eerdmans, 1979), 487.

[17] Dale C. Allison, *Jesus of Nazareth: Millenarian Prophet* (Minneapolis: Fortress Press, 1998), 77.

[18] Berry, *Jayber Crow,* 52.

[19] Karl Barth, *Evangelical Theology: An Introduction,* trans. Grover Foley (New York: Holt, Rinehart, and Winston, 1963), 126–29.

message seems weak compared to the wisdom of the world in economics, natural science, and technology, and less than the sublimity of the fine arts. In contrast, the Church is plagued with the legacy of crusades, burning of witches, and Barth would add, I'm sure, most recently, clergy malpractice. The individual Christian existence, moreover, if one looks at it frankly, quite often fans the fuel for doubt through fanatical excesses in asceticism or the study of theology at the exclusion of life's other concerns! The inevitability of the vicissitudes of life sows a fertile field of doubt, such as the perennial question of why a good and all powerful God would take away a loved one.[20]

From the Realism of Faith

Faith, it is argued, has its own place, if not necessity for, doubt. Tennyson's well-known aphorism, "that more faith lives in honest doubt than in half the creeds," is a testimony to the relationship between faith and doubt. Without doubt, faith loses vitality.[21] Without doubt, there is no place for religious tolerance, for a person with complete certainty would have no reason to tolerate a different viewpoint.[22] Such a view does not respect the mystery of faith. Its devotee's "wonderless belief" can offer only "wonderless love," according to Macgregor, which is "blasphemy" and an expression of narcissism rather than an outpouring of love. Doubt is at the heart of genuine religion, in this view. A vital faith is characterized by admitting that doubt is theoretically possible. Thus, genuine faith is demonstrated in a willingness to act in a way that reflects one's beliefs.[23] A thinking person must begin as a skeptic, yet that skepticism can lead to either belief or unbelief. In T. S. Eliot's words, "Every man who thinks and lives by thought must have his own skepticism . . . that which ends in denial, or that which leads to faith and which is somehow integrated into the faith which transcends it."[24] Doubt

[20] James Torrance, *Worship, Community, and the Triune God of Grace,* 44.
[21] Macgregor, "Doubt and Belief," 429.
[22] Ibid., 430.
[23] William James, "The Sentiment of Rationality" in *The Will to Believe and Other Essays in Popular Philosophy* (London: Longmans, Green, and Co., 1912), 90.
[24] T. S. Eliot, "Introduction" to Blaise Pascal, *Pascal's Penseés* (New York: Dutton, 1958), xv. See also Taylor, *The Myth of Certainty,* 80.

is a stepping stone, a "ladder of ascent" into faith, the darkness on the mountain of Moses that is necessary for the light, as in Gregory of Nyssa's *Life of Moses.*

It can be argued that there is a pastoral necessity to admit the virtue of doubt. Genuine faith does not disdain those who doubt, but listens to them, empathizes with them, and recognizes that in God's providence genuine faith may be forged out of the furnace of doubt. The apostle Thomas is praised in "the Sunday of Thomas" of the Orthodox liturgy:

> O how praiseworthy and truly awesome is Thomas' undertaking! For daringly he touched the side that doth flash forth with the lightning of the divine fire. Thou hast proved the disbelief of Thomas to be the mother of belief for us; for by Thy wisdom, Thou dost provide for all things that are to our profit, O Christ, since Thou art the Friend of man.[25]

Doubt takes seriously that God himself is not distanced from suffering, including the suffering of doubt.[26] This is contrary to the kind of "faith" found in Jayber's professors. They could not minister to Jayber because they had never considered his questions. Jayber's doubt leads him to abandon what he had perceived to be his call, in order to be open to his true calling, to be a barber, a member of the Port William community, and to love Mattie. Jayber also demonstrates the difficulty of faith. His honesty with the Bible creates difficulties for him, but they are the difficulties of faith ("And if He said not to pray in public, how come we're all the time praying in public?").[27] Love also means suffering. In his love for Mattie, at times he feels great joy and a welcoming of the "sacrifice."[28] At other times, however, faith is not "the assurance of things hoped for . . ." (Heb 11:1), but living in a desert with "no joy . . . no hope . . . Then I

---

[25] The Sunday of Thomas, *The Pentecostarion,* 75–76.

[26] Alan E. Lewis, *Between Cross and Resurrection,* 98: "There is a 'faith' which has forgotten what it is to doubt; a way of hearing which no longer listens to the silence; a certainty that God is close which dares not look into eyes still haunted by divine remoteness; a hope for some glory other than a crown of thorns."

[27] Berry, *Jayber Crow,* 53.

[28] Ibid., 247.

lived by faith alone, faith without hope." Suffering is one part of the "the law of undulation" according to C. S. Lewis.[29] Life is filled with "a series of troughs and peaks" that both the devil and God seek to use. In fact, God relies on the troughs more than the peaks since he wants to make "little replicas of himself" through the development of human free will. God "cannot ravish. He can only woo." The devil's cause then is in the most danger "when a human, no longer desiring but still intending to do our Enemy's will, looks round upon a universe from which every trace of Him seems to have vanished, and asks why he has been forsaken, and still obeys." Doubt is undoubtedly involved in those "troughs." Indeed, does not knowledge of God seem to be the most profound in both the deepest blessing and the darkest abyss?

The Vice of Doubt

Doubting God's Word

Despite all the claims for the virtue of doubt, the New Testament does not seem to acknowledge them. Jesus' teaching on the faith that can throw a mountain into the sea is coupled with the admonition, "and if you do not doubt in your heart but believe that what you say will come to pass, it will be done for you" (Mark 11:23). Doubt involves wavering and inconsistency (Jas 1:6; 2:4), and uncertainty of faith (Rom 14:23). The essence of doubt in the New Testament seems to be the doubting of God's word that he can do what he has promised to do.[30] Philosophical questioning is not the issue here, but insubordination, originating in the serpent's question in Gen 3:1, "Did God say, 'You shall not eat from any tree in the garden'?"[31] Here is no mere vacillation, but a rhetorical device seeking to create vacillation, yet founded on a plain denial.[32] The doubt

[29] C. S. Lewis, *The Screwtape Letters and Screwtape Proposes a Toast* (New York: Macmillan, 1972), 37–39.

[30] F. Büchsel, *"diakrinō"* in *TDNT,* 1: 947.

[31] D. J. Tidball, "Doubt," in *New Dictionary of Theology,* eds. Sinclair Ferguson, David F. Wright, J. I. Packer (Downers Grove, Ill.: InterVarsity Press, 1988), 209.

[32] J. S. Feinberg, "Doubt," in *Evangelical Dictionary of Theology,* ed. Walter A. Elwell (Grand Rapids: Baker, 1984), 333.

was planted in the woman. The goal was to place vacillation in the mind of Eve, to make her of "two minds" (the Latin word *dubito,* the root of "doubt").[33] Such a hesitation is seen later with Peter's lack of faith during the storm at sea (Matt 14:31).[34] Jesus, having to rescue Peter from drowning, does not mince words: "You of little faith, why did you doubt?" Even after the resurrection of Jesus, some worshipped him, "but some doubted" (Matt 28:17). There is no commendation for such a doubt. Kierkegaard cites Hamann's exhortation that doubt should be dismissed with a simple, "Bah!"[35] Like Barth's view of evil, doubt has no right to exist and is to be dismissed with scorn. Its presence should be viewed as an "embarrassment" by the Christian since it questions God and therefore the very motive for theology.[36] Its root is in the estrangement between God and humanity.

Why is doubt to be dismissed so readily and with such scorn? Because, it is argued, its character is only evil, an evil that is tricky and full of guile like the serpent. Kierkegaard at one place can speak of doubt as "sly and guileful, not at all loudmouthed and defiant," crafty in its suggestions to Adam and Eve.[37] Yet in another place Kierkegaard will grant a "vociferousness" to doubt because it has nothing else to offer since it has no being or essence.[38] Either way, doubt comes in for an unqualified condemnation from the Dane. Doubt is dishonest; not really allowing doubt to be doubted, just as one rarely sees someone who writes humbly about humility![39] Whereas some might claim that the suffering of doubt creates spiritual maturity, Kierkegaard views doubt as placing a question before the necessity for hardship in the Christian life.[40] Doubt wants to

---

[33] Macgregor, "Doubt and Belief," 425.
[34] Alister E. McGrath, *Doubt: Handling It Honestly* (London: InterVarsity, 1990), 30.
[35] Søren Kierkegaard, *Stages On Life's Way,* ed. and trans. Howard V. Hong and Edna H. Hong (Princeton: Princeton University Press, 1988), 92.
[36] Barth, *Evangelical Theology,* 124.
[37] Søren Kierkegaard, *Eighteen Upbuilding Discourses,* ed. and trans. Howard V. Hong and Edna H. Hong (Princeton: Princeton University Press, 1990), 41.
[38] Søren Kierkegaard, *Kierkegaard: Letters and Documents,* ed. and trans. Henrik Rosenmeier (Princeton: Princeton University Press, 1978), 143.
[39] Søren Kierkegaard, *Judge for Yourself!* in *For Self-Examination and Judge for Yourself!,* ed. and trans. Howard V. Hong and Edna H. Hong (Princeton: Princeton University Press, 1990), 119.
[40] Søren Kierkegaard, *Upbuilding Discourses in Various Spirits,* trans. Edna H. Hong (Princeton: Princeton University Press, 1993), 296.

keep us from the joy of the only certainty: that we are to suffer, by suggesting that the road of discipleship can be walked without suffering. Jayber Crow's crisis with Jesus' prayer in Gethsemane raises that question as well. If Jesus' prayer that the cup be taken from him was not answered, then what of us? We, too, must suffer. At that time, Jayber could not preach that message, so he gave up his call to be a preacher. But he will suffer, suffer in his love for Mattie, yet have the joy of certainty in suffering of which Kierkegaard speaks. For Jayber to continue to doubt would rob him of that suffering love (Is this the risk of love?).

The tragic irony of doubt is that though its very nature prohibits any certainty, yet it espouses its only reason for existing is the quest for certainty![41] Humility has become inverted in the modern world, according to Chesterton.[42] One used to be doubtful about oneself and possess convictions about the truth. The opposite has now occurred. The contemporary person (particularly in a postmodern sense) is certain about one's own convictions yet not so with any objective truth. But can doubt ever lead on to the truth? Is not methodological doubt, the legacy of Descartes, a *cul de sac*? The God that can be doubted is a God that can be destroyed by doubt, an option that was never made available to the people of Israel or the Church of the New Testament. Doubt, as such, is only technically distinct from unbelief. The minute one doubts, the minute one asks the question of *possibility,* one surrenders the *actuality* of God. So it is not surprising that doubt may grow from such sins as impatience or apostasy.[43] Clarence Wilmot's wife, in Updike's *In the Beauty of the Lilies,* is still a believer although her pastor husband has forsaken the faith.[44] She views him as selfish since he did not simply brush aside his doubts and get along with life. She would like Ray Anderson's father, a life-long South Dakota farmer, in Anderson's telling of their periodic tending of the cemetery graves.[45] His father's conversations during that time were only

---

[41] Søren Kierkegaard, *Concluding Unscientific Postscript to Philosophical Fragments,* Vol. 1, ed. and trans. Howard V. Hong and Edna H. Hong (Princeton: Princeton University Press, 1992), 335.

[42] G. K. Chesterton, *Orthodoxy* (Garden City, N.Y.: Image, 1959), 31. See also Os Guinness, *In Two Minds* (Downers Grove, Ill.: InterVarsity, 1976), 126.

[43] Guinness, *In Two Minds,* 283–84.

[44] Updike, *In the Beauty of the Lilies,* 350–51.

[45] Ray S. Anderson, *Unspoken Wisdom: Truths My Father Taught Me* (Minneapolis: Augsburg, 1995), 111–12.

in the form of questions, not expecting any answers, but reciting the history of the community: "Yes, and here is the two-year-old Peterson boy. He was kicked in the head by a cow and died that very night." But there was no accusation, anxiety, or complaint here. "Death and God were the two subjects never questioned. Both were assumed to be beyond doubt and therefore, beyond question." Was he just a typical inexpressive male? Or did Anderson's father realize how futile and unnecessary doubt is? (Perhaps our ever-growing separation and alienation from the rural lifestyle is contributing to our increasing pathology of doubt.)

False Views of Faith

The presence of doubt, it is argued, also reveals the shallowness, inadequacy, and falsity of our ideas of faith. It seems that we have yet to learn from Karl Barth's critique of "religion as unbelief."[46] Our views of faith are shallow because our views of unbelief are inadequate, not including religion as the attempt of humanity to create its own god, a temptation that Christianity as well can fall into. "In religion man bolts and bars himself against revelation by providing a substitute, by taking away in advance the very thing which has to be given by God."[47] A substitute has been made. The vicarious humanity *of Christ* has been replaced by the vicarious humanity *of religion*.

Faith is demonstrated by action, an action that doubt is unable to make. Wallowing in its vacillation, doubt might refuse to stop a murder because it might be justifiable homicide.[48] The moral consequences of the lack of faith demonstrate how one cannot afford the luxury of doubt in real life.

One certainly has reasons to doubt the very meaningfulness of the world. Randomness and waste abound in nature and history. Nihilism seems to be a most natural philosophy.[49] The only Christian affirmation of the world comes from a Higher Source, outside of our consciousnesses,

[46] Barth, *CD,* I/2, 297–324.
[47] Ibid., 303.
[48] James, "The Sentiment of Rationality," in *The Will to Believe and Other Essays in Popular Philosophy,* 109.
[49] Barth, *CD,* III/1, 346.

a source that has spoken to us. If so, then doubt should be forbidden. To doubt would be to ignore the Word spoken to us, the Word of God's self-revelation in Jesus Christ that challenges and confronts our ideas.[50] From a philosophical point of view, perhaps Descartes was right to question the existence of the world, as silly as the beginning philosophy student thinks that is. Yet the Christian must affirm the world, along with God, without doubt. This is true faith and obedience, an "echo and response" to the Creator's self-disclosure.[51] Faith recognizes our total incapacity for knowledge and therefore cannot begin to entertain doubt seriously without becoming a fool.[52]

The true nature of faith is not based on certainty, but anxiety and paradox, it is argued from a Kierkegaardian perspective. The story of Abraham and Isaac is a story of terror, the terror in trusting God although God even seems to command what is immoral. Abraham is no hero, no "knight of infinite resignation," doing the right, heroic thing, but he is a comic figure, taking Isaac up Mount Moriah to be sacrificed because of God's command (Genesis 22). Only in this way is he Kierkegaard's "knight of faith." There is no room for doubt here. If Abraham begins to doubt, then he never takes a step up the mount. "But Abraham had faith and did not doubt; he believed the preposterous. If Abraham had doubted, then he would have done something else, something great and glorious."[53] He could have plunged the knife into himself. Certainly he would have been applauded for this self-sacrificing gesture. But, Kierkegaard contends, that would not have been an act of faith. Faith involves the anxiety of the Abraham who loves his son yet is about to sacrifice him because of the command of God.[54] The young Jayber Crow is not able to live with the paradox of faith. He is motivated by the "fearful uncertainty" that he might miss the call of God and therefore makes a rash decision, just to be on the safe side.[55] His problem with the Gethsemane prayer is a problem with the paradox between the first part of the prayer of Jesus, "Remove this cup from me," and the second part of the prayer, "nevertheless, not

---

[50] Ibid., 348.

[51] Ibid., 349.

[52] Ibid., 350.

[53] Kierkegaard, *Fear and Trembling,* 20–21.

[54] Ibid., 28.

[55] Berry, *Jayber Crow,* 43.

my will, but thine be done." His doubt is that these two parts can be reconciled, the paradox of how we can ask God of things and still be resigned to his will.[56] The anguish in Jayber's doubt reminds us that doubt is not the benign experience that Paul Tillich seems to think it always is.[57]

Faith as paradox reminds us that faith must be grounded in itself, not on any outside criteria of reason, tradition, ideologies, feelings, or intuition. Doubt springs forth when faith ties itself to outside criteria, making itself liable to be criticized by reason, tradition, etc.[58] A false view of faith surrenders the freedom of faith to be grounded in that which is beyond itself, into that which it attests. Therefore, faith should be free from the anxiety that doubt produces. Certainty is not absent, however, since faith is grounded on the external Word of God, so doubt does not have a leg to stand on.[59]

The Vicarious Doubt and Faith of Christ

"Faith Seeks Understanding" vs. "Did God Say . . ."

Is doubt a vice or a virtue? We have presented two conflicting positions. Where do we go from here?

What if we went back to our Christology? Did Jesus' faith include doubt or was his faith utterly exclusive of doubt? How does his doubt and/or faith relate to our doubt and faith?

Perhaps one misunderstanding can be seen in the confusion between a faith that seeks understanding (from Anselm's famous saying, *fides quaerens intellectum)* and the cynical question of the serpent in Genesis 1, "Did God say . . . ?" The proper heritage of the great eleventh-century theologian is to explore the limits of faith but not to go beyond them.[60] In

Faith : Reason

[56] Ibid., 50–51.

[57] Frank Rees, *Wrestling with Doubt: Theological Reflections on the Journey of Faith* (Collegeville, Minn.: Liturgical, 2001), 97.

[58] Barth, *CD,* III/3, 403.

[59] Barth, *CD,* III/1, 350.

[60] Karl Barth, *Anselm: Fides Quaerens Intellectum: Anselm's Proof of the Existence of God in the Context of His Theological Scheme* (Pittsburgh: Pickwick, 1975), 21. See also St. Anselm, "Proslogium" in *Basic Writings,* trans. S. M. Deane (La Salle, Ill.: Open Court, 1962), 47.

contrast to this is the modern age that assumes the phenomenon of faith but really values going beyond faith into the achievements of reason.[61] Faith is elementary at best, superstitious at worst. At any rate, we must go beyond it, the modern world claims. This was not Anselm's agenda, although his subsequent use of reason was obviously profound. Going beyond faith assumes a certain critical stance that faith can be judged as wanting. The serpent's cynicism is not far behind.

If faith is not discarded for the sake of reason, then reason has a humility that confesses at times "I don't know" instead of "I know better."[62] Perhaps this is one way to understand the ignorance of the Son concerning the "day or hour" of the eschatological events (Mark 13: 32), a point of perennial trouble in upholding the deity of Christ. God has voluntarily restricted his knowledge in the person of the incarnate Son. The Son does not need to know, for in his humanity he possesses a faith that continually seeks understanding. The Son seeks understanding, as we know from his earliest days in the temple, where he was both "listening to them and asking them questions" (Luke 2:46), increasing "in wisdom and in years" (Luke 2:52). The Epistle to the Hebrews, indeed, speaks of the Son who "learned obedience through what he suffered" (Heb 5:8). Jesus' faith was the kind that sought understanding, in clear contrast to the skepticism and cynicism of one who abandons faith for a supposedly neutral objectivism.[63]

The Solidarity of Doubt in Love

As the one who "listened" in the temple, the one who "questioned" the Father, the Son is able to question us. His questions did not end with the temple. His very last question was, "My God, my God, why have you forsaken me?" (Mark 15:34), the cry of abandonment.[64] This is often

---

[61] Kierkegaard, *Fear and Trembling,* 7, 9, 122–23.

[62] Barth, *Anselm,* 27.

[63] See the criticism of objectivism in epistemology and science in Michael Polanyi, *Personal Knowledge: Towards a Post-Critical Philosophy* (Chicago: University of Chicago Press, 1958); and T. F. Torrance, "The Place of Michael Polanyi in the Modern Philosophy of Science" in *Transformation and Convergence in the Frame of Knowledge* (Grand Rapids: Eerdmans, 1984), 107–74.

[64] T. F. Torrance, "Questioning in Christ" in *Theology in Reconstruction,* 117.

cited as evidence that Jesus doubted, and therefore, doubt is essential to faith. But if one views this cry in a *vicarious* sense, it is a cry not just of Jesus but also on behalf of and in place of all humanity. Otherwise, such a cry is not remarkable. It is simply another poor soul crying Psalm 22:1. In a vicarious sense, however, Jesus is crying out for all of us, making our questions his own.[65] Here is the depth of *fides quaerens intellectum*.[66] There is a danger of the anguish of doubt, as we have seen. Doubt is not the cheery act of courage as Tillich suggests. It can be one step away from unbelief. Psalm 22:1 is dangerous to pray. There needs to be a strong prior faith in order to pray it. The difficulty of Jewish belief, especially since Auschwitz, is evidence enough. Jesus' faith enables him to pray the cry of abandonment for us and in our place. We are not able to pray it. It is too dangerous for us. Despair and then destruction can easily be the next steps. Only God can pray this prayer for us![67] (We have not left the deity of Christ behind.) Only God possesses the love that dares to embrace the doubts of doubting creatures through providing the faith they need in the faith of Jesus Christ.[68] Love does not fear doubt, Ray Anderson suggests, because love springs from reality not reason. The reality here is God's compassion and mercy, the outward manifestation of his inward trinitarian being (John 17:26).

Since God has taken up our questions, he can then begin to question us. Here is the beginning of genuine knowledge, not when we question the truth, but when the truth questions us, the supreme question being asked by Jesus to all humanity, "Who do you say that I am?" (Matt 16:15).[69] These are the questions that doubt cannot raise, for doubt is predicated on the sovereignty of the individual thinking, doubting self (Descartes).[70] Yet, the compassion of God will not allow our doubts to go ignored. He will take them upon himself on the Cross, not as an example of "deeper"

---

[65] T. F. Torrance, *Theology in Reconstruction,* 117.

[66] Ibid., 118: "In doing that [the cry of abandonment] Jesus not only determined for us in himself the true mode of religious and theological questioning but constituted himself as the very centre of reference for our questions about God."

[67] Ibid., 119.

[68] Ray S. Anderson, *Soulprints: Personal Reflections on Faith, Hope and Love* (Huntington Beach, Ca.: Ray S. Anderson, 1996), 72.

[69] T. F. Torrance, *Theology in Reconstruction,* 121.

[70] Ibid., 123.

faith, but as an act of mercy for our desperate condition. We are not left to even answer the questions by ourselves. Jesus himself is the answer to God. The vicarious humanity of Christ can become our humanity; his faith can become our faith.

This kind of faith is not triumphalistic. Like love, it is "not envious or boastful or arrogant" (1 Cor 13:4). It realizes that its proper service is to confess that it is "incompetent" to grasp its object.[71] Here is the "apophatic" theology of the Greek Fathers, language about God that realizes its limitations within a genuine knowledge of God.[72] This is portrayed strikingly in the contrast between the faith of Job and Job's friends. With all of his wrestling with God, Job does not try to defend him as his friends do.[73] They might be seen at first to be the faithful ones, but that is not the case. Job is the true witness to God because he does not cease to seek him; his is a faith that seeks understanding. The friends torture him by pretending to speak for God. Job does not speak for God, but he does bear witness of God in the midst of his struggles. Job realizes all too well (existentially!), that the task of theology is never completed.[74] We live "between the times." But that is not to be equated with doubt, as is often the case. The serpent in the garden is a theologian. He believes in God. But he is an evil theologian who tries to get humanity to doubt God's word.

Job is the witness of God that prefigures the perfect Witness of God, Jesus Christ, in his vicarious humanity.[75] Jesus bears witness to God and his goodness when we are unable to do so. This is the meaning of his history of solidarity with us; in baptism, temptation, by fulfilling the Law for us as a demonstration that the Law is made for humanity, not humanity for the Sabbath (Mark 2:27). His emotional solidarity reaches its crescendo with the cry of abandonment.

Did Jesus, then, doubt? No, not in the sense that doubt is contrary to absolute faith in the Father and his purposes. Yes, he did, in the sense that he took upon our doubt, our fallen human nature, in order to heal and

---

[71] Hilary of Poitiers, *On the Trinity,* II.11, NPNF, second series, Vol. IX, 55.

[72] T.F. Torrance, *Reality and Scientific Theology,* pp. 124–25; John of Damascus, *The Orthodox Faith,* NPNF, second series, I.2., Vol. IX, 1–2.

[73] Barth, *CD,* IV/3, first half, 457.

[74] Barth, *Evangelical Theology,* 121.

[75] Barth, *CD,* IV/3, first half, 368–433.

redeem it through solidarity with us. In a similar sense, Christ became guilty, not because he sinned, but because the Father "made him to be sin who knew no sin, so that in him we might become the righteousness of God" (2 Cor 5:21). He was, in Bonhoeffer's words, "guilty without sin."[76] *Stellvertretung* ("vicarious representative action" or "deputyship") is the word Bonhoeffer uses for the relation of the vicarious humanity of Christ to our discipleship.[77] A "deputy" does for one what one is unable to do for oneself. This has a plain representative and substitutionary flavor. Deputyship itself stands under the nature of the responsible life. In becoming guilty for us, Christ performed the responsible act of the deputy, doing for us what we are unable to do for ourselves. In a similar fashion, Christ took upon our doubt, taking it seriously (in contrast to Hamann's "Bah!") yet not giving it the stature that Tillich desires, in order to transform it by the faith and obedience of Christ, even through the depth of the Cross.

The Triumph of Faith Over Doubt

The vicarious faith of Christ provides a triumph of faith over doubt. The illness of the son compels the father to bring the child to Jesus (Mark 9:14-29). He admits, however that he believes and does not believe: "I believe; help my unbelief!" The man is of two minds, yet he does not revel in that situation. He wants to be delivered from his unbelief: "*help* my unbelief!" Doubt is not a virtue for him. Doubt, like evil, does not have being. Standing against the reality of God and the goodness of what God creates, doubt has no right to exist.[78] Yet he is not ashamed to admit his doubt. And Jesus is not ashamed to act on his behalf despite his doubt (and despite the disciples' inability to heal, v. 28).

Jesus' faith is enough, however, to be the foundation for the faith of those who follow him. He explicitly reprimands Peter, "You of little faith,

---

[76] Bonhoeffer, *Ethics,* trans. Reinhard Krauss, Charles C. West, and Douglas W. Stoff, 275.

[77] Ibid., 257–60.

[78] Paul Fiddes, *Participation in God: A Pastoral Doctrine of the Trinity* (Louisville: Westminster John Knox, 2000), 166.

why did you doubt?" when Peter's fear of the sea wind caused him to sink (Matt 14:31). In contrast to Peter is the faith of Jesus that enables him to walk on the water (Mark 14:25).[79] Here is a distinction between those of "little faith" that Jesus chastises (Matt 8:26; 14:31; 16:8; Mark 14:31; Luke 12:28) and the faith of a mustard seed, the smallest of the seeds, that Jesus commends (Luke 17:6; Matt 17:20; Mark 4:21). Ultimately, Jesus' faith defeats the doubt of the cry of abandonment with the victorious, "Father, into your hands I commend my spirit" (Luke 23:46).

What is Jesus' faith but a kind of certainty in the context of paradox? He is crucified as a criminal, seemingly abandoned by God, the just man who unjustly suffers, yet he goes to his fate with a determination of certainty ("The Son of Man must undergo great suffering, and be rejected by the elders, chief priests, and scribes, and be killed, and on the third day be raised." Luke 9:22). The certainty longed for by religious people of all ages takes a different twist with the Crucified Messiah. So it is not easy to simply condemn or recommend doubt. The paradox of the Crucified God is one who takes upon all of our sufferings, including our doubts, and triumphs over them by his faith, not ours. There is certainty in the faith of Jesus in that we can lean on his faith, not our own, for that certainty. If Jesus is wrong about God, heaven, resurrection, etc., then it is his burden, not mine! We can have a "paradoxical certainty" because of the certainty of the faith of the Crucified One. The foundation of that faith is the love of the Son for the Father through the Spirit. Why is it that in an age of uncertainty, doubt, and skepticism about everything else, the lover is certain about one's love? That may be irrational for us, but it may be a key to understanding the power of the certainty of Jesus' love for God that was demonstrated time and time again. "Here at last is a man who loves the Lord with all his heart and soul and mind and strength and his neighbor as himself."[80] He did not come to abolish the law but to fulfill it (Matt 5:17). His fulfillment is in doing what we have been unable to do: love God and our neighbor. In a similar vein, he has conquered doubt; something we try in vain to abolish through determined effort or rationalizing it as an essential part of faith.

---

79 Wallis, *The Faith of Jesus Christ in Early Christian Traditions,* 39.

80 Smail, "Can One Man Die for the People?," 87.

God as Advocate

More important than the question of whether doubt is a virtue or a vice is the question of what side God is on. This is the question about God. Job, however, does not answer it from a position of neutrality. He knows God, therefore he is able to complain: "Why is light given to one who cannot see the way, whom God has fenced in?" (Job 3:23).[81] The Lord will have his own criticism of Job (ch. 38), yet it does not compare with his criticisms of Job's friends ("for you have not spoken of me what is right, as my servant Job has," 42:7). Job's friends are confident that they are advocates of God's law of cause and effect: If Job is suffering, he must have sinned. The reader knows that is not the case. The friends are limited to their own knowledge.[82] Their advocacy is not of God but of their own circumscribed knowledge, some "timeless truths" abstracted from the living God. In contrast, Job appeals to the living God, even if there needs to be an advocate between the two ("There is no umpire between us, who might lay his hand on us both," 9:33). Job is no doubter, but one who seeks for an advocate. What he does not know is that God will become his advocate (even against God! . . . "My God, my God, why have you forsaken me?"). "We have an advocate with the Father, Jesus Christ the righteous" (1 John 2:1). Job is awaiting the coming of the Messiah. In this anticipation there is (dare we say it) both the presence and absence of God.[83] There is enough knowledge of God so that Job, and the rest of humanity, are without excuse (Rom 1:20). Doubt is not a necessity, but it does prey upon the paradox of God being present yet also absent, as seen in Job's experience. Job needs that Umpire, that Advocate.

Job's doctrine of God is in bad shape. The Christian message is not just one of redemption but also of revelation, revelation of the Triune God. This God will be a shock, however. He will be different from the Pure Power that Job expects or the Cold Judge of his friends. He will be Father, Son, and Holy Spirit, "one in essence and undivided."[84] Yet even

[81] Todd H. Speidell, *Confessions of a Lapsed Skeptic: Acknowledging the Mystery and Manner of God* (Eugene, Or.: Wipf and Stock, 2000), 45.

[82] Barth, *CD,* IV/3, first half, 458.

[83] Speidell, *Confessions of a Lapsed Skeptic,* 45.

[84] *The Divine Liturgy of Our Father Among the Saints John Chrysostom,* 111.

in the incarnation there will be a "presence within absence," for the glory of the kingdom of God has not come in all of its fullness. Christians still pray, "Your kingdom come" (Matt 6:10). This is not a sign of a defeatist Christianity but one that takes seriously the mercy of God towards those who suffer, including those who are suffering under doubt. Doubting, being "of two minds," is indeed a "presence within absence" existence. Without a doctrine of God that acknowledges that phenomenon, we can very easily throw people back upon their own resources: "Just have more faith!" No, the God who is in the midst of "presence within absence" is the God who can be our advocate in the midst of our trials.

Unbelief promotes a God who cannot be the Crucified Messiah.[85] Here is the first-century stumbling block to the Jews and folly to the Gentiles, "Christ crucified" (1 Cor 1:23). Unfortunately, Christians of all traditions throughout church history are tempted not to identify God with the death of Jesus.[86] But the key issue is whether or not God's love is deep enough to become one of us even unto death, even into our godlessness, coming as, in Alan Lewis' words, "a servant Lord, a guilty Judge, a wounded healer."[87] Otherwise, the Church surrenders to its critics that God cannot take on perishability and the desperate straits we have plunged so deeply within. Has God revealed himself in identity with the perishability of the man Jesus?[88] So the death of Christ should not be separated from the cry of abandonment. The timing of the cry and the death are too close, of course. The loneliness and desolation of the cry already begins with the disciples sleeping in the garden of Gethsemane (Mark 14:37), their abandonment of Jesus (Mark 14:50), Peter's denial (Mark 14:54ff.), and the mocking of the crowd as he is on the cross (Mark 15:29ff.).[89] At this point of forsakenness, and certainly at death, our philosophical, mythological, and folk ideas of God have no place to dwell. "How could God the infinite and everlasting, be one with so vulgar an

[85] Alan E. Lewis, *Between Cross and Resurrection,* 91.

[86] The early Fathers, such as Tertullian, were not as skittish about referring to "the passion of my God" (Ignatius, *Romans 6:3*) or the God who has suffered (Melito) as the later Fathers. See G. L. Prestige, *God in Patristic Thought* (London: SPCK, 1952), 76–78.

[87] Alan E. Lewis, *Between Cross and Resurrection,* 91.

[88] Jüngel, *God as the Mystery of the World,* 187.

[89] Gérard Rossé, *The Cry of Jesus on the Cross: A Biblical and Theological Study,* trans. Stephen Wentworth Arndt (New York: Paulist, 1987), 64.

expression of carnality and time as the *buried* man of Nazareth?"[90] Alan Lewis adds that this is why we ignore Easter Saturday, the burial of Jesus. But a God who can take on death is also able to take on doubt. And he does this from the side of humanity. He is faithful and "obedient to the point of death—even death on a cross" (Phil 2: 8).

Our doubts remain; not only about God, but also about ourselves and the world. But they remain only as we are also continuing to pray, "Thy kingdom come," the only real response we should have to doubt according to Karl Barth.[91] Most of all, it is Jesus himself who continues to pray, "Thy kingdom come." In solidarity with us, Christ offers our prayers, such as the cry of abandonment, to the Father, along with our desires, including our desire to be delivered from doubt.[92] The one who offers our prayer for deliverance from doubt is well acquainted with undulation, the troughs and the highs, the one who lives "presence within absence" in a world "between the times." Jesus doubts, yet without sin, for he takes our doubts and faithfully presents them to the Father. He is God the Advocate in his vicarious humanity. As Advocate "he cannot ravish. He can only woo."[93] Our doctrine of God is affected radically by the God who becomes our Advocate, so our view of doubt towards this God should change as well. (This will be the theme of chapter four.)

God our Advocate is the God of fellowship, of communion, expressed most of all at the Lord's Table. Communion speaks boldly of this "presence within absence" as his body and blood is broken for us (presence) and yet at the same time absent in that he is the ascended Christ who prays for us as our High Priest, continuing to share in our humanity, enabling us to participate in his thanksgiving (Eucharist) to the Father.[94] Communion is thus the power of the presence of God in the midst of his absence, such as can be felt profoundly in times of doubt.

Doubt is not necessary to growth in faith, although God may use it thus in his freedom, as he brings good things out of the most horrendous evils. That never justifies the evil, however. Interestingly, both Barth and Tillich, despite their distinctive views on doubt, view faith as believing

[90] Alan E. Lewis, *Between Cross and Resurrection*, 92.
[91] Barth, *Evangelical Theology*, 125.
[92] James Torrance, *Worship, Community, and the Triune God of Grace*, 46.
[93] C. S. Lewis, *The Screwtape Letters*, 38.
[94] James Torrance, *Worship, Community, and the Triune God of Grace*, 87.

"in spite of" appearances and circumstances, in the spirit of Heb 11:1: "Now faith is the assurance of things hoped for, the conviction of things not seen." For Barth, "Christian faith" is "the gift of the meeting" between God and humanity in Jesus Christ, "the word of grace" heard "in spite of all that contradicts it."[95] Tillich also believes "there is no faith without an intrinsic 'in spite of . . .'."[96] Doubt is a vice, but it can be used by God, for just as only a believer has a "problem of evil," because one believes in a good and all-powerful God, so also God, through Christ, may transform our hesitations into his full-flowered faith.[97] Despite himself, "the disbelief of Thomas" can become "the mother of belief for us."[98] Again, this is still not to say that doubt is *necessary* for faith. The perfect faith and obedience of the Son of God argues against that. Yet, the "in spite of" is the sign of the grace of God.

The certainty of the paradox in the Crucified Messiah takes our doubt in the context of his faith, even revealing the true nature of the transcendence of God, as Ray Anderson suggests. The twin prayers of one, abandonment ("My God, my God, why have you forsaken me?"), and two, commitment ("Father, into your hands I commend my spirit"), both reveal the nature of the transcendence, or distinctiveness of God, "that prayer is possible from the 'far side' of estrangement, as well as from the 'near side' of intimacy."[99] We need to be careful not to be offended by God using our doubt. Jesus is, as Anderson says, "the Man who is for God," who, nonetheless, "utters the God-forsaken cry," creating the perfect response to God's covenant with humanity.[100]

The vicarious doubt of Christ that takes upon our doubt is released into the vicarious faith of Christ. Who the God is that Christ has faith in will continue to be important to us: in our knowledge of him, in what his nature is, and in his actions towards us in a world of evil and suffering (chapters three through five).

---

[95] Barth, *Dogmatics in Outline,* 15.

[96] Tillich, *Dynamics of Faith,* 21–22.

[97] On the problem of evil, see T. F. Torrance, *Divine and Contingent Order* (Oxford: Oxford University Press, 1981), 113–28.

[98] The Sunday of Thomas, *The Pentecostarion,* 75–76.

[99] Ray S. Anderson, *Historical Transcendence and the Reality of God* (Grand Rapids: Eerdmans, 1975), 178.

[100] Anderson, *Historical Transcendence and the Reality of God,* 175.

3

Jesus Knows God For Us and In Our Place

For you know the grace of our Lord Jesus Christ,
that though he was rich, yet for your sakes he
became poor, so that you through his poverty
might become rich.
2 Cor 8:9 (NIV)

He himself gave up his own Son as a ransom for us—
the holy one for the unjust, the innocent for the guilty,
the righteous one for the unrighteous, the incorruptible
for the corruptible, the immortal for the mortal. For
what could cover our sins except his righteousness? In
whom could we, lawless and impious as we were, be
made righteous except in the Son of God alone? *O
sweetest exchange!* O unfathomable work of God! O
blessings beyond all expectation![1]
Epistle to Diognetus (c. 200)

[1] *Epistle to Diognetus* 9 in *Early Christian Fathers,* ed. Cyril C. Richardson (New York: Macmillan, 1970), 220–21 (emphasis mine).

How powerful, and even lovely, is the sentiment expressed here in this early Christian writing, *The Epistle to Diognetus,* concerning the atonement of Christ. Reflecting the biblical teaching on ransom and redemption (2 Cor 8:9; Mark 10:45; 1 Tim 2:6; Tit 2:14; Rom 5–8), this early Christian sees the heart of the matter: Becoming like us, we now become as Christ; we share in his blessings.

However, often these blessings are simply restricted to removal of guilt. What about our problem of doubt? How does the atonement of Christ affect our doubting selves? How does the atonement affect our very knowledge of God? Here is, once again, where the vicarious humanity of Christ becomes fruitful. The gospel proclaims that Jesus knows God, on our behalf and in our place. There is a vicarious *knowledge* of Christ as well as a vicarious *atonement* of Christ.

Since Jesus knows God and we can participate in his knowledge of God we can go beyond doubt as only a problem in a skeptical, postmodern age. Many questions may be raised about the historical Jesus, but it is hard to doubt that Jesus believed in God and in his special relationship with him (Matt 11:25-27). This may be just enough for us. A "sweet exchange" has taken place, not just in terms of the righteous for the unrighteous, but of the one who knows God for the ones who do not know God. Jayber Crow the "lost traveler" is progressively replaced in the novel by Jayber Crow the man who is called to love and to have faith. A sweet exchange is taking place throughout the story of Jayber Crow. Here is what is needed for our doubt: something this deep and far-ranging, at the level of our being. This sweet exchange speaks of both *boundaries and limits* of the knowledge of God, because we begin with our ignorance of God (Acts 17:23), as well as the *frontiers and horizons* of the knowledge of God, because we may now participate in the Son's knowledge of God (John 17:25).

The "Sweet Exchange": Boundaries and Limits in the Knowledge of God

Limits to Our Knowledge: Ignorance and Sin

The "sweet exchange" is needed because from our side there is no knowledge of God. Despite the tradition of natural theology, we are "without hope and without God in the world" (Eph 2:12, NIV). We live in ignorance, even (and maybe particularly) if we are religious. The postmodern critique is too strong: The multiplicity of religious viewpoints speaks loudly of the cultural and social origins of religion. Even those of most fervent faith believe so often from an abysmal ignorance, such as the college English student I heard of who described her "born *against*" (!) religious experience in her term paper. The nature of faith itself seems to speak of that which is theoretically possible not to be true. Doubt cannot be far behind.[2] The voices of Hume, Russell, and other modern philosophers have long reminded us of how ignorant we really are of God. The vast expanse of knowledge (made even more frustratingly accessible by the information age) only reminds us of how little we know. Simply on an informational level we are very little beings. At the beginning of the scientific revolution, Pascal saw humanity as only "blind" and "wretched" before "the whole silent universe":[3]

> When I see the blindness and the wretchedness of
> man, when I regard the whole silent universe, and
> man without light, left to himself, and, as it were,
> lost in the corner of the universe, without knowing
> who has put him there, what he has come to do,
> what will become of him at death, and incapable
> of all knowledge, I become terrified . . .

Humility, regarded as a virtue when it comes to knowledge, is just a reminder of our ignorance. He was a humble man, Churchill is reported to have said about someone, because he had much to be humble about! Is not this true of the entire human race, when it comes to knowledge of God? If we are humble, we will admit the multiplicity of motives that go into our religiosity: acceptance, security, ethnic connection, etc. We do not have to sneer at the beliefs of others. We can look at ourselves. We are our own worst enemies.[4] Like Sarah's womb, we are barren. Our religions often seek more for power and status than service and worship. Our

---

[2] James, "The Sentiment of Rationality" from *The Will to Believe,* 90.
[3] Pascal, *Pensées,* 198. See also Taylor, *The Myth of Certainty,* 10.
[4] Barth, *The Epistle to the Romans,* 506.

relationships are smothered in idealism and romanticism about the beloved, threatening to obscure the knowledge of the real person. Jayber is at least honest in facing that question concerning his knowledge of Mattie. Yet love is fickle. Feelings change. "I've changed and you haven't," the bored spouse says to the discarded partner. The passionate love affair of two movie stars who wear a vial of their blood mixed together soon disintegrates. The human heart is hard to know and hard to trust.

Ignorance is difficult to admit. Who wants to say, "I don't know" when one wants to be respected? The remarkable feature of Jayber Crow's professor Ardmire is his willingness to set Jayber free to admit his ignorance and go forth on a journey that will take maybe more than his lifetime.[5] He possesses questions to which answers cannot quickly be given. He will have to "live them out—perhaps a little at a time." Jayber will have to be patient, a much neglected virtue in our age.[6] He will have to live with his limits, live with being ignorant. Like Moses before Pharaoh, Jayber needs to realize his powerlessness, that he starts from "nothing," an *ex nihilo,* as Ray Anderson explains.[7] An "exchange" is needed because of our ignorance. But that *ex nihilo* is created by the Word of God, whether it comes to Abraham, Moses, or us. Abraham faces the death of his own possibilities when Ishmael was refused as God's choice (Genesis 17). No, God's promise would come through the barrenness of Sarah.[8] "The grace of God must kill before it can make alive."[9] Why are we surprised and shocked by this statement of Ray Anderson's? In a lighter vein, one might remember the advice of the great American theologian Clint Eastwood, "A man's got to know his limitations!"

Recognizing our ignorance about God is not just a modern invention of the "masters of suspicion" like Marx, Nietzsche, and Freud.[10] Biblical religion makes it plain that humanity's ignorance of God is reflected in its idolatry, creating its own gods (Isa 44:9-20; Jer 10:1-16).[11] The teaching

---

[5] Berry, *Jayber Crow,* 54.

[6] See David Baily Harned, *Patience: How We Wait Upon the World* (Cambridge: Cowley, 1997).

[7] Anderson, *The Soul of Ministry,* 35–42.

[8] Ibid., 46.

[9] Ibid., 47.

[10] See David Tracy, *The Analogical Imagination: Christian Theology and the Culture of Pluralism* (New York: Crossroad, 1981), 53.

[11] Barth, *CD,* I/2, 303–7.

of the Reformation also declares that there is nothing we can bring to God to establish a relationship with him.[12] Why do we assume that our minds are in harmony with the mind of God? Whatever similarities there are between God and humanity ("the image of God"), there needs to be *some* distinction between the Creator and the creature! The sin of humanity only exacerbates this chasm.[13] Someone needs to take our place in knowing God.

Love reveals our ignorance, paradoxically, and then the reality of our limits comes crashing down upon us. This was true of some of the disciples who "disbelieved for joy" when they saw the risen Lord (Luke 24:41). What is going on here? We can understand disbelief. We can understand joy. But how can they respond with both? Perhaps they want to believe but are so fearful of disappointment.[14]

The disciples might have been expressing the fear of love. Loving someone opens one to the risk of disappointment, so doubt and hesitation about one's love, or about the possibility of that love being returned, can creep in. Love weakens, wanes, and then disappears. This barrenness leaves us lonely. Love involves both pain and risk, as Hosea demonstrates. Hosea's unfaithful wife mirrors the unfaithfulness of Israel to Yahweh (Hos 11:1-3).[15] Israel's unfaithfulness reveals her ignorance of the depth of God's love that will not leave her even when she strays. God suffers the pain of risking the rejected of the beloved, yet his love is not thwarted. Still, genuine love is not coercive. "Knowing one's neighbour is inseparable from an attitude of non-possession."[16] The "empty hands" of faith are akin to the lover that has to admit that one can do *nothing* to force a beloved to love or to stay loving one.[17] Love, like Luther's view of faith, is a "passive righteousness." Bonhoeffer's words from prison ring all too true: "Life in a prison cell may well be compared to Advent; one waits, hopes, and does this, that, or the other—things that are really of no consequence—the

[12] William Stringfellow, *Count It All Joy: Reflections on Faith, Doubt and Temptation Seen through the Letter of James* (Grand Rapids: Eerdmans, 1967), 50.
[13] Colyer, *How to Read T. F. Torrance,* 93; T. F. Torrance, *Reality and Evangelical Theology* (Philadelphia: Westminster Press, 1982), 84–97; *God and Rationality,* 139–53.
[14] Os Guinness, *In Two Minds* (Downers Grove, Ill.: InterVarsity, 1976), 171–72.
[15] Fiddes, *Participation in God,* 165.
[16] Clément, *The Roots of Christian Mysticism,* 272.
[17] On the "empty hands" of faith see Barth, *CD,* IV/1, 631.

door is shut, and can be opened only *from the outside.*"[18] To be loved is out of our control . . . we can only wait and hope, ultimately, for God's grace and love.

Love, however, does not mean the obliteration of the individual. Our boundaries and limits are not overturned by embracing a pagan view of community in which one's individuality is seen to be inferior to the herd. Paul speaks of the incarnation as a *kenosis,* in which Christ "emptied *(ekenosen)* himself" (Phil 2:7). Countless volumes have been written asking what was it that Christ "lost." Did he surrender his deity, in fact? Or did he empty himself *into* humanity, demonstrating that his deity is a reality in the world of hurting people?[19] Some theories of spirituality tend to stress that Christian discipleship is simply renunciation, a *kenosis* of our individuality. This can sound more Buddhist than Christian at times. Kenosis does not mean a "self-renunciation" that is "a shrinkage of ourselves."[20] Our effort to destroy our individuality for the sake of the community actually becomes our desperate last attempt to assert our sovereignty. Throwing oneself into the herd is too common in the history of fascism, communism, and certain expressions of mysticism. Boundaries and limits to the knowledge of God mean that the individual has value. A boundary means, "This is your creaturely limitation." The obvious example of this are the limits set in the Garden of Eden (Gen 2:15-17). The boundaries and limits of human ignorance are demonstrated in God doing what humanity is unable to do, in Christ.[21] God goes where we cannot go (the vicarious humanity of Christ), so the human creature does not have to be the "one" sacrificed for the "many." That is Jesus' job! Christian discipleship is not simply being the hero who sacrifices himself for the sake of the many, but rather to have faith in God, despite its absurdity.[22] The former is John Wayne; the latter is Abraham.

---

[18] Dietrich Bonhoeffer, *Letters and Papers from Prison.* ed. Eberhard Bethge, trans. Reginald Fuller et al. (New York: Macmillan, 1972), 135.

[19] Anderson, *Historical Transcendence and the Reality of God,* 146–86.

[20] Contra Alan E. Lewis, *Between Cross and Resurrection,* 301.

[21] Alan. E. Lewis, *Between Cross and Resurrection,* 431.

[22] See the contrast between "the knight of infinite resignation" (a heroic, courageous figure) and "the knight of faith" (Abraham about to sacrifice Isaac) in Kierkegaard, *Fear and Trembling.*

Ignorance becomes tied together with sin. There are none "who seek after God," the psalmist sighs. "All have gone astray" (Ps 14:2-3). If God's existence is based on Descartes' "I think therefore I am," is not this God simply another creation of the minds of humanity?[23] Such a willful action is reflected in our constant idol-making. So go the gods of much of the modern world. A god who is simply a reflection of our minds is not the living God. Who is to say that we postmoderns are not without our own idols? These idols begin with our abstract, generalized ideas of God disconnected from God's covenant relationship in Israel culminating in Christ. Job's friends are good examples of pious people whose knowledge of God is limited by their "timeless truths" about God.[24] If Job is suffering, Job must have sinned. That is their "timeless truth." Their God is merely an Architect, Guarantor and Executor, the subject of clichés, but not the God whom Job wrestles with and complains to because he is the living God in living, fresh encounter with Job. Boundaries and limits to our knowledge of God begin with the *ex nihilo,* recognizing our "nothingness," our incapacity for knowing God, even what we "worship in ignorance" (Acts 17:23). Ultimately, such creations of the Cartesian thinking mind simply remind us of our loneliness, cut off from history, tradition, and others.[25] The emotional impact of such ignorance and sin can be devastating.

A "self-demonstration" of God is needed. Such a "self-demonstration" will not be satisfied with only a thundering Word from above, but also a faithful response from below. Knowledge of God is not possible without reconciliation with God.[26] What is true for atonement will also be true for knowledge of God. We are not far here from the vicarious humanity of Christ.

The "self-demonstration" of God in Jesus Christ affects us through the baptism of Jesus, a vicarious baptism that we participate in through our baptism. Paul has to remind the Romans that they were buried with Christ through baptism into Christ (Rom 6:3,4).[27] They have fallen back

---

[23] Barth, *CD,* III/1, 360.

[24] Barth, *CD,* IV/3, first half, 458–59.

[25] Jüngel, *God as the Mystery of the World,* 116–26.

[26] T. F. Torrance, *The Mediation of Christ,* 25–26, 79. See also Colyer, *How to Read T. F. Torrance,* 109.

[27] Alan E. Lewis, *Between Cross and Resurrection,* 447.

into their previous ignorance, so they can perversely think that if they sin, grace will abound (Rom 5:20). The ignorance of our minds, our alienated minds, has been sanctified by the perfectly obedient mind of the Son.[28] Not only the soul and the will, but the mind is converted through the vicarious humanity of Christ.

Jayber Crow recognizes his ignorance: he becomes the self-described "lost traveler."[29] Not many of us are willing to be so honest with ourselves. Not only is he "lost," but Jayber also recognizes that he cannot avoid still "traveling," still making choices, still living life. He is going somewhere, but not knowing where (Abraham?). Is Jayber really that far, then, from being a man of faith, even at this point?

Perhaps Jayber is at least aware that not any answer, but an appropriate answer; not any response, but an appropriate response, is needed.[30] Recognizing "our nature's inability to gain life . . . [God] showed the Saviour's power to save even the powerless."[31] The knowledge of God is revealed most profoundly in the deepest blessing and the darkest abyss. No natural theology can create the appropriate response that comes purely *sola gratia* as the unique response of the Son to the Father, doing what we cannot do for ourselves.[32] The proper function of our faith, therefore, is to acknowledge its "incompetence" to comprehend its object, God.[33]

---

[28] T. F. Torrance, *Karl Barth: Biblical and Evangelical Theologian* (Edinburgh: T. & T. Clark, 1990), 231. See also T. F. Torrance, "The Greek Christian Mind" in *The Christian Frame of Mind: Reason, Order, and Openness in Theology and Natural Science* (Colorado Springs: Helmers and Howard, 1989), 1–16.

[29] Berry, *Jayber Crow,* 52.

[30] Colyer, "A Scientific Theological Method," in Colyer, ed., *The Promise of Trinitarian Theology,* 111. See also Daniel W. Hardy, "Thomas F. Torrance," in *The Modern Theologians: An Introduction to Christian Theology in the Twentieth Century,* Vol. 1 (Oxford: Blackwell, 1989), 77–79. T. F. Torrance acknowledges that "in and through all my stumbling word and acts, I rely on the crucified and risen Lord Jesus himself who is present fulfilling his own ministry." "Thomas Torrance Responds" in Colyer, ed., *The Promise of Trinitarian Theology,* 322.

[31] Epistle to Diognetus, 9.

[32] T. F. Torrance, *Karl Barth: Biblical and Evangelical Theologian,* 143.

[33] Hilary of Poitiers, *On the Trinity,* II.11, NPNF, second series, Vol. 9, 55.

Limits to Our Knowledge: Reason

Our barrenness, our inability to know God continues despite the presence of that most remarkable human facility: reason. The desire of many to possess certainty in religion is often tied to seeking a harmony between faith and reason. Valiant attempts have been made throughout the ages to establish reason as a means of at least some knowledge of God (Thomas Aquinas' "five ways" for proving the existence of God by reason alone), yet experience teaches us that the most valuable relationships are not limited by reason: relationships with a spouse, a friend, beauty, art, or nature all go beyond rational categories.[34] The poet wrestles for words to say things one does not yet understand.[35] Jayber Crow is not a study in the rational, scientific, technological man who develops a project in how to have perfect relationships with the earth, other people, and God! Quite the contrary. Jayber is encountered by grace as he proceeds down the lonely highway of the "lost traveler." In contrast to his college professors, Jayber does not see certainty as his god but takes the risk of love, with all the consequences.[36] Free to love, Jayber does not fear doubt since love is based on reality, not reason (Anderson). One aspect of Jayber's reality is Mattie, who opened up love in Jayber for the world and for God. His "relationship" with Mattie is certainly not "reasonable," and even questionable from an ethical standpoint. The fruit, however, is in the love. Falling in love is hardly a virtue in itself. The question is (as Screwtape slyly puts it) whether or not the love leads us to God or to the devil.[37] Being led to God does not mean blissful indifference to human love, as if *agapē* is opposed to *eros,* or that all human *eros* is ultimately subsumed by divine *eros.*

Jesus was "the man of sorrows, acquainted with grief" as well as the triumphant resurrected savior. So the presence of doubt is not the last word. God in Christ takes the doubt to himself. Yet we will never rid ourselves of doubt by seeking a false certainty or even "absolutes."[38] So certainty is a slippery category when it comes to God. As we have suggested, if we must speak of certainty it must be the certainty of the paradox. "It is

---

[34] Taylor, *The Myth of Certainty,* 70–71.
[35] Norris, *Amazing Grace: A Vocabulary of Faith,* 66.
[36] Taylor, *The Myth of Certainty,* 71.
[37] Lewis, *The Screwtape Letters,* 88–89.
[38] Taylor, *The Myth of Certainty,* 78–79.

not certain that it [religion] is," admits Pascal, and he adds, "but who will venture to say that it is certainly possible that it is not?"[39]

Reason's limits are discovered when we realize that the human mind is finite and interpretative (contributions of both modern and postmodern philosophy). There is no necessary connection between the human mind and reality.[40] A "sweet exchange" is needed between our limited minds of reason and the mind of Christ, a mind of faith in God the Father. The quest for certainty is admirable because one should be confident in what one knows of oneself, the world, or God. But the knowledge of the Son reminds us of a knowledge from within God, within the triune relationship of Father, Son, and Holy Spirit. Knowledge is possible when obstructions have been removed and the mind can participate in the reality of the object.[41] Genuine knowledge is communion, particularly of persons and the personal. Therefore, our knowledge of God begins by acknowledging the uselessness of taking refuge in some principle outside of *God's self-knowledge*, which we know only by grace.[42] We need to look away from ourselves, the last thing the priority of reason wants to do. Religious pluralism also pleas for a turn from an anthropocentric view to a "reality-based" center, yet how can one even speak of God as love if God in himself is unknown (a Kantian presupposition)?[43] A generic "lowest common denominator" such as love may bring unity to the study of religions and yet may beg the question of where is this love. In contrast, the truth of Christianity will always come from within God's self-revelation, otherwise the claims of unbelief have already won out.[44]

Skepticism, God, and the Dogmatism of Unbelief

The boundaries and limits of knowledge of God may immediately encounter the great wall of skepticism and unbelief. The certainty of all

---

[39] Pascal, *Pensées,* 69.

[40] Colyer, *How to Read T. F. Torrance,* 93.

[41] T. F. Torrance, *The Mediation of Christ,* 25–26. See also Colyer, *How to Read T. F. Torrance,* 109.

[42] Barth, *CD,* I/2, 357; cf. I/1, 196 and Alan J. Torrance, *Persons in Communion,* 27.

[43] See the discussion in Charles Hughes, "Pluralism, Inclusivism, and Christology," in Meyer and Hughes, *Jesus Then and Now,* 154–69.

[44] Barth, *CD,* I/2, 357.

knowledge, save mathematics, is questioned by many.[45] On a popular level, the comedian George Carlin is amazed that people are taught to believe in an "invisible man" when their everyday perceptions of reality argue otherwise. Why pursue something that might not be there?

Are we back to the risk of love? Jayber takes that risk with Mattie. He has no certainty he will bear any fruit from that love in a "normal" way. Mattie will not even know that he loves her. She might not return his love. Yet he still loves; loves as an action, an act of the will, unconditionally.

Jayber is aware of the gift and urgency of life that demands a choice.[46] Not to choose is a decision! The pragmatic necessity is a boundary and limit to the knowledge of God. There will be implications to belief or unbelief that are significant.[47] The skeptic about moral matters may have trouble ever admitting that a murder, not just a killing, has been committed, yet Pascal's wager is not dead.[48] We will live differently if we believe there is a God, afterlife, etc.

The question then becomes, We may *want* to believe, but do we have the *strength* to believe? A "sweet exchange" is needed. A "first step," a "preliminary faith," in William James' words, or a participatory knowledge that Torrance and Polanyi speak of is needed to believe.[49] Someone must take the first step in knowing God: "Jesus, the pioneer and perfecter of our faith" (Heb 12:2). Skepticism is not discounted out of hand because we do live in ignorance of God (Eph 2:12).The genuine skeptic, however, is open to the possibility of faith.[50] Grace reveals to one, not the mystery of whether or not to believe, the mystery of our responsibility, but the mystery of God, the God who is only known by grace.[51] The skeptic should be skeptical of religion since it is the fruit of unbelief, our attempt to create God in our own image, an attempt of humanity to have faith in itself. The true skeptic is skeptical of that deception as well as others. Because religion is unbelief we need the "sweet exchange," the knowledge

---

[45] Such as Bertrand Russell, cited in Macgregor, "Doubt and Belief," 428.

[46] Donald M. Baillie, *Faith in God and Its Christian Consummation* (London: Faber and Faber, 1964), 140. See also James, *The Will to Believe.*

[47] James, *The Will to Believe,* 20.

[48] Ibid., 109.

[49] Ibid., 25

[50] Eliot, "Introduction to Pascal's *Pensées,*" Pascal, *Pensées,* xv.

[51] Barth, *CD,* I/2, 314.

of the Father possessed by the Son in the Spirit, through the vicarious humanity of Christ.

The "Sweet Exchange": Frontiers and Horizons in the Knowledge of God

A Vicarious Way of Knowing

The boundaries and limits of us "lost travelers" in the search for knowledge of God are now evident. We need help. A "sweet exchange" of our lack of knowledge of God for the Son's knowledge of God is the good news of the gospel. Atonement and knowledge of God are wedded together in the vicarious knowledge of Christ. How is this to be done?

At the beginning of the *Philosophical Fragments,* Kierkegaard introduces a "thought-project."[52] His question is, "Can the truth be learned?" Socrates' "pugnacious proposition" in the *Meno* puts it well: How can a person seek to know something, unless he already knows it? "He would not seek what he knows, for since he knows it there is no need of the inquiry, nor what he does not know, for in that case he does not even know what to look for."[53] Socrates, of course, responds with the way of recollection as the answer. But Kierkegaard is interested in something else.

What does the learner need in this situation? The learner needs a teacher. And the kind of teacher one needs is particularly important. This teacher needs to be a "midwife."[54] As the traditional role of the midwife is to assist in the birth of the child, "drawing out" the child, literally, so also the teacher needs to assist the learner in "drawing out" the truth. The learner is not able to do this by himself. In fact, the teacher has a divine commission.[55] The god has told Socrates that he was not to give birth, but simply to deliver *(maieuesthai).* The maieutic relationship is the highest between one human being and another. To give birth belongs to the god.

---

[52] Kierkegaard, *Philosophical Fragments,* 9.

[53] Plato, *Meno,* 80e, *Plato: The Collected Dialogues,* eds. Edith Hamilton and Huntington Cairns (Princeton: Princeton University Press, 1961), 363.

[54] Kierkegaard, *Philosophical Fragments,* 10.

[55] Plato, *Apology,* 21–23b, 28e–30, 7–9, 14–16; *Theatetus,* 149–50c, 853–55.

The teacher himself is only an "occasion," because truth can only be discovered by oneself.[56] This is true even if the teacher is a god. In this process, the teacher must not only bring the truth, but also "the condition for understanding it." The learner is in dire straits. He needs help. The proper teacher, however, steps out of the way and only becomes the "midwife" of the truth. We need to realize this desperate situation. As Socrates explains in the *Phaedo,* we should not despair of seeking the truth. The truth is not the problem. *We* are the problem. It is our arguments that are not sound, not the truth.[57] But because of this situation we need help. This help is not found in attaching oneself blindly to a teacher, even to a Socrates, as Socrates himself teaches his disciples: "If you will take my advice, you will give but little thought to Socrates but much more to the truth."[58]

What earnest schoolteacher has not struggled with the difficulty of creating an environment in which learning truly takes place? What earnest teacher has not been frustrated in all of one's attempts to encourage learning? In my own experience as a college teacher, some of the most exasperating moments are when, after a week teaching on eschatology, some wide-eyed student will ask, "What is eschatology?"

What has happened? I try my best at repetition. That shouldn't fail. But even repetition can fail if the *condition* for learning is not there. If the student is so concerned with the instructor, the truth cannot be embraced. I need to be a midwife. I need to assist in the student's discovery of the truth for himself, so it is literally a "birth" of new knowledge that will change the student's life; just as a newborn changes the lives of one's parents.

In the same way, what parent does not feel the exasperation of repeated moral exhortations that go through one ear and out the other? Can a parent be a midwife of truth? Isn't there a limit to moral exhortation? Socrates realizes that with his students. So, in his questioning, he seeks to be the midwife, to draw the truth out of his disciples. Can a parent do the same? I think Socrates would say yes. What he is suggesting through his *maieutic* ("delivering") method is a *vicarious* way of knowing. It is vicarious in the sense that one is standing in the place of another, the teacher doing

---

[56] Kierkegaard, *Philosophical Fragments,* 14.
[57] Plato, *Phaedo,* 90e, 73.
[58] Ibid.

for the student what the student is unable to do for oneself. But notice! The vicarious teacher respects the integrity of the learner's humanity. The teacher is not satisfied with simply shouting cognitive, moral exhortations. One rather provides the "condition" by which the student discovers the truth oneself. Is not this what Christ has done for us? Indeed, the vicarious way of knowing provides the basis for our genuine knowing. Because Jesus believes for us does not exclude the imperative for us to believe! The "condition" has been provided so that we can discover the truth for ourselves. In our utter need and despair, the eternal Son of God, beloved of the Father, has revealed the Father (Matt 11:27). But that revelation was not shouted nakedly from the rooftops. The Son is the Word who was made flesh (John 1:14). He has assumed our fallen human nature so that we might participate in his exalted human nature (Phil 2:5-11). This is the "condition" Christ has provided for us. Therefore, we do not initiate our knowledge of God. We are not alone in our knowledge of God. A "sweet exchange" has taken place.

The Son's Knowledge of God as Faith

Christian faith is something different than simply pious hopes or sentimental feelings. Faith is not the opposite of knowledge, but is a kind of knowledge itself, "a firm and certain knowledge of God's benevolence toward us, founded upon the truth of the freely given promise in Christ, both revealed to our minds and sealed upon our hearts through the Holy Spirit" (Calvin).[59] In contrast to the false alternatives of either faith vs. reason (Tertullian) or faith and reason as "separate but equal" (Thomas Aquinas), faith's relationship with reason is better seen as not counter to reason but as "the illumination of reason."[60] Reason can now be set free, but not based on our faith. It has to begin with the faith of Jesus. Our faith is too fragile and too fickle. Not only does our faith need to be shaped by the faith of the Son, our knowledge of God needs to be shaped by that same faith. "The knowledge of God is the knowledge of faith" (Barth).[61] The uniqueness of faith as the means of knowledge of God is

[59] Calvin, *Institutes,* 3.2.7. See also Macgregor, "Doubt and Belief," 427.

[60] Barth, *Dogmatics in Outline,* 22.

[61] Barth, *CD,* II/1, 12.

demanded by the uniqueness of God.[62] This unique character is dependent on the knowledge that the Son has of the Father through the Spirit. Faith is fragile, yet the Son of God has taken our faith upon himself. "He places our faith in question."[63] Such a substitutionary work again goes far beyond simply paying the penalty for our sin. The cry of abandonment, "My God, my God, why have you forsaken me?," is in solidarity with our cries of abandonment, therefore we can say that our faith is established by the Son letting faith be taken from him (Barth).[64] We do not have to lose our faith! *Jesus has lost our faith for us!* As we have suggested, Jesus was perfectly faithful to the Father, yet took our doubts upon himself, so that doubt is not imperative for us anymore. "The necessary temptation of our faith has already taken place in Jesus Christ and . . . it is removed in Him."[65] Our faith is given to us. Here is a frontier and a horizon of faith, only made possible because "we must not only believe *in* the risen Christ. We must believe *with* the risen Christ . . ."[66]

What is the knowledge that Christ has in faith? It would be a mistake to simply limit it to the existence of God. "Even the demons believe—and shudder" (Jas 2:19). As knowledge of the Father through the Spirit, the Son's knowledge is essentially relational.[67] Beyond our speculations and flutterings about the existence and reality of God, the intimacy of the relationship between Jesus and God as Father *(Abba)* is immediate and profound.[68] The only God that Jesus presents to his disciples is the one who is his Father.[69] Christ has faith like Abraham (Galatians 3), yet his faith is different. Otherwise, why would the advent of Christ be necessary? Why not just imitate Abraham's faith?[70] Jesus is able to trust the Father in

---

62 Barth, *CD,* II/1, 14: "For although God has genuine objectivity just like all other objects, His objectivity is different from theirs, and therefore knowledge of Him—and this is the chief thing to be said about its character as the knowledge of faith—is a particular and utterly unique occurrence in the range of all knowledge."

63 Barth, *CD,* II/1, 253.

64 Ibid.

65 Ibid.

66 Ibid.

67 F. LeRon Shults, "Sharing in the Divine Nature: Transformation, Koinonia and the Doctrine of God" in *On Being Christian . . . and Human,* ed. Speidell, 112.

68 Thomas A. Smail, *The Forgotten Father* (Grand Rapids: Eerdmans, 1980), 30–46.

69 Guinness, *In Two Minds,* 270.

70 Richard B. Hays, *The Faith of Jesus Christ: The Narrative Substructure of Galatians 3:1—4:11,* second edition (Grand Rapids: Eerdmans, 2002). See also M.D. Hooker, *"Pistis Christou," New Testament Studies* 35 (1989), 321–42.

a way he did not trust the crowds who allegedly "believed" *(episteusan)* in him. Jesus refuses to "entrust" *(episteuen)* himself to them, "for he himself *knew* what was in man" (John 2:25, RSV). Epistemology and faith *(pistis)* are closely related![71]

Knowledge of God raises the hermeneutical problem: How do we interpret the Word of God? How dare we presume that we understand rightly? How dare that Jayber think that his love for Mattie is any more than just trying to satisfy an emotional and physical need? How do we interpret our feelings for another? How dare we speak of love . . . of another . . . or of God?

The Bible is enough of a hermeneutical conundrum for Jayber. The contradictory messages the Bible sends to Jayber become a catalyst for his doubt.[72] Instead of being able to blithely ignore the problems in the Bible, every time Jayber opens the Bible it sets off "a great jangling and wrangling of questions that almost deafened me."[73] The paradox of the Old Testament holy wars and Jesus' command to love your enemies simply becomes an inconsistency to Jayber, a challenge to any genuine knowledge of God. But it is Jesus' own prayer that is most troubling to Jayber. Jesus' prayer was refused. The cup was not taken from him. Jesus had to suffer, and so will we. How then can we have the strength to pray, "Thy will be done"?[74]

Where is Jayber going to find the strength? How will he know the will of God? Someone else needs to have the strength; someone else needs to know the will of God. Jayber is not able to live with the contradictions between the holy wars of the Old Testament and the command to love your enemies. But Jesus is. The Bible has no authority of its own. The Bible has genuine authority because Jesus reads it with us today (Anderson).[75] Knowledge of God, divine revelation, is essentially discovered

---

71 Shults, "Sharing in the Divine Nature . . ." in Speidell, ed., *On Being Christian . . . and Human,* 112.

72 Berry, *Jayber Crow,* 49.

73 Ibid., 50.

74 Ibid., 51.

75 Ray S. Anderson, "Real Presence Hermeneutics: Reflections on Wainwright, Thielicke, and Torrance with Some Implications of the 'Real Presence' of Christ in the Hermeneutical Task," *TSF Bulletin* 6, no. 2 (November/December, 1982), 5–7; "Practical Theology as Christopraxis: Hermeneutical Implications" and "The Resurrection of Jesus as Hermeneutical Criterion" in *The Shape of Practical Theology* (Downers Grove, Ill.: InterVarsity, 2001), 47–60, 77–101; "Does Jesus Think About Things Today?" in *Dancing with Wolves While Feeding the Sheep* (Huntington Beach, Ca.: Ray S. Anderson, 2001), 35–48.

in the humanity of Christ, the "real text" of revelation (Torrance).[76] Jesus is able to hold together our questions without nervously depending on an "Encyclopedia of Bible Difficulties" to resolve them!

The burden is ultimately on Jesus' "articulation of reality."[77] Such a movement should lead irresistibly to the worship of the Father by the Son ("I thank you, Father, Lord of heaven and earth . . ." Matt 11:25). Knowledge of God, faith, and worship all become wrapped in each other. Revelation is not just information about God, provided by the instrumentation of Jesus, but Jesus himself in his own knowledge, worship, and faith in the Father is the substance of revelation.[78]

The Son's Faith as Risk and Rest: The Vicarious Mysticism of Christ

The Son's knowledge of the Father through faith is relational, a relation of love. As such, with any relationship, there is an element of risk. Dare we say that if the Son is *homoousios* with the Father (the Nicene Creed), just as much God as the Father and the Spirit? Not only risk is involved, however, but rest. The faithful and obedient Son now rests, sitting at the right hand of God (Matt 26:64; Mark 14:62; Col 3:1). Jesus is the High Priest who has enabled us to enter God's rest, the rest that Israel was not able to enter into (Heb 3:11; 4:1-16). Such a relationship with the Father is so immediate and intimate that we may even speak of the vicarious *mysticism* of Christ. Therefore, there is a place for mysticism, if we begin with the mysticism of Christ, not our own or others' achievements.

The Son takes the risk of the knowledge of God, a risk that because of our biases and prejudices, our selfish motives for being religious, we would be unwise to take. We can only say that we have the true religion if Christ

---

[76] T. F. Torrance, *Theology in Reconstruction,* 138; *Reality and Evangelical Theology,* 93. See also the problem of rationalism in some versions of "verbal inspiration" and "consulting Holy Scripture apart from its centre" in Barth *CD,* IV/1, 368.

[77] Alan J. Torrance, *Persons in Communion,* 360.

[78] T. F. Torrance, *Karl Barth: Biblical and Evangelical Theologian,* 230. Ray S. Anderson, "Christopraxis: the Ministry and the Humanity of Christ for the World" in *Christ in Our Place: The Humanity of God in Christ for the Reconciliation of the World: Essays Presented to Professor James B. Torrance,* eds. Trevor A. Hart and Daniel P. Thimell (Allison Park, Pa.: Pickwick, 1989), 12–13.

takes our place.[79] The minute we leave Christ's faith, his risk, we can plunge into the abyss of either hubris and arrogance on the one hand, or uncertainty and doubt on the other. The doctrine of election, far from being a source of smugness and self-assuredness, should be seen as the end of our self-confidence: we are what we are in Christ solely by God taking the first step, choosing us in Jesus Christ.[80] "What is truth, if it is not this divine affirmation"?[81] The relational theme is evident here as well. Here is the basis of true certainty, the certainty of paradox that does not depend on our logical abilities. The certainty of paradox is the certainty that is established only as certainty is first abolished, such as in Barth's critique of "religion." For Barth, "the revelation of God" is "the abolition of religion."[82] Yet, as Geoffrey Bromiley observes, the German word translated "abolition," *Aufhebung,* can mean elevating as well as abolishing.[83] So Barth discusses "The Revelation of God as the Abolition of Religion" (section 17) under both subsections of "Religion as Unbelief" as well as "True Religion." Certainty can be viewed in a similar way. Certainty needs to be abolished in order to be elevated. God takes the "risk" of "abolishing" religion by becoming human, therefore destroying the wall between the "natural" and the "supernatural," the "profane" and the "sacred," the "this-worldly" and the "other-worldly," the only justification for religion (Schmemann).[84]

There is forgiveness of sins for our religiosity, then, because of the true faith and obedience of Jesus Christ.[85] Apart from this faith and obedience, our faith is simply a charade. With his faith and obedience we participate in the Son's human nature and are nourished by his body and blood in communion with him.[86] These are all relational realities. Without this relationship, the Church is in greater danger than any other religion,

---

[79] Barth, *CD,* I/2, 346.

[80] Ibid., 350.

[81] Ibid.

[82] Ibid., 280.

[83] Geoffrey W. Bromiley, *Introduction to the Theology of Karl Barth* (Grand Rapids: Eerdmans, 1979), 29.

[84] Schmemann, *For the Life of the World,* 93.

[85] Barth, *CD,* I/2, 355.

[86] Ibid., 356.

Barth argues. "It has its justification either in the name of Jesus Christ, or not at all."[87]

Since the Son takes the risk of faith, we can take the risk with him. With nothing more than "the faith of a mustard seed" we may simply work out the pragmatic effects of faith through what Dostoevsky calls "active love." This is the advice for doubt given by the elder in Dostoevsky's novel: "Try to love your neighbors actively and tirelessly. The more you succeed in loving, the more you'll be convinced of the existence of God and the immortality of the soul."[88] But isn't that our problem with faith? We want to believe and we can't. So also we may want to love and we can't. True, yet the risk taken by the Son gives us the freedom to use our will by simple acts of love. We are set free from "the bondage of the will" by the will of Christ.

"Do not waste time bothering whether you 'love' your neighbour; act as if you did," C.S. Lewis is famous for saying.[89] This can lead to affection, Lewis argues. So also, Kathleen Norris relates the response of the Orthodox theologian to the seminarian who has trouble affirming parts of the Creed.[90] His counsel is just keep saying it, and the belief will come. Perhaps, but one cannot help but think that an action or speech is not motivated by anything but duty until the affection or genuine faith arrives. And this arrives with Jesus, the pioneer of our faith. Christian discipleship is more than "The Little Engine That Could": "I think I can . . . I think I can . . ." Christ loves before we love. He takes the risk of love. Then we can enter with him into the practical movement and consequences of that faith and love. Faith is a risk, a wager in Pascal's sense that has pragmatic benefits. Yet it is not one that we are left to risk alone.

The faith of the Son is not only risk but also rest. The Son as the revelation of the Father (John 14) is not knowledge based on any other criterion than God's own initiative.[91] As a divine burden, not ours, it is meant to bring an end to doubt. There is genuine rest here in the divine burden that is born by the Son, a rest we can share in. Because his response is the response of a particular person, the particular is now affirmed in all

[87] Ibid.

[88] Dostoevsky, *The Brothers Karamazov,* 56.

[89] C. S. Lewis, *Mere Christianity,* 116.

[90] Norris, *Amazing Grace,* 65.

[91] Barth, *CD,* III/1, 365

of its diversity.[92] The temptation of mysticism to absorb all things into God can be avoided because God has provided the final "rest" in the faithful and obedient response of Jesus of Nazareth, an historical figure in space and time.

The vicarious humanity of Christ is the "sweet exchange" of God taking our *risk* so that we might participate in his *rest.* Jayber Crow's risk of loving Mattie creates the unusual rest and peace he feels about his life. Within the humanity of Christ is a *perichoresis,* a mutual indwelling of risk and rest unknown to us, based upon the *perichoresis,* the relationship between the Father and the Son through the Spirit. Like any deep relationship it involves the risk of plunging into it, not knowing all that is involved.[93] This makes sense then of the passages that speak of the Son's "ignorance" ("But about that day and hour no one knows, neither the angels of heaven, nor the Son, but only the Father." Matt 24:36 = Mark 13:32), despite the Fathers' resistance to any ignorance of the Son.[94] God takes a risk in becoming human, a risk of even voluntarily limiting his knowledge in the humanity of Jesus.

The relational nature of the risk and rest of the Son is reinforced when one recognizes that the dynamic between the Father and the Son through the Spirit involves the worship of the Father by the Son (Matt 11:25).[95] Thus, worship itself is not simply a reflection of subjective piety

[92] Fiddes, *Participation in God,* 209.

[93] Norris, *Amazing Grace,* 66.

[94] Dale C. Allison, "The Historical Jesus and Contemporary Faith" in Miller, ed. *The Apocalyptic Jesus : A Debate,* 148.

[95] Alan J. Torrance, *Persons in Communion,* 224–25. The issue of the worship of the Father by the Son was raised in the Christian East during the twelfth century. The obvious question is whether or not this invites the charge of tritheism. Eustratius, Metropolitan of Nicaea (c. 1114), had argued that the Son worships the Father, although he later recanted under the pressure of a synod in 1117. His genuine concern was to safeguard the humanity of Christ as "real and fully distinct from the divinity," although John Meyendorff believes that as a result he "had lost contact with the positive value of the hypostatic union." This controversy was later revised by the condemnation by two synods at Constantinople (1156 and 1157) of the teaching of the patriarch-elect of Antioch, Soterichos Panteugenos, who believed that the sacrifice of Christ was offered strictly to the Father and not to the whole Trinity. Meyendorff, in his criticism, expresses the nervousness of those who stress the unity of the divine and human in Christ at the expense of a genuine humanity that worships the Father and a reality of worship that does not begin with our response. This is in contrast, it seems to me, to the liturgies of

but a gift of God's grace.[96] There is a vicarious *worship* by Christ on our behalf and in our place. Here is the context for genuine *theosis* or *theopoiesis* (becoming like God) that can avoid the temptation of either being absorbed into God or denying our true humanity.[97] The Trinity is not just three "masks" God wears at different times, but three eternal Persons. These are persons in unity *(perichoresis),* yes, but we should not be afraid of the persons' distinct realities, such as the worship of the Father by the Son.[98] The entire Epistle to the Hebrews testifies to the importance of the worship by Christ as our great High Priest. As Chrysostom's liturgy proclaims, "It is he who offers and it is he who is offered."[99] The Eucharist becomes our participation in his once and for all offering.

Here we are deep into the vicarious *mysticism* of Christ. If the religious person has been judged, what should be the ideal for religious experience? Mysticism, defined simplistically as an immediate rather than mediated relationship of the one with the whole, should not be discounted easily. Mysticism does take seriously the relational and the intimate, the place where we can participate in that union between the Father and the Son through the Spirit (Eph 2:18). Also, the tradition of Christian mysticism particularly emphasizes the ineffability of God first of all, and ecstatic

---

Basil and Chrysostom cited by Meyendorff himself: "For it is Thou who offerest and art offered, who receivest and art Thyself received." *Christ in Eastern Christian Thought* (Crestwood, N.Y.: St. Vladimir's Seminary Press, 1975), 196–98. Meyendorff is not alone is his anxiety. I remember well at a ministers' conference several years again when my university sponsored a well-known evangelical advocate of worship renewal. After his lecture I suggested to him the liturgical, theological, and spiritual riches of the worship of the Father by the Son, particularly as advocated by James Torrance. His only response was, "Oh, that's Arianism."

[96] Alan J. Torrance, *Persons in Communion,* 314.

[97] Kenneth Paul Wesche paraphrases the classic patristic formula as, "God became human (without ceasing to be God) that humanity might become God (without ceasing to be human)." The parentheses, Wesche believes, emphasize what was assumed by the Fathers because of the christological controversies. "Eastern Orthodox Spirituality: Union with God in Theosis," *Theology Today* 55 (1999), 1, 8, n. 1. One wonders, particularly in an age of New Age pantheism, whether a renewal of *theosis* teaching can maintain Wesche's qualification. The vicarious humanity of Christ provides a means to reinforce the teaching of *theosis* through our exaltation with Christ in which the vicarious element stresses the distinction yet relation between Christ's response and our response.

[98] Alan J. Torrance, *Persons in Communion,* 324.

[99] Schmemann, *For the Life of the World,* 35.

experiences only secondarily.[100] Such a view of mysticism directs us immediately to the knowledge of the ineffable Father by the Son alone (Matt 11:25-27).

I confess a genuine lack when it comes to a mystical experience. Emotional or spiritual ecstasy, a richly intimate union with God is not my usual experience. In a way I envy those who have such deep experiences. Is there something wrong with me because I do not have this experience (the same can be said for a charismatic experience)? The danger of a faith based on rationality is all too real for me.

But I am left with faith, "the assurance of things hoped for, the conviction of things not seen" (Heb 11:1; cf. Rom 8:24; 2 Cor 5:7), a faith based on the faith of the Son. The Son's mysticism can be vicarious even, for my sake and substituting for my inability to have such an experience.

The intimacy of the relationship of the Son with the ineffable Father is mystical, and can only be something given to us by grace. Therefore our knowledge of God will be checked and critiqued by the only one who brings together intimacy and ineffability: Jesus Christ. Such a christocentric mysticism maintains the concern of the Christian tradition of mysticism for apophatic theology, a theology that is "extra-logical," in Torrances's words, refusing to claim positive knowledge of God (*kataphatic*) apart from acknowledging what God is not.[101] Yet such a christocentric mysticism also avoids the problem of apophatic theology when it, in effect, can define God based on our ideas of what he is not, a subtle natural theology that can introduce a God who is all-powerful based on our ideas of power and bypass the christological indicative of knowing God. The Arians, Athanasius claimed, by calling God "the unoriginate," were defining God according to his works. " Piety and truth are therefore better served by describing God in relation to the Son and calling him 'Father' than by naming him in relation to his works alone and calling him 'unoriginate.'"[102]

---

[100] Ralph Norman, "Rediscovery of Mysticism," in *The Blackwell Companion to Modern Theology,* ed. Gareth Jones (Malden, Mass.: Blackwell, 2004), 449–84.

[101] T. F. Torrance, *Reality and Scientific Theology* (Edinburgh: Scottish Academic Press, 1985), 123–24.

[102] Athanasius, "Against the Arians," I.34, in Maurice Wiles and Mark Santer, eds., *Documents in Early Christian Thought* (Cambridge: Cambridge University Press, 1975), 30. See also T. F. Torrance, *The Trinitarian Faith,* 49.

Jesus' "mystical union" with the Father is also a critique of reducing the relationship between Christ and the Christian to only a "moral union' in which the sole relationship is that of the follower to the moral commander, whether it is Jesus or Hitler.[103] Mysticism can help us avoid the problem of reducing the union with Christ to only the imitation of Christ, especially in its cruder forms as in defining the Christian life by simply asking the question, "What would Jesus do?"[104]

In contrast, for Paul, the Christian life is to be motivated by a living union with Christ, living in the same place as Christ, a place found in daily living, not just mountaintop experiences.[105] Euodia and Syntyche are exhorted by Paul to "be of the same mind in the Lord" (Phil 4:2; cf. 2:5).[106] Paul would agree with Matthew that the place of Christ is wherever two or three are gathered in his name (Matt 18:20). Here is the "high" of the "low" Church!

The foundation of this experience with Christ is Christ's own experience. Christ's vicarious life of "mysticism," if you will, his unmediated relation to the Father, is given to us, for us, and in our place, representing us. Most of us are unable to become mystics. The mystical experience, as much as it is valued by some, is rare. We should not discount it, however, because we can participate in the mystical experience of Jesus. He is the mystic for us. We are brought to God to worship, adore, and serve, participating in the deep "Abba" experience of the Son, his immediacy

---

[103] James S. Stewart, *A Man in Christ: The Vital Elements of St. Paul's Religion* (London: Hodder and Stoughton, 1935), 165. Love in a relationship is moral, Stewart says, yet it is based on the "true inwardness and intimacy of this union." Our fear of both inwardness (Kierkegaard) and intimacy (Buber's "I-Thou") may have disastrous effects. (Stewart's book is a model of the integration of exegesis, theology, and pastoral sensitivity that once again deserves a wide circulation.)

[104] See also Daniel P. Thimell, "WWJD: What *Is* Jesus Doing?" in *On Being Christian . . . and Human,* ed. Speidell, 70–86.

[105] Stewart, *A Man in Christ,* 161–62. Stewart comments that extraordinary experiences were uncommon for Paul (2 Cor 12:1-2). Notice that it had been "fourteen years" since he had been caught up to "the third heaven."

[106] Ibid., 159: "It is as though he said to those two Christians who had unhappily become estranged 'Remember your common union with Christ.' Remember that it is not in two different spheres that your spirits are living: the two spheres coincide, there is but one, and it is Christ. Realize this and act on it, and your present differences will vanish. *In the Lord* you will agree."

and intimacy with the ineffable Father (Matt 3:17; 6:9; 11:25-27; Mark 14:35-36; Luke 23:46; Rom 8:15; Gal 4:6), a relationship that we have been unable to live (see the example of ancient Israel).[107]

Such an intimacy, without a lapse into pantheism, finds a welcome expression in medieval mystics such as William of St. Thierry (c. 1085–1148). For William, commenting on Mark 20:22, "to love and to fear God and to obey his commands is nothing else but to be one spirit with him."[108] This "one spirit" is accomplished through the Holy Spirit, creating a trinitarian basis for William's spirituality.[109]

The importance of such intimacy becomes corrupted, however, with the temptation to monism or pantheism such as found in some women mystics of the thirteenth and fourteenth centuries. The analogy between the intimacy of sexual love and the relationship of Christ and the Church is popular in various twelfth-century commentaries on the Song of Solomon, such as the sermons of Bernard of Clairvaux (1090–1153).[110] While seeming often to denigrate physical sexual love by seeking to replace it, the usage of the intense eroticism of the Song of Songs speaks powerfully of the possibility of passionate intimacy in union with Christ. With some women mystics, however, this developed also into a practical obliteration of the individual, merging into the being of God. "The madness of love," as Beatrice of Nazareth (1200–1268) calls it, seeks to break down the ordinary boundaries of consciousness and selfhood.[111] This is the "no-self" of the true God that is beyond human abilities to comprehend, a startling implication for the doctrine of God found in fruition in the

[107] Smail, *The Forgotten Father,* 39.

[108] William of St. Thierry, *De Contemplando Deo* 11, cited by Bernard McGinn, *The Presence of God,* Vol. 2: *The Growth of Mysticism* (New York: Crossroad, 1994), 265.

[109] William of St. Thierry, *De Contemplando Deo* 11, cited by McGinn, *The Presence of God,* Vol. 2: *The Growth of Mysticism,* 266; cf. James M. Houston, "Spirituality and the Doctrine of the Trinity" in *Christ in Our Place,* eds. Hart and Thimell, 48–69.

[110] Bernard of Clairvaux, *On the Song of Songs,* 4 vols. (Kalamazoo, Mich.: Cistercian Publications, 1971–1980).

[111] Bernard McGinn, *The Presence of God* Vol. 3: *The Flowering of Mysticism* (New York: Crossroad, 1998), 157, 174. See also 190, which cites Beatrice's powerful identity with Jesus on the cross: "My body will hang with your body, nailed on the cross, fastened, transfixed within four walls. And I will hang with you and nevermore come from my cross until I die—for then I shall leap from the cross into rest, from grief into joy and eternal happiness. Ah Jesus, so sweet it is to hang with you" *(The Wohunge of Ure Lauerd,* 36*).*

thought of Meister Eckhart (c. 1260–1327), in which the distinction between the Creator and the creature is obliterated.[112] So one must be purged even of the thought of God as Trinity and move into that which is "the Abyss," the "Source," or the "Silent Desert."[113]

The problems with this pantheism are obvious. But they are also instructive. They demonstrate how necessary a trinitarian-incarnational foundation is to spirituality.

What happens to the belief in God as Lord? Yet, can we speak of a *Christian* understanding of intimacy with God apart from lordship? Lordship can be spoken of in the context of union with the Christ who takes upon himself our humanity, not just a moral example, but also in a vicarious sense, for us and in our place. He expresses his lordship in this vicarious act, in this "sweet exchange" in which he receives as well as gives the knowledge of God. This is not the lordship of an arbitrary sovereign, but a lordship that grants us the grace of participation in the intimate union between the Father and the Son through the Spirit, the "condition" the Son creates for us (John 17:10, 18-23, 26; Eph 3:16-17). The vicarious humanity of Christ is absolutely essential in order to maintain both lordship and intimacy, not one without the other.[114] Intimacy without lordship

[112] Cyprian Smith and Oliver Davies, "The Rhineland Mystics," in *The Study of Spirituality*, eds. Cheslyn Jones, Geoffrey Wainwright, and Eduard Yarnold (New York: Oxford University Press, 1986), 317.

[113] Smith and Davies, "The Rhineland Mystics," in *The Study of Spirituality*, eds. Jones, Wainwright, and Yarnold, 318. The tendency for contemporary "New Age" thought to equate the evolution of the soul as a development of its divinity is criticized by Ray S. Anderson in *The New Age of Soul: Spiritual Wisdom for a New Millennium* (Eugene, Ore.: Wipf and Stock, 2001), 24.

[114] See also Barth, *CD*, IV/3, second half, 538: "As Jesus Christ speaks with man in the power of the Holy Spirit, His vocation is *vocatio efficax*, i.e., effective to set man in fellowship with Himself. For the gift and work of the Holy Spirit as the divine power of His Word is that, while Jesus Christ encounters man in it with alien majesty, He does not remain thus, nor is He merely a strange, superior Lord disposing concerning him in majesty from without. On the contrary, even as such, without ceasing to be the Lord or forfeiting His transcendence, but rather in its experience, He gives and imparts Himself to him, entering into him as his Lord in all majesty and setting up His throne with him." "Fellowship" is the operative word here for Barth, a fellowship that should not mean the identification of the follower with the leader. This is part of Barth's argument against mysticism (539). "Fellowship" also safeguards "the freedom of the human partner. Indeed, it is genuinely established and validated" (540). However, one might add to Barth that

means a God who is less than worthy of worship. Lordship without intimacy means a God who cannot understand the emotional experiences of being human, such as the love that Jayber has for Mattie.

Such a "sweet exchange "of the knowledge of God for our lack of knowledge of God is the act of God's grace. Grace is not simply the reality of salvation, but just as important for the knowledge of God. Just as we have no ability to save ourselves, so also, we have no ability to know the Holy One of Israel (Exod 3:4). As Torrance reminds us, the knowledge of God is neither based on nature (Roman Catholicism), nor on our own subjective piety (Protestant liberalism, and, I might add, American evangelicalism).[115] God provides the One from the human side who already knows God. This is an act of God's grace as much as salvation is.

The Son's Knowledge and Our Knowledge of God: "The Unassumed Doubt is the Unhealed Doubt"

Yes, the Son has knowledge of God. But do we have knowledge of God? It is one thing to speak of the mutual knowing between the Father and the Son through the Spirit. It is another thing to speak of our knowledge. And even if our knowledge is connected vicariously to the knowledge of

---

this is not only because of the lordship of Christ but also due to his vicarious humanity, his perfect faith and obedience lived on our behalf, in our place. Therefore, there is no place for us to stand in presumption of equality, let alone, identification with Christ. As Barth states, the union with Christ is not what the mystic often is tempted to see it as, that is, as "the product of work of his own skill" but "only as the creation of the call of Christ" (539). Barth's "call" should be developed, not just as a pronouncement by a sovereign lord, but as a command that is fulfilled by the commander himself, which even enables the follower to imitate him! See also Paul in Rom 7:15: "I do not understand my own actions. For I do not do what I want, but I do the very thing I hate." Our problem is not just ignorance of the right thing to do, but the problem of how to do the right thing. See Dale C. Allison, *The Sermon on the Mount: Inspiring the Moral Imagination* (New York: Crossroad, 1999), 170. Barth sees both mysticism and atheism as failed critics of religion, which can only be truly challenged by revelation. *CD,* I/2, 319–25. For Barth, Christian mysticism is always in danger of anthropocentrism, emphasizing putting ourselves to death spiritually, rather than the death that we already share in Christ's death. *CD,* IV/4, 16.

[115] T. F. Torrance, *Theology in Reconstruction,* 134.

the Son, is there a necessity for us to believe if the Son has already believed for us?

The Fathers are fond of speaking of the dynamic relation between the humanity of the Son and our humanity in their famous saying: "The unassumed is the unhealed."[116] So we may say the same about doubt. Our doubt needs to be healed and it can only be healed by the eternal Word of God assuming our humanity to the point of assuming our doubt: "The unassumed *doubt* is the unhealed doubt." Our doubt is healed, we suggest, when we participate vicariously in the knowledge that the Son has of the Father.

This knowledge is a two-way track: from the Father to the Son, certainly, but also from the Son back to the Father.[117] Human knowledge is not left up to our department. The first human knowledge is the knowledge of the Son. Thus possibilities of other sources of knowledge of God should be ignored; but not out of arrogance.[118] Quite the contrary, to pass them by is simply to allow people to go on their way. A refusal to encounter other positions seriously is not a matter of intolerance but of single-mindedness in looking to Jesus, the author and perfecter of our faith (Heb 12:1,2). We are too aware of our own feebleness to waste a second on possibilities or even to cast doubt on other possibilities.

The source of our knowing is not in ourselves but in the triune God.[119] There is no knowledge of God apart from his triune knowing. The relational nature of the knowledge of God again returns to us. The triune God communicates himself as the Word of God not contingent on our abilities but as an accomplished event in history.[120] So James encourages his readers to "welcome with meekness the implanted word that has the power to save your soul" (Jas 1:21). In contrast to this are those who see themselves in a mirror yet forget who they are. Such are those who are not "doers of the word" and "merely hearers who deceive themselves."

Jayber Crow refuses to divide hearing and doing of the word, yet at great cost. His knowledge of his love for Mattie is by faith, often faith

[116] Gregory Nazianzen, *Ep.* 101, cited by T. F. Torrance, *The Trinitarian Faith,* 164.
[117] T. F. Torrance, *The Mediation of Christ,* 7. See also Colyer, *How to Read T. F. Torrance,* 61.
[118] Barth, *The Epistle to the Romans,* 506.
[119] Shults, "Sharing in the Divine Nature: Transformation, Koinonia, and the Doctrine of God," in *On Being Christian . . . and Human,* ed. Speidell, 114.
[120] Stringfellow, *Count in All Joy,* 73.

without hope, destined to being "married and yet live alone."[121] So he lives a life of undulation: sometimes welcoming the sacrifice; sometimes in the desert, not even remember his old feelings! There is a cost to not only hearing but also doing the word, since that is the experience of Jesus. The disciple is not above the master.

The word for Jayber is the word that not only speaks but intercedes for us as well.[122] The two-way movement is so important. The second movement is a movement of intercession, of pleading for us, doing for us what we are unable to do for ourselves. But intercession does not leave us. We can believe now because he believes, because we can join together with the Son in his knowledge of God despite our doubt. A hearing has taken place that is true hearing: hearing and doing inextricably combined in harmony and rhythm. Jesus does not know hearing without obeying. We cannot say as much. The hearing and the doing is not just our part, but the place of the Son. We can now be "caught up together" with him, "not as co-workers, but as recipients" (Barth).[123] A co-worker can only give one's due share, according to one's abilities. A recipient is one who receives what one needs desperately. Having received, however, means that a wellspring of gratitude can now flow forth.

What is faith in Christ, then, if the faith *of* Christ is significant? Here is not a continuation of Christ's faith by our imitation, but a genuine following of Jesus.[124] Such following is an actual following Jesus down his road, but realizing that he always goes before us. He is the "pioneer" (Heb 12:2), the Kit Carson, the Daniel Boone of our faith. So walking behind him is a genuine walking, a genuine faith, but not without him going first … always. He replaces our attempts to blaze our trails, even to help ourselves.[125] Still, we are enabled then to walk the trail. We are enabled to actually have the knowledge of faith, yet it is faith in the "exchange of status" between us, the "sweet exchange" of his life for ours. Such a faith replaces doubt, the kind of doubt that, with "a murderous intention" seeks to prove or disprove, the kind of faith from which Jayber mercifully spares

121 Berry, *Jayber Crow,* 247.

122 Barth, *CD,* I/2, 221, 226.

123 Ibid., 237. But see Barth's reworking of "cooperation" in *CD,* IV/3, second half, 602–3.

124 Barth, *CD,* I/2, pp. 118, 277.

125 Ibid., 368; cf. IV/1, 458–78.

himself.[126] Yet it is still a faith that does not depend on our independent abilities, indeed that criticizes our own attempts at knowledge of God.[127] Even our worship has been established now, not by our natural proclivities for religion but by the praise of the Father by the Son.[128]

Is the human knower then obliterated by the response of the Son? No, because the humanity of Christ actualizes the knowledge of the human nature that he has taken upon himself, our human nature, so his knowledge can become our knowledge.[129] We share in the intimacy of relationship in the Son's knowledge of the ineffable Father through the Spirit. This is our "adoption" as sons and daughters of God (Gal 4:4-7).[130] Through this participation we are genuinely connected to, but not identified with, the Son. Just as God's deity was not obliterated when he became human, so also our humanity is not destroyed as we participate in the vicarious humanity of Jesus. No longer is our salvation to be seen in terms of an *ordo salutis,* an order of salvation in which Christ is only an instrument that leads to our acts of justifying faith and sanctifying works. It is Christ who has become for us "wisdom from God, righteousness and sanctification and redemption" (1 Cor 1:30).[131] Sanctification is not to be seen as only "our part."

The knowledge of God is now an accomplished two way street: God not only being on the side of revelation, but also on the side of response, replacing the sinful response of religion with the Son's human response. Thus, there is now a foundation and ground for our proper response. God's questions to us *and our questions to God* are now answered in the perfect, obedient responses of Jesus Christ.[132] We may not receive the answers we expect; but they are answered, firmly and decisively in the

---

[126] Anderson, *Unspoken Wisdom,* 120.

[127] Andrew Purves, "The Christology of Thomas F. Torrance," in Colyer, ed., *The Promise of Trinitarian Theology,* 71.

[128] Barth, *CD,* I/2, 424.

[129] T. F. Torrance, *The Christian Doctrine of God,* 34.

[130] J. I. Packer made an impression on me years ago through his chapter, "Sons of God" in *Knowing God* (Downers Grove, Ill.: InterVarsity, 1973), 181–208.

[131] T. F. Torrance, "The Atonement: The Singularity of Christ and the Finality of the Cross: The Atonement and the Moral Order" in *Universalism and the Doctrine of Hell,* ed. Nigel M. Cameron (Grand Rapids: Baker, 1993), 233; "Karl Barth and the Latin Heresy," *SJT* 39 (1986) 230. See also Colyer, *How to Read T. F. Torrance,* 112.

[132] Barth, *CD,* III/2, 439–40.

gratitude of the Son to the Father (Matt 11:25). Only through this response can there be the communication among God's questions, our questions, and God's answers in the context of a genuine human response. Our knowledge of God is now wrapped up within Jesus' knowledge of God, just as Paul lives because "Christ lives in me." Paul still lives, yet his life is lived by the faith *of* the Son of God, the one "who loved me and gave himself for me" (Gal 2:20).[133] The Son who actively trusts in the Father is also the one who "loved me and gave himself for me."

To speak of "Christ living in me" is the heart of the Christian life, but should also be the heart of our knowledge of God in terms of our participation in his knowledge of the Father. This mystic union speaks of that which is ontological rather than moral, a deep connection between the uncreated Truth of God and the created truth of this world.[134] Such a relationship can only be known through the Holy Spirit who makes the power and presence of the continuing life and ministry of Christ the life-giving source for a ministry that can critique both human manipulation and human control.[135] The Greek Fathers' teaching on *theosis* (deification) should not be accepted in terms of a deified humanity but the Spirit uniting us with the vicarious humanity of Christ, not obliterating our humanity since we participate in his knowledge by grace.[136]

Humanity that can know God through the knowledge of the Son is not a solitary humanity, but in ontological connection with others: the Church. So the Creed should be said, Kathleen Norris suggests, first of all because it belongs to the Church, not to an individual.[137] This certainly reflects the nature of the triune God, the one whose being is in community.[138] The Church as the body of Christ is ontologically related to Christ, therefore it can participate in the knowledge of the Father through the Son in the Spirit. Yet, the Church must constantly be reminded

---

[133] See the arguments for the subjective vs. the objective genitive use of *pistis Christou* in Luke Timothy Johnson, "Romans 3:23-26 and the Faith of Jesus," *Catholic Biblical Quarterly* 44 (1982), 83.

[134] T. F. Torrance, *Reality and Evangelical Theology*, 125.

[135] Ray S. Anderson, "Reading T. F. Torrance as a Practical Theologian" in *The Promise of Trinitarian Theology*, ed. Colyer, 167–68. See also Colyer, *How to Read T. F. Torrance*, 230.

[136] Colyer, *How to Read T. F. Torrance*, 178–79.

[137] Norris, *Amazing Grace*, 65.

[138] Colyer, *How to Read T. F. Torrance*, 251.

that it is only the body, not the head, not having a source of knowledge within itself. Therefore, the source *of doubt* is not in the Church as well! The luxury of solitary doubt has been stolen from us by the vicarious faith of Christ.

The actual human participation of the Eucharist affirms that Christ's vicarious humanity involved our actions as well, yet not without the ontological relationship to Christ, since the Eucharist, as real presence, is the body and blood of Christ. We are only joining in with Christ in his continual High Priestly offering, not as a repetition, but as "participation, manifestation, and witness," a participation in the "perfect tense" of Christ's one offering.[139]

It is wrong, however, to view the Eucharist as simply our response to God's grace. The sacrament should not be divorced from the knowledge of God. The foundation of any response to God is based on a knowledge of the one, triune God. This is the knowledge only the Son possesses (Matt 11:25-27). Therefore, in the Eucharist, we have the continual response of the Son to the Father in the Spirit. Jesus is "the perfect Eucharistic Being" (Schmemann).[140] As such, there is no preparation for communion apart from the prior intercession of the Son on our behalf.[141] "To be in Christ means to be like Him, to make ours the very movement of His life."[142] He is the one who "always lives to make intercession" for us (Heb 7:25). His Eucharistic Prayer becomes summed up in the Lord's Prayer that he gives to us in order to make it our prayer, for it is Jesus who alone knows God![143] In Gethsemane, he alone prays, "Thy will be done!"[144] He alone fulfills the petition, "Thy will be done, on earth as it is in heaven," but he fulfills it so that it might become our prayer as well.

The whole person cannot avoid making decisions about ultimate questions, as William James reminds us.[145] The intellect cannot be surgically removed from the will and the emotions in order to make a cold, calculating

139 George Hunsinger, "The Dimension of Depth: Thomas F. Torrance on the Sacraments," in *The Promise of Trinitarian Theology*, ed. Colyer, 147, 151.

140 Schmemann, *For the Life of the World*, 37.

141 Ibid., 45.

142 Ibid., 44.

143 Ibid., 45.

144 Barth, *CD*, IV/1, 632.

145 James, "The Sentiment of Rationality" in *The Will to Believe*, 92.

decision. We have been taught that from Polanyi to postmodernism. So also, Jesus Christ who knows God on our behalf is the whole man of Nazareth who is also the eternal Son of God, one who is not just a mere "Christ Principle" but our Brother Man, our High Priest carrying our sorrows and questions, interceding for us with the Father (1 John 2:1).[146] If this is so, then our doubt is no longer our own. "The whole man would not have been saved, unless he had taken upon himself the whole man" (Origen).[147] The whole man includes our doubt: The unassumed *doubt* is not healed. Christ assumes our doubt when he assumes our humanity. We belong to the whole Christ in the whole of our humanity and can no longer live for ourselves: "The Lord has become everything for you, and you must become everything for the Lord."[148] A place is made for our genuine response of obedience, not apart from Christ but in Christ. Here again is "the vicarious mysticism of Christ," the High Priest who offers "His every word, His every feeling, His every thought, His every labor and His every tear, who finally offers Himself to God completely as a man, on behalf of man."[149] There is no mysticism, there is no knowledge of God, apart from Christ. To follow him is to abandon any claim, even of "self-emptying," for the Son is the one who has emptied himself already (Phil 2:5). A mystical self-emptying is not the preparation for grace, a religious act that can only seek to justify ourselves.[150] "Following Jesus"

[146] James B. Torrance, "The Place of Jesus Christ in Worship" in *Theological Foundations for Ministry,* ed. Ray S. Anderson (Edinburgh: T. & T. Clark, 1979), 348, 367. See also Todd H. Speidell, "Trinity, Community, and Society," in Speidell, ed., *On Being Christian . . . and Human,* 196.

[147] Origen, "Dialogue with Heraclides" in *Alexandrian Christianity,* eds. Henry Chadwick and J. E. L. Oulton (Philadelphia: Westminster, 1954), 442; cf. Athanasius, *Ad Epictetum* 7: "But the Saviour having in very truth become Man, the salvation of the whole man was brought about . . . But truly our salvation is not merely apparent, nor does it extend to the body only, but the whole man, body and soul alike, has truly obtained salvation in the Word Himself," NPNF, second series, Vol. 4, 572–73; T. F. Torrance, *The Trinitarian Faith,* 152: "If the humanity of Christ were in any way deficient, all that he is said to have done in offering himself in sacrifice 'for our sakes,' 'on our behalf,' and 'in our place' would be quite meaningless," and Ware, *The Orthodox Way,* 85.

[148] St. John of Kronstadt, cited by Ware, *The Orthodox Way,* 85.

[149] St. Nikolai Velimirovich, *The Prologue of Ohrid,* vol. 1 (Alhambra, Ca.: Serbian Orthodox Diocese of N. America, 2002), 100.

[150] See also Barth, *CD,* IV/1, 628–29: In faith in God, "we do not have here a directive to mystical self-emptying, to entrance into the night of quiescence, of silence, of an

means not to imitate his self-emptying, but to be with him.[151] To be with Jesus is to take up one's cross, to deny oneself, yet not apart from his cross and his self-denial (John 12:26). Knowledge of God no longer has to be a terrible burden we postmodern people have to bear alone. We can be with Jesus. Karl Barth's words are encouraging: "It is good to be with Jesus and not elsewhere. This is good because there God Himself is good for us."[152]

artificial anticipation of death; not even (and more especially not) when such experiments appeal expressly to the example of the death and passion of Christ and are portrayed as the mystic's imitation of this event . . . There is nothing, nothing at all, to justify the belief that God has created us for the practice of this self-emptying, or that it has to be recognized and adopted as the way to reconciliation with God. When a man ventures to make this experiment, where does he find himself but in the enclosed circle of his proud being and activity? If faith in its negative form is indeed an emptying, then it is certainly an emptying of all the results of such practices of self-emptying. It begins at the point where all the works of man are at an end, including his quiescence and silence and anticipatory dying. Christian faith is the day whose dawning means the end of the mystical night." For a sourcebook referencing the Fathers as the source for a distinctive Christian mysticism, see Clément, *The Roots of Christian Mysticism.*

151 Barth, *CD,* II/2, 570.

152 Ibid.

4
Who is the God Whom Jesus Knows?

The vicarious way of knowing through the vicarious humanity of Christ leads us irresistibly to the question, Who is this God whom Jesus knows? Asking, Who is God? may become the last taboo in western society. We have been let down by denominations that have simply become secular social service agencies devoid of spirituality and transcendence. We have been scandalized by the sleaze and hypocrisy of many televangelists. Even the political parties express the increasing split between the religious and the secular in American society. Secular America seems increasingly suspicious of those who wear religion on their sleeves. Is not religion best left as a private affair? Does not everyone have one's own idea of God (postmodernism)? As we have noticed, the phenomenon of the awareness of global religious pluralism greatly energizes such doubts. Even if we admit that there must be something that gave us existence, what person can ever say who or what God or this Source is? Would not that be the height of arrogance?

I agree. We can say too quickly who God is and too quickly reveal that our God is simply a reflection of our highest values or our deepest paranoia. We too easily make God into our own image (Feuerbach). One must be very careful when speaking of God! Our doubts demand this. But, more than our doubts, God, because he exists, might even demand it.

Jesus Knows Who God Is

Jesus Knows God as Father

Doubt stares into our faces with the taunt of the serpent, "Did God say . . . ?" Such a taunt seems only possible because the human subject is imperfect, lacking in something.[1] Descartes will continue to argue from this "lack" for the existence of a Most Perfect Being: "Why would I know that I doubt and I desire, that is, that I lack something and that I am not wholly perfect, if there were no idea in me of a more perfect being by comparison with which I might acknowledge my defects?"[2] A Most Perfect Being, however, may be cold comfort on winter nights.

Jayber Crow has a different idea.[3] All of his life he has heard preachers expound on John 3:16: "For God so loved the world, that He gave His only begotten Son, that whosoever believeth in Him should not perish, but have everlasting life." The preachers emphasize the "believeth" part, but Jayber comes to recognize the significance of the first part: "For God so loved the world . . ." This is the world, Jayber contends, with all of its faults, loved by God even before Bethlehem; loved like a father loves a wayward child whom he cannot forget. Jayber begins to see God, not as a "First Cause" or a "First Mover," but as Father, with all that implies: "the love, the compassion, the taking offense, the disappointment, the anger, the bearing of wounds, the weeping of tears, the forgiveness, the suffering unto death."

God as Father

Jesus agrees with Jayber. The one who has seen the Father (John 6:46) invites his disciples to pray with him, "Our Father . . ." (Matt 6:9). The disciples know that for Jesus, God was Father, so that God should be Father to them as well: "But go to my brothers and say to them, 'I am

[1] Buckley, *At the Origins of Modern Atheism*, 86.

[2] Descartes, *Meditations* 3, 30.

[3] Berry, *Jayber Crow*, 251.

ascending to my Father and your Father, to my God and your God'" (John 20:17).[4] Jesus desires to share the knowledge of this God with his followers, in fact to reserve "Father" for God alone (Matt 23:9). As Father, God cares for his creation (Matt 6:26; Luke 12:6, 7), yet gives the warning that they are not to deny Jesus so that he will not deny them before "my Father" (Matt 10:26-33; Luke 12:2-9).

What does it mean for God to be Father? At the very least it means that he has a *personal* nature. As Jayber observes, he can love as well as be disappointed, forgive as well as suffer. The vicarious faith of Jesus reveals God as Father, a personal being involved in relationships of love, trust, and obedience.[5] God as Father is not just a "Supreme Being," but one who is free to love (Barth).[6] The God of Jesus will enable men and women to become born again by God's Word and Spirit in order to become covenant-partners with God. Such a miracle is constrained and limited by an abstract concept of a "Supreme Being." Rather, here is the God who is not just an object, but is and remains the Subject, a living, active, personal Subject, the Father who will not forget his wayward children. Jesus knows this Father for us, despite our doubts, skepticism, cynicism, and rebellion.

"Father" of course immediately raises all sorts of questions (and objections) as a name for God. Does this mean that God is a male? What if one has had an abusive human father? Would not that make it impossible to pray to God as Father? Are not "Mother" or "Creator" alternatives that at least have as much weight as Father?

Our doubt cries out in desperation. We need help. Jesus responds by encouraging us to pray, "Our Father . . ." Perhaps we will be surprised at the implications of what God as Father means for Jesus, as he prays for us and in our place. In fact, given bad experiences of fathers by many, there may be a necessity for Jesus to pray "Our Father" for us! Nonetheless, he has left us no other alternative but to call on God as Father if we want help in the desperation of our darkest doubt.

"Person" may be a problem for us when we speak of God because of the modern view of "person" as an individual psychological entity.[7] One

[4] Guinness, *In Two Minds,* 270.

[5] Christopher Kaiser, *The Doctrine of God* (Westchester, Ill.: Crossway, 1982), 22.

[6] Barth, *CD,* IV/3, first half, 447–48.

[7] Here is the problem Karl Barth has with using "person" in the Trinity; see Barth, *CD,* I/1, 355–58.

does not want to speak of the Trinity as three "persons" and imply three gods. But, as with all language about God, we need to let God define what he means. This is true with "Father" as well as how we would use "person." The Father, the Son, and the Holy Spirit are persons in the sense that as they personally relate to each (the Greek Fathers' doctrine of *perichoresis*), they also establish their distinction from one another.[8] There is no Father apart from his relation with the Son and the Spirit, and vice versa. God from all eternity is freely engaged in a relationship of love. Therefore, we are dependent upon the Son (for the Father and the Spirit are not incarnate) to know the Father and the Spirit (Matt 11:15-27; Romans 8).

We are dependent upon the Son to know God as Father. One might say that there are limitations to speaking of God as Father, as in any language about God. God is incomprehensible in his essence, it is argued.[9] We certainly are confronted by the temptation to read our preconceived ideas of father into God as Father. But are not both problems faced by God's initiative of grace? Do we have genuine knowledge of God in the face of Jesus or not? Knowledge of God will never be exhaustive or total knowledge, but how can the Son claim that "all things have been handed over to me by my Father" (Matt 11:25) if what he reveals is only a cultural, patriarchal metaphor that can easily be replaced in the postmodern era?[10] If God is able to become human, is he not able to reveal who he truly is,

[8] T. F. Torrance, *The Christian Doctrine of God,* 157.

[9] Ibid.

[10] Athanasius admits that "one must use a poor simile drawn from tangible and familiar objects to put our idea into words, since it is over bold to intrude upon the incomprehensible nature [of God]." *In Illud Omnia* (On Luke X.22 [Matt XI.27]) 3, NPNF, second series, Vol. 4, 89. See also John Chrysostom, "On the Incomprehensible Nature of God," *FC,* vol. 72. However, we should not restrict all the meaning that God puts into human words. In fact, without that divine intention, we are bereft of any revelation of God at all. Torrance speaks rightly that "we are unable to pierce behind what God has revealed of himself as he addresses us in the language of the Holy Scriptures" but qualifies this by adding, "to what he is in himself apart from his self-revelation to us." (*The Christian Doctrine of God,* p. 159). But is there not a distinction between having total or exhaustive knowledge of God (which we cannot have) and the existence of a God "in himself" apart from the personal revelation in Jesus Christ? Is there lurking behind this a Platonic form that can be viewed as the "real" God, a God we cannot know, which Torrance in other places criticizes as "a God behind the back of Jesus"? We will always be doubting our knowledge of this God! See also T. F. Torrance, *The Mediation of Christ,* 59–62.

not simply a "part" of God or our impressions of God? The personal nature of the intimacy between the Father and the Son is what we partake in through the Holy Spirit. What we participate in is no less than a relationship, since we are adopted as sons and daughters (Gal 4:5).[11]

The Father/Son relationship is not simply a convenient cultural expression nor only a concession to human limitation but, rather, that which falls within the very being of God.[12] Still, to avoid projecting our ideas of "Father" and "Son" onto God, we must maintain a "healthy doubt," respecting both God's freedom to name himself, providing the content of that name, and God's inexhaustible nature. A self-evident God, a God whom we can deduce from our own logic or perceptions of creation, is not God at all, but a projection of our egocentricity. Such is the proper place for "mystery" in the faith; not in the sense of a Kantian agnosticism about who God is, but in the sense of maintaining a sense of wonder, a child's wonder before one's parent and indeed the immensity of the world's mystery.[13] Gerard Manley Hopkins' words are classic: "You do not mean by a mystery what a Catholic does. You mean an interesting uncertainty . . . But a Catholic means by mystery an incomprehensible certainty."[14] This is the kind of certainty, sometimes even a paradoxical certainty, which respects the "sheer ineffability" of God.[15] Knowledge of the Father includes ineffability as well as intimacy. Only the Son of the Father knows this

Mystery

[11] According to Aristotle Papanikolaou, John Zizioulas argues for personhood, not the energies of God, as the eucharistic connection in *theosis* (becoming like God). In contrast, Vladimir Lossky, Papanikolaou claims, rejects Karl Rahner's equation of the immanent and the economic Trinity because of the priority of apophatic knowledge of God. "Divine Energies or Divine Personhood: Vladimir Lossky and John Zizioulas on Conceiving the Transcendent and Immanent God," *Modern Theology,* 19 (2003) 357–85.

[12] T. F. Torrance, *The Trinitarian Faith,* 119. See also Colyer, *How to Read T. F. Torrance,* 75.

[13] Geddes Macgregor, *Christian Doubt* (London: Longmans, 1952), 137. The more modern, Kantian view of mystery is found in Gordon D. Kaufman, *In Face of Mystery: A Constructive Theology* (Cambridge: Harvard University Press, 1993). See also the rather different approach of the eastern Church Fathers such as Clement of Alexandria and Symeon the New Theologian in Bishop Hilarion Alfeyev, *The Mystery of Faith: An Introduction to the Teaching and Spirituality of the Orthodox Church* (London: Darton, Longman and Todd, 2002), 27, 40–41.

[14] Gerard Manley Hopkins, *The Letters of Gerard Manley Hopkins* (Oxford: Oxford University Press, 1935), 187–88; cited by Macgregor, *Christian Doubt,* 141.

[15] T. F. Torrance, *The Trinitarian Faith,* 213.

God.[16] Only he can "comprehend him," yet we can "apprehend" him (Torrance).[17] Since the Father/Son relationship falls within the being of God, however, we can know the essence of God, yet not exhaustively.[18] We have genuine knowledge, but only as the Son reveals the Father to us (". . . and no one knows the Father except the Son and anyone to whom the Son chooses to reveal him." Matt 11:27).

By calling God "Father," Jesus is calling our doubt into question; not its emotional significance to us (for he is in solidarity and identification with us—see the cry of abandonment) but by providing an alternative to our doubt—his knowledge of God as Father, with all of his "love, compassion, the taking offense, the disappointment, the anger, the bearing of wounds, the weeping of tears, the forgiveness, the suffering unto death." God's identity then becomes manifest in the freedom of this act towards us in Jesus Christ. This confronts our doubt with the freedom of God's love; love based on reality, not reason alone (Anderson).

Is this not the same way in our relationships with a beloved? For Jayber, Mattie never loses her "incomprehensible" nature, for he refuses to idealize her or their relationship. He accepts it as it is "with twisted face and pocket full of seeds," like the farmer in the Edna St. Vincent Millay poem who responds to a natural disaster with both the realism of the tragedy (with "twisted face") yet still with hope for the future (with "pocket full of

---

[16] John Chrysostom preached against the Anomoeans or Eunomians who believed that they possessed the same knowledge of God that the Son possessed. St. John Chrysostom, *On the Incomprehensible Nature of God,* trans. Paul W. Harkins, *FC,* Vol. 72 (Washington, D.C.: The Catholic University of America Press, 1984). Granted we do not know God exhaustively as the Son, does the platonic heritage of Chrysostom's day keep him from stressing our participation in the Son's knowledge of the Father, a genuine yet not exhaustive knowledge?

[17] T. F. Torrance, "The Christian Apprehension of God the Father" in *Speaking the Christian God,* ed. Kimel, 136.

[18] Contra T. F. Torrance, who differs between saying, "What God ultimately is in the essence of his eternal being we cannot know, but we are given by God to know *who* he is" and that "Fatherhood and Sonship belong to the eternal and unchangeable being of God." "The Christian Apprehension of God the Father" in *Speaking the Christian God,* ed. Kimel, 136–37. However, can this distinction hold true? If Fatherhood and Sonship belong to God's "eternal and unchangeable being," and we know the Father and the Son by God's grace, then would we not also know the being or essence of God, although not exhaustively? Who is this God whose eternal essence we cannot know? This creates the potential for a pool of doubt concerning whether we really know God.

seeds").[19] Yes, it is important for God to remain incomprehensible; otherwise we are in danger of the presumption that by knowing all there is to know about God we can control him.

At an important point, the analogy between Jayber and God breaks down. Jayber is convinced that he possesses real knowledge of who Mattie is in her essence. "Intact and clear within herself . . . she had the lightness of a girl, a woman's gravity in her eyes." Jayber watches her with the Vacation Bible School children, "free with children as if she had been a child herself—as free as a child but with a generosity and watchfulness that were anything but childish. She was just perfectly there with them in her pleasure."[20] Notice that this knowledge of Mattie is only from observation. Observation can only tell us a limited amount about another person. The observations of Jesus, the carpenter of Nazareth, by his contemporaries (including his family) often misconstrued who he truly was. Jayber believes he knows Mattie in her essence yet not totally. Jesus knows God in his essence, and God has revealed himself in the relationship between the Father and the Son through the Spirit. We have genuine yet not exhaustive knowledge of God in the face of Jesus, but only by the grace of God, by God's self-initiative. We would have no knowledge of God's essence apart from his act of grace. Jayber cannot claim that of his knowledge of Mattie. He can love Mattie, but he needs to remember that the only knowledge of the essence of Mattie (or anyone else) comes from one's self-disclosure, an act of grace on one's part towards another. There is no evidence in *Jayber Crow* that Mattie has ever extended that grace to Jayber. His love for Mattie remains a risk: Does he know the real Mattie? Ultimately this is up to her. (The end of the novel may provide the only answer.)

Here is one significance of the icons of Christ: they genuinely communicate both the deity and the humanity of Christ (contra Karl Barth!), for we know no deity apart from the flesh of Jesus of Nazareth.[21] The icon is sufficient in bearing witness of Christ (a theological category Barth would approve), but not a necessity (a tendency in the Christian East); the New Testament is silent in portraying what Jesus looked like in

[19] Cited by Anderson, *Unspoken Wisdom,* 54.

[20] Berry, *Jayber Crow,* 241, 283, 191.

[21] Barth, *CD,* II/1, 666. According to Barth, portraying the face of Christ should be given up "for the sake of God's beauty."

his earthly existence (one need not be either an "iconoclast" or an "iconophile"). But here is the one person in whose faith we can know God as Father, through whom we can know the essence of God yet not exhaustively, and cling to his knowledge in the midst of our doubts.

To be personal is to be *relational,* as the *perichoresis,* the mutual indwelling between the Father, the Son, and the Holy Spirit, explains.[22] *Perichoresis* means that the relationship among the persons of the Trinity is characteristic of the nature of God (dare we say "essence"?). Practically speaking, each person of the Trinity is God. The intimacy between Abba, Father, and the Son proceeds from *perichoresis.* In this mutual love there exists a oneness (John 10:30; 14:11; 17:11).

What does it means for the Father and the Son to be one? At the least it means that they both possess "the divine mind" as John McLeod Campbell suggests.[23] The mind of God is not simply an all-encompassing intellect manifesting all knowledge and power but the eternal expression of mutual intimacy between the Father and the Son in the Spirit. The action of the Son reveals the heart of the Father who sends him, the great sorrow of the Father over our sins, a sorrow so great that the Son becomes incarnate in order to provide the "perfect repentance" on behalf of humanity, "a perfect Amen in humanity to the judgment of God on the sin of man."[24] That the Son provides the "perfect repentance" demonstrates that there is no division between the Father and the Son, but a reflection in the incarnation of the intense intimacy, the oneness of mind in the Holy Trinity.

This personal, relational nature of God the Father is made manifest in his actions toward humanity, in his freedom to love, who as the sovereign nevertheless determines to make humanity his covenant-partner.[25] God

---

[22] T. F. Torrance, *The Christian Doctrine of God,* 174–75.

[23] John McLeod Campbell, *The Nature of the Atonement* (Edinburgh: Handsel and Grand Rapids: Eerdmans, 1996), 19.

[24] Campbell, *The Nature of the Atonement,* 118.

[25] Barth, *CD* III/1, 364–65. "For the God of grace discloses Himself to the creature as the One who is, and in so doing discloses the fact that the creature is . . . And it is the recognition of this co-existence of the Creator and the creature, characterised by the mutual implication of creation and the covenant, which we have had in mind in all that we have so far said. Only on this basis can there be a clear distinction between what we say to ourselves on the ground of our awareness of ourselves and the world, and what must be said to us by a higher Judge if it is to be valid, between assumptions and

the Son is the Word of God, signifying that the being of God is "divinely eloquent" in communicating not just information, but his very being to humanity in Jesus Christ.[26]

Distinctions between the persons are not dissolved, however; in fact, they are established in the mutual indwelling.[27] Jayber's knowledge of Mattie is most real when he recognizes his distinction from her. It is as if he realizes that we only become truly close to someone when we realize our distinction from another.[28] In fact, almost their entire relationship is lived in separation from each other, only to meet by "accident" occasionally at a favorite place. He maintains the distinctions by respecting her marriage and by not revealing the depth of his feelings to her. Jayber is taking a risk, but it is the risk of love. Allowing the otherness of the other person to exist can risk alienation.[29]

Perichoresis, although it speaks of a mutual indwelling, respects the distinctions among the Father, the Son, and the Holy Spirit. While some distinctions in the incarnate Son are only the result of his solidarity with human nature (the *economic* Trinity) (e.g., being a male), the characteristics of the Son that reflect his relationship to the Father must be seen as a

A Son by virtue of the Father, etc.

probabilities, rooted in our own mind; between our consciousness of God and God's unfailing self-disclosure; between the human idea of an existent God in whom all existence is grounded and the existence of this God Himself implying that of man and his world, between the circle of our consciousness and being and the confrontation of this circle by God in whom consciousness and being are not two but one." In "the self-disclosure of God" in creation and covenant there is "the basic end of all doubt."

[26] T. F. Torrance, *The Trinitarian Faith,* 131. See also Colyer, *How to Read T. F. Torrance,* 75.

[27] See Alan J. Torrance, *Persons in Communion,* 324: There must be an "inner connection between the ontology of grace and the vicarious humanity of Christ" in order to "appreciate the interrelationship between the *Deus ad intra* and the *distinct* divine appropriations. Failure here can only lead to our reducing the trinitarian event of communion as it constitutes the very grammar of an integrated and integrative understanding of worship, worthship, and epistemic communion to what will at best be simply an ethical or exemplary *principle* of communion or an epistemically crippled *structure* of revelation or divine Self-communication." Fear of Nestorianism should not dissuade us at this point.

[28] Fiddes, *Participation in God,* 243. See also Ray S. Anderson, *On Being Human: Essays in Theological Anthropology* (Grand Rapids: Eerdmans, 1982), "Humanity as Determined by the Other," 44–54.

[29] Fiddes, *Participation in God,* 244.

reflection of the eternal, essential nature of God (the *immanent* Trinity).[30] Certainly the obedience of the Son is involved here, as strange as it may seem to us to speak of an "obedience" in God.[31]

One important distinction between the persons is found in the worship of the Father by the Son. Doubt creeps in often in terms of the feelings of worship: its boredom, its routine, the endless disagreements among Christians concerning worship, from the significant to the silly. Is all this effort at worship worth it? Then Jesus enters into the sanctuary and it is *he* who is worshipping the Father through the Spirit. His intimate (Abba) relationship with the Father desires to pray to and praise the Father (Matt 11:25; Luke 10:21-22; John 3:35; 17:2; 13:3; 7:29; 10:14-15; 17:25). Someone else has desired God before we have. Therefore, a desiring has already been given to us.[32] One has already worshipped the Father. Our prayers then become an "echo" of his.[33] This is in stark contrast with a doctrine of God that bypasses the vicarious humanity of Christ for either an immediate relationship with God shared by all humanity (a "unitarian" perspective) or a Christian approach centered on our acts of faith, not the faith of Christ (an "existential, experience" model).[34] No, Jesus' worship

---

[30] See the discussion of the immanent and economic Trinity especially as ignited by Karl Rahner in Karl Rahner, *The Trinity*, trans. Joseph Donceel (New York: Crossroad Herder, 2003). See the discussion in Roger E. Olson and Christopher A. Hall, *The Trinity* (Grand Rapids: Eerdmans, 2002), 95–115 and T. F. Torrance, "Towards an Ecumenical Consensus on the Trinity," *Theologische Zeitschrift* 31 (1975), 337–50. Paul D. Molnar argues that "Rahner's Rule," the identity between the economic Trinity and the immanent Trinity, should not be read to imply that the being and freedom of God are limited to what we know through human experience. See *Divine Freedom and the Doctrine of the Immanent Trinity: Dialogue with Karl Barth and Contemporary Theology* (London and New York: T. & T. Clark, 2002).

[31] Contra T. F. Torrance, *The Christian Doctrine of God*, 180. Torrance denies that there is a God "in the depths of his eternal Being other than what he has revealed of himself in the Gospel as the Father of the Son," yet "we are unable to pierce behind what God has revealed of himself as he addresses us in the language of the Holy Scriptures to what he is in himself apart from his self-revelation to us." *The Christian Doctrine of God*, 159. Yet, who is this God who is "*what he is in himself* apart his self-revelation to us" (emphasis mine)? Might he not be a different kind of God? Barth's argument for an "obedience in God" against Torrance is discussed in Kettler, *The Vicarious Humanity of Christ and the Reality of Salvation*, 94–97.

[32] Alan J. Torrance, *Persons in Communion*, 319.

[33] James B. Torrance, *Worship, Community, and the Triune God of Grace*, 14.

[34] Ibid., 25–26.

of the Father, his prayers, obedience, and faith involve a unique relationship that we are only invited to participate in.[35] Only the Son is *homoousios* with the Father.[36] The worship by the Son, far from being an indication of the Son as inferior to the Father, is a manifestation of the perichoretic relationship in the Holy Trinity that expresses God in his eternal being as love. "What God is toward us in these relationships, he is in his innermost being" (James Torrance).

The incomprehensibility or ineffability of God, his "otherness," is not a God behind the back of Jesus that fills us with paranoia and doubt. The God who reveals himself simultaneously hides himself, but what is "hidden" overflows in action and resurrected glory toward us (cf. the Transfiguration) in the ministry of *leitourgia,* the "service" first to God (worship), and then to humanity by word and deed.[37] What is hidden is the inexhaustive nature of God yet his being is known to us as the Lord who can even become the servant, as the faithful and obedient one who can believe and obey for us in the midst of our failings in order to create a community of reciprocity reflecting the eternal harmony among the Father, the Son, and the Holy Spirit.[38] In Christ, God's otherness becomes a manifestation of his lordship and the end of our rebellious, silly autonomy, including our doubt, since it is Jesus who is able to keep "the faith we did not keep," acting "once and for all in our place."[39]

For God to be Father means for God to be personal. The personal relationship between the Father and the Son through the Spirit is a direct challenge to our skepticism and our doubt. Jesus has faith and obedience, daring us to be skeptical, daring us to doubt.

It is not enough, however, simply to say that God is personal. God's personhood is unique to his ineffable deity. He is personal in that he confronts my humanity by his vicarious act, believing when I am unable to believe. Here is a "real presence" that makes a demand upon me, for I cannot escape the act done on my behalf. Whether or not I choose to

---

[35] Ibid., 30.

[36] Ibid., 32

[37] See also T. F. Torrance, *The Christian Doctrine of God,* 242 and Barth, *CD,* II/1, "The Hiddenness of God," 179–203.

[38] See also T. F. Torrance, *Trinitarian Perspectives: Toward Doctrinal Agreement* (Edinburgh: T. & T. Clark, 1994), 3.

[39] Barth, *CD,* I/1, 391.

embrace it, become thankful for it, it will always be with me, prodding me, seeking to persuade me of the love that the Vicarious One has for me.[40] God remains as Subject, standing against the vicissitudes and variances of my feelings and emotions. Does not the dark side of doubt begin at the moment when we no longer know God as Subject and he only becomes an object in our eyes? This is true of any love relationship. So Luther was said to have shouted in the midst of his deepest doubts, "I have been baptized!", i.e., a vicarious act has been done, a personal act, an act on his behalf.[41] Jesus believes when I am unable to believe. Jesus acts when I am unable to act. Jesus loves when I am unable to love. Jesus forgives when I am unable to forgive. Jesus lives when I am dead in my sins. That is the power of truth become personal, the power of a vicarious life.

A vicarious life is a life that can be shared with others. The worship of the Father by the Son in the Spirit is but a part of a complete life of faith and obedience to the Father that in turn offers to us a share in this intimate communion between the Father and the Son in the Spirit.[42] The Son indeed "sanctifies" himself, sets himself apart for a holy use, for our sakes: "And for their sakes I sanctify myself, so that they also may be sanctified in truth" (John 17:19). "For the one who sanctifies and those who are sanctified all have one Father. For this reason Jesus is not ashamed to call them brothers and sisters . . ." (Heb 2:11). In light of our doubts about the goodness of God, the Son steps up and proclaims that God as Father is a God of holy love by offering his own blood as a seal of the covenant between God and humanity.[43] Jesus, in teaching us to pray "Our Father . . . ," is himself "the living embodiment of that prayer."[44] All true prayer is but a participation in the prayers of our great High Priest to God the Father, whose prayers continue to this very moment (Heb 7:25). He is continually drawing us to God the Father, enabling us to share in his

---

[40] See also Barth, *CD,* IV/1, 682: "What would be the result if His real presence as the living and speaking Lord was genuinely accepted, if it was not merely maintained but allowed to become an event in the form in which it is earnestly believed?"

[41] Roland H. Bainton, *Here I Stand: A Life of Martin Luther* (London: Mentor, 1950), 287.

[42] James B. Torrance, *Worship, Community, and the Triune God of Grace,* 48.

[43] Ibid., 48–49.

[44] Ibid., 84.

precious communion with the Father.[45] His intercession, then, is the only preparation for the Eucharist, since it is his communion that is the basis of our communion.[46]

The problem of humanity, and therefore of God's creation, is its corruption due to sin, resulting in death. The Father of Jesus, however, is not afraid of the contradictions in his creation.[47] The crazy quilt of our world of woe can bring us so easily to doubt and despair, but the Son knows the Father who has sent the Son to bear the contradiction on the cross. Since the Son is of one essence *(homoousios)* with the Father, this contradiction is now not alien to God's own being. God has made the problem of creation his own problem in sending the Son in the power of the Spirit. He has taken our place. Can we say then that the problem of evil and suffering in a world created by an all-powerful and loving God is no longer our problem? This is what Christ's vicarious faith proclaims.

Jesus is the "faithful witness" of the Father in a world of suffering and woe.[48] He is "the faithful witness" (Rev 1:5), who is "faithful and true" (Rev 19:11; cf. 3:11). Jesus' witness is faithful because he knows his origin and goal: "Even if I testify on my own behalf, my testimony is valid because I know where I have come from and where I am going, but you do not know where I come from or where I am going" (John 8:14).[49] As the faithful one, he bears witness even unto death.[50] He witnesses to the Father's holy love when we are unable to do so. God is both, therefore, "the Author and the Witness" of our faith.[51]

What becomes of my doubt then? My doubt is then relieved of its power to destroy. It may remain, even in a positive sense, but not to be

[45] Ibid., 93, 125.

[46] Schmemann, *For the Life of the World,* 45.

[47] Barth, *CD,* III/1, 380–81.

[48] Hilary of Poitiers, *On the Trinity,* NPNF, second series, II.6, Vol. 9, 54: The Father "is unbegotten, everlasting, inherently eternal. To the Son only is He known . . . Therefore, since no one knoweth the Father save the Son, let our thoughts of the Father be at one with the thoughts of the Son, the only faithful Witness who reveals Him to us." See also Wallis, *The Faith of Jesus Christ in Early Christian Traditions,* 209 and Barth, *CD,* IV/3, first half, "The True Witness," 368–433; second half, 612–14.

[49] See also Bonhoeffer, *Ethics.*

[50] Wallis, *The Faith of Jesus Christ in Early Christian Traditions,* 173.

[51] Hilary of Poitiers, *On the Trinity,* NPNF, second series, Vol. 9, 70.

energized by the introspective possibilities of my failings and finitude. Jesus is Victor! An objective reality now exists that is stronger than the shifting sands of my subjectivity and emotional life. So Christ believes regardless of whether anyone else ever has faith. Certainly he desires us to have faith, yet there is no guarantee, coercion, or *ex opere operato* action of God that will create faith in unwilling subjects. (Indeed, there is the cryptic, rhetorical [?] question of Jesus, "And yet when the Son of Man comes, will he find faith on earth?" [Luke 18:8]). The vicarious humanity of Christ, however, lifts the burden from us to obtain and sustain objective knowledge of God, and places it squarely upon Jesus. The emotional and spiritual benefits of this release are powerful indeed.

The Father Knows the Crucified Jesus

The Son knows the Father; but the Father also knows the Son (Matt 11:27). Who is the Son that the Father knows? Who is this one who has faith when we are unable to have faith? He is no one less than the Crucified One. A crucified man is able to believe in God when we are unable to believe! But who better has the right to protest and say, "No! There is no God! If there is, this God is not good!"? The one who is crucified is, nonetheless, the Word and Son of God. We know no other Word or Son of God than the man on Golgotha.[52] However, Jesus is the Word of Man as well as the Word of God. As the Word of Man he is the Faithful Witness to God, but also the epitome of the place where humanity should be: patient before God in a world of turmoil and tragedy. In Jesus Christ, God has relinquished his power in order to be patient for us![53] God waits for us in the waiting of Jesus.

Jesus This man who meets us is not impressive. He is not the "successful man."[54] Jesus was not counted among the bright and the beautiful of his day. His life was not viewed as a success. One who is successful has no guilt. He has achieved what he has wanted to achieve in the eyes of the

[52] Barth, *CD,* IV/3, first half, 396.

[53] Harned, *Patience,* 122.

[54] Bonhoeffer, *Ethics,* trans. Reinhard Krauss, Charles C. West, and Douglas W. Stott, 88–91.

world. Christianity is a failure in the eyes of the world. However, this is not surprising to the Crucified Jesus. His concern is not with success or failure but in accepting God's judgment on sin.[55] He accepts the judgment we have been unable to accept because of our sin and "unmasks us as liars."[56] We do not have good news and what we think is good news is a lie: the nice middle class status quo (Jayber's dream of a nice wife and plenty of food in his parish!) or a life full of "meaning" in artistic or intellectual achievement. As such, we miss what it means to be truly human: the freedom to be obedient to God.

Jesus the crucified is the one who is the faithful and true witness.[57] The resurrection does not make us forget that the One who was resurrected is the Crucified One. "The risen Christ is and remains the crucified Christ" (Moltmann).[58] The Father knows only the one who was crucified who nonetheless believes, knowing the Father's risk of misunderstanding if he entrusts knowledge of God to the Crucified One.[59] What kind of God would they believe in that is so weak and powerless? And the resurrection doesn't even appear to help (at least immediately . . . look at church history!). In Bonhoeffer's words, we live before God as if God does not exist *(etsi Deus non daretur)* but only because "God lets himself be pushed out of the world on to the cross."[60] How difficult is it for us to say this! The good news is that Jesus says this for us because he participates in our godforsakeness. We are not godforsaken alone.

In crying, "My God, my God, why have you forsaken me?," the cry of abandonment, the one known by the Father is revealed as one who addresses the Father even in abandonment as "my God." He still trusts in

---

[55] Ibid., 90.

[56] Barth, *CD,* IV/3, first half, 390–91.

[57] Ibid., 391: On the cry of abandonment: "My God, my God, why have you forsaken me?" (Mark 15:34): "What does it mean that it is only as this One who is rejected and abandoned by God that He is His Elect and therefore the true Witness of the kingdom of God come in His person? Can we really accept the fact that it is this man who meets us today, with no answer to the scorn naturally heaped upon Him, and with only that question to His and our God on His lips? How wonderfully high must be the truth attested by Him, and how terribly deep the human falsehood which He unmasks!"

[58] Jürgen Moltmann, *Theology of Hope,* trans. James W. Leitch (New York: Harper and Row, 1967), 171.

[59] Barth, *CD,* IV/3, first half, 379.

[60] Bonhoeffer, *Letters and Papers from Prison,* 360.

the Father in the midst of the agony of abandonment.[61] Herein the question of transcendence raised by the ineffability of God takes on a new character: God's transcendence is not known apart from this cry of agony.[62] The Son known by the Father is not known apart from this mission of abandonment for our sakes. He is only known through the darkness of the grave, so God is only known through the darkness of the grave. Therefore, the second day, the burial must not be ignored and remembered along with the first day (of death) and the third day (of resurrection).[63]

Doubt and unbelief quickly pounce upon the Christian claims of a crucified God as a "stumbling block" and as "foolishness" (1 Cor 1:23).[64] Ironically, as Alan Lewis observes, Christians who have problems with a God who is a "servant Lord, a guilty Judge, a wounded healer," that is, a God who suffers, play right into the hands of the critics.[65] However, it is at such a place, Lewis continues, that God goes, the place where we are most vulnerable, where human existence is exposed for the transient whiff that it is: in death. Such a place seems to be the last place to find God![66] The achievement of Jesus is not that of a religious genius or a poet but of one who, despite all odds, waits upon God, where God becomes "present only in questioning about Him" (Barth).[67] God's weakness is divine, yet it

---

[61] Wolleb in Heinrich Heppe, *Reformed Dogmatics: Set Out and Illustrated from the Sources.* Revised and edited by Ernst Bizer, trans. G. T. Thomson (Grand Rapids: Baker, 1978), 464.

[62] Anderson, *Historical Transcendence and the Reality of God,* 178: "If at that moment, the estranged flesh was brought into that space between the Son of God and the Father, so the face of the Father was eclipsed from the face of the Son, we are given a new and terrible glimpse of the depths of divine transcendence."

[63] Alan E. Lewis, *Between Cross and Resurrection,* 78.

[64] Ibid., 91.

[65] Ibid.

[66] Ibid., 92, asks the question, "'How could God, the infinite and everlasting, be one with so vulgar an expression of carnality and time as the *buried* man of Nazareth?' Perhaps this is why we pass over Easter Saturday with such silence and embarrassment."

[67] Barth, *The Epistle to the Romans,* 96–97 on Rom. 3:22: "By the knowledge of Jesus Christ all human waiting is guaranteed, authorized, and established; for He makes it known that it is not men who wait, but God—in His faithfulness . . . All human activity is a cry for forgiveness; and it is precisely this that is proclaimed by Jesus and that appears concretely in Him . . . The life of Jesus is perfected obedience to the will of the faithful God. Jesus stands among sinners as a sinner; He sets Himself wholly under the judgment under which the world is set; He takes His place where God can be present only in

is not powerlessness, for the sake of exalting humanity into the divine life.[68] But the Son whom the Father knows has been there; in fact, he has descended into hell.

Here is the freedom of the triune God of love: the Father sees the mirror of his face in the death and burial of the Son, the Son who goes down to our depths, to our lowest points not the least including our doubts, even today.[69]

The death and burial of the Son teaches a "presence within absence," a presence of God that is not afraid of absence.[70] Such a presence is not afraid of the claims of doubt and unbelief that assumes absence is a veto against God. Yet, there is a cost. To pray to the crucified God is to pray to death and, therefore, death to oneself, a radical commitment of which we are all too afraid.[71] We will not be able to escape the surrender of self-centeredness if we participate through the Spirit in the dependency of the Son on the Father, revealed in the earthly life of the vicarious humanity of Christ. This is the only Son the Father knows. "God *is* dependence rendered infinite, unable to be the Father without the Son, or Son without the Father" (Alan Lewis).[72]

The Father knows this one who wagers on God.[73] Of no one else does he testify, "You are my son, Beloved; with you I am well pleased" (Mark 1:11). As such he cares for him and guides him (Ps 23:5; 103:4). They

---

questioning about Him; He takes the form of a slave; He moves to the cross and to death; His greatest achievement is a negative achievement. He is not a genius, endowed with manifest or even with occult powers; He is not a hero or leader of men; He is neither poet nor thinker—*My God, my God, why hast thou forsaken me?*"

[68] As Alan E. Lewis comments, Barth, in *CD* IV, "overturns the Christological tradition as a whole by interpreting Christ's weakness and humiliation as a *divine* event and his exaltation as a *human* happening. By thus placing God in the 'far country' Barth bypasses the obstacle of impassibility and is able to carry to its conclusion the thought of divine suffering in the incarnation from which the Fathers of Chalcedon ultimately shrank." *Between Cross and Resurrection,* 192, n. 93.

[69] Alan E. Lewis, *Between Cross and Resurrection,* 99.

[70] Ibid., 91.

[71] Ibid., 303.

[72] Ibid., 414. See also T. F. Torrance: "Whatever is said of the Father is said of the Son except Fatherhood, and whatever is said of the Son is said of the Father except Sonship." "The Christian Apprehension of God the Father" in *Speaking the Christian God,* ed. Kimel, Alvin F. (Grand Rapids: Eerdmans, 1992) 134.

[73] Barth, *CD,* IV/3, first half, 379.

will stand together. The Son's testimony, in turn, is that there is no other God, and our substitutes (religious and non-religious) are exposed as false and all humanity as liars.

The God Jesus Knows Is Free

God's Freedom Is to Send Jesus for Our Sake

Doubt may wrestle mightily with a crucified God. An omnipotent God is difficult enough to believe in at times. The word of the cross, however, is that which challenges doubt, interrupting a God that doubt likes: a purely omnipotent, abstract, immovable, impassible Being, with another understanding of the Being of God: the triune God who is eternally in a relationship of love. Therefore the word of the cross is a challenge not just a stumbling-block to our doubt. The Son bears witness in his vicarious humanity to a different kind of God than we might expect, upsetting the applecart of our doubt. The Son bears witness as well that this God is free, free to love.[74]

John 8:32

God is free. How enticing it is to think of God as free because of how much we value freedom. Freedom is a byword of being a modern person. So Walker Percy's character Dr. Tom More asks rhetorically,

> What does a man live for but to have a girl, use his mind, practice his trade, drink a drink, read a book, and watch the martins wing it for the Amazon and the three-fingered sassafras turn red in October?[75]

Not a bad kind of life, say . . . but not particularly Christian? Maybe. Maybe not. But we do value our freedom (perhaps more specifically, autonomy) in "the land of the free, the home of the brave."

God values freedom, too, but according to his own definition. God's freedom reveals who he is, his loving, dynamic, acting being.[76] Yet he has

---

[74] Barth, *CD,* II/1, 257–321.

[75] Walker Percy, *Love in the Ruins* (New York: Ivy Books, 1971), 288.

[76] T. F. Torrance, *The Ground and Grammar of Theology,* 67.

his aspirations, just like Dr. Tom More, to live his kind of life. God's difference is that his kind of life is in relationship: between the Father and the Son through the Spirit.

In the sending of the Son in the power of the Spirit the Father demonstrates his absolute independence from all of our perceptions, bias, prejudices, and cultural creations that postmodern thinking rightly charges color our ideas of God, whether it be our ideas of power, goodness, or, especially, love.[77] But what a joy to "cleave freely to this free God"![78] What a means to be freed from sin (and doubt) by cleaving to the God who is not mastered by our culture, presuppositions, and assumptions. The modern heresy is that we can make ourselves free. How can those in bondage, however, free themselves? Plato's "Allegory of the Cave" makes that point all too well: those chained to the cave are not accustomed to "the dazzle and glitter of the light," such as the idea of the good.[79] They must be helped, gradually, with skill. But who will and who can help us?

The God Jesus knows is the God who is free to act on our behalf. This is not true of all ideas of God! Job's friends, Barth comments, present a doctrine of God who appears to be sovereign but who really is unfree.[80] They assume that Job's sufferings come from God because of his sins. This appears to be a sovereign act of a God who is able to punish sin. However, there is no freedom here. Job's friends believe in a God held captive to a law of retribution, expressed only in terms of well-worn clichés. Their God never acts *gratis,* out of love, freely, yet only reacts to the sins of humanity. This God is his own prisoner.[81] Such a God is not free to love as the triune God can, free to go outside of himself.[82] God's interaction with Israel demonstrates the freedom of Yahweh to love.[83] In contrast to this is Job's view of God as the living and active Subject with whom he can argue and complain. Indeed, the God of Job's friends would never have the freedom to do what the God and Father of our Lord Jesus Christ

---

[77] Barth, *CD,* IV/3, first half, 446. See also Kaiser, *The Doctrine of God,* 115.
[78] Barth, *CD,* IV/3, first half, 447.
[79] Plato, *The Republic,* 514–15.
[80] Barth, *CD,* IV/3, first half, 459.
[81] Ibid., 460.
[82] T. F. Torrance, *The Christian Doctrine of God,* 4, 166.
[83] T. F. Torrance, *The Mediation of Christ,* 1–46.

does: hand himself over to the world.[84] This is what the Father has done in sending the Son for our sake, making himself vulnerable to our doubt but also alive to the faith of Jesus.

What has God's freedom, however, got himself into? Jesus "was put to death in the flesh, but made alive in the spirit, in which also he went and made a proclamation to the spirits in prison . . ." (1 Pet 3:18-19). Is this merely a proclamation of the gospel to those before Christ or is this proclamation really the "descent into hell" that the Creed speaks of? How far are we from taking the death of Jesus as a genuine death that transpires within the life of God unless we see this depth to this vicarious humanity?[85] Dare we even say that here is the freedom of God expressed as the freedom of God to *fail* even his Son (the cry of abandonment) (Alan Lewis)?[86] Are we so afraid of a genuine dynamic love among the three persons of the Trinity that such language as *failure* is unthinkable? But what love is truly free if it does not have that freedom to fail? (Is the doctrine of hell very far behind?) Can we really be honest then, and view the cry of abandonment on the cross as a real, not just felt abandonment, and therefore take our feelings of abandonment more seriously, including our doubts?[87] When we look at the issue of evil and unjust suffering, the Son's protests may be stronger than ours!

God's freedom is the actuality that creates the possibility of human freedom. Christians, of all people, should be most aware of our "unfreedom," our bondage due to sin. We should not be afraid of God's "sovereignty" in the sense of his freedom to set humanity free. Certainly this begins with God determining the freedom of the Son. Where is our hope in the midst of our doubts if not in God's ability through the Son to live a life of complete faithfulness to the Father?[88] Dependence on our own freedom is only the unfreedom of doubting God. God has decided that the man Jesus is not a puppet but a genuinely free man who will perfectly have faith, not doubt, in the Father.[89] So Jesus' prayers are not

[84] Harned, *Patience,* 122.

[85] Alan E. Lewis, *Between Cross and Resurrection,* 39, n. 43.

[86] Ibid., 54.

[87] Ibid., 54–55.

[88] Barth, *CD,* II/1, 595.

[89] Barth, *CD,* II/2, 178. See also 180: "If Jesus Christ was that man, if from the very beginning He was elected man, then we have to say that God's eternal will has as its end the life of this man of prayer."

play-acting. He really prays, really weeps, really possesses faith, even on the cross.

Scripture testifies that God both "gave up" his Son (John 3:16) and Jesus gave himself up for us (Gal 1:3-4). God is in charge, but he is not in control. He has voluntarily become powerless in the Son, voluntarily depriving himself of freedom![90] Divine freedom is not reflected in coercive power that forces humanity to believe, but in the loving union with our humanity in the incarnation, the king who becomes a peasant in order to win the peasant girl's love (Kierkegaard).[91] God's freedom is to be the person who is the free, active Subject in loving, for what love can be genuine if it does not issue from the freedom of the lover, as well as respect the freedom of the beloved? In fact, the Trinity reveals that God as Person is truly free, much in contrast to our creaturely, fallen, damaged examples of freedom, so often confused by what "freedom" means.[92]

Divine freedom sets us free

Jesus' Freedom Is to Love the World for God's Sake

Jayber Crow discovers his calling but he becomes something unexpected: a barber.[93] Events around him can be said to move him in that direction, yet ultimately there is a genuine decision on Jayber's part to stay in Port William, the obscure Kentucky rural town, buy the barber shop, and love Mattie. Jesus is victor over sin and death only because he goes willingly to the cross.[94] Atonement is not child abuse! His voluntary life of suffering is his active choice to obey the Father in the power of the Spirit in loving humanity, ultimately because of the filial bond with and for the sake of the Father.

The actions of Jesus are the foundations of our actions. Because he acts, we can act. This is no mere imitation, however. The free God has

---

[90] Barth, *CD*, II/2, 490.

[91] Kierkegaard, *Philosophical Fragments*, 26–30.

[92] Barth, *CD*, I/1, 138–39. See also 138: "The doubtful thing is not whether God is a person, but whether we are" and Alan J. Torrance, *Persons in Communion*, 35. The modern equation of freedom with autonomy is obvious in Langdon Gilkey, *Message and Existence: An Introduction to Christian Theology* (Minneapolis: Seabury, 1979).

[93] Berry, *Jayber Crow*, 54.

[94] Christina Baxter, "Jesus the Man and Woman's Salvation" in *Atonement Today*, ed. Goldingay, 133.

freed us through the free acts of the Son. Something has happened to us and in us. (Here is Luther's "passive righteousness").[95] Since the actions of the Son continue through all eternity (the *perichoresis* and the continual high priestly ministry of the Son), we are not left to act on our own, even simply to be "enabled" by grace. Our union with Christ is too close. The opposite of this is the religion that is actually unbelief, a manifestation of faith in oneself.[96] Jayber is, in contrast, remarkably free from lamenting that he did not more carefully plan his life in order to be something more "successful" than a barber. He is transferring the mystery of his responsibility to the mystery of God.[97] Belonging to the faith of the Son means the surrender of our autonomy but not of our freedom.[98] Our doubt has been taken from us but we now live in freedom having been "transferred … into the kingdom of his beloved Son" (Col 1:13), a new kind of root, soil, and country. Belonging to him means that we can participate in his faith, the faith we have been unable to keep. One has to question if our futile works of piety and spirituality have been judged if they are done apart from this "root, soil, and country" we now live in.[99] Our actions are to be characterized by truly living in this new country. Then habits of virtue can reinforce the new kingdom we live in.[100] Apart from this kingdom, that is, the Son's continual faith and service, we simply live in the lie of our autonomy, open to a life of perennial doubt. And why not? Our autonomy can always think of a new question, a new problem, a new wrinkle. It has nothing else to do in its loneliness.

"'All of grace' does not mean 'nothing of man,' but precisely the opposite: *all of grace means all of man,*" T. F. Torrance is fond of saying.[101]

---

[95] Barth, IV/3, first half, 447.

[96] Barth, *CD,* I/2, 314. Human faith in oneself "makes the mystery of his responsibility his own mystery, instead of accepting it as the mystery of God. It is this faith which is religion."

[97] Barth, *CD,* I/2, 314.

[98] Ibid., 391.

[99] Ibid., 392.

[100] C. S. Lewis, *The Screwtape Letters,* 60–61.

[101] T. F. Torrance, *The Mediation of Christ,* xii. See also Thomas Merton, *The New Life* (Farrar, Strauss, and Giroux, 1961), 180: "We cannot become sons of God by an obedience that is merely a blind renunciation of our own autonomy. On the contrary, spiritual freedom consecrates our autonomy to Christ and, in Christ, to the Father, so that we may love the Father with His own Spirit of freedom, or, so to speak, with His own autonomy."

Logically, all of grace would mean nothing of humanity, yet logic is limited because the Son reveals the Father in his ineffability, his inexhaustible nature that we cannot comprehend in its totality including his working with humanity.[102] The prayers of the Son to the Father can become our prayers because the Father to whom the Son prays is the inexhaustible God who in his mystery takes our prayers into the prayers of the Son through the intercession of the Spirit (Rom 8:15-16, 26).[103] Jesus has a genuine freedom to love humanity for God's sake since he has taken upon the totality of the human condition ("the unassumed is the unhealed"), including our faith, displacing the loneliness, desperation, and arrogance of the doubt that persists in our alienated minds.[104]

Jesus is free to be obedient. Therefore, obedience is not to be seen as simply the complement to faith (Rom 1:5; 5:19; 16:26; Phil 2:6-11).[105] Obedience and dependence are not to be viewed as foreign to the being of God if one takes the economic Trinity seriously. The freedom of Jesus is to be dependent on the Father and in that dependency he loves humanity in its plight. Waiting on the Father himself, Jesus demonstrates the imperative for us to wait rather than to always assume the mantle of activity.[106]

---

[102] Colyer, *How to Read T. F. Torrance,* 120; cf. 122: "When you think of the times in your life when you are most fully aware of the love of God, the grace of the Lord Jesus Christ and the communion of the Holy Spirit, are you not the mostly fully personal and fully human being God has created and redeemed you to be, though this is only a foretaste of what is to come? Is it not the case that all of Christ and all of you are fully compatible? And does this not propel you out of self-centered selfishness into love for and relations with God and others?" See also T. F. Torrance, *Christian Theology and Scientific Culture* (Belfast: Christian Journals Limited, 1980), 128–32, a masterful discussion on predestination and election.

[103] Alan E. Lewis, *Between Cross and Resurrection,* 306, n. 72. It is too strong to say with Lewis that "Our dependence unbridles the God whose own dependence is redemptive and transforming . . ." (p. 307). Lewis is subject to the danger of the "openness" theologians who, while admirably speaking of God's relational being, shackle the freedom of God with a dependence on our actions. The vicarious humanity of Christ, the freedom of the Son to be dependent upon the Father, in contrast, enables us to be freely dependent upon God.

[104] T. F. Torrance, *Karl Barth: Biblical and Evangelical Theologian,* 235.

[105] Johnson, "Romans 3:21-26 and the Faith of Jesus," *Catholic Biblical Quarterly,* 85–89.

[106] Harned, *Patience,* 15. Glenn Tinder argues provocatively for the virtue of patience in Christian social ethics in *The Political Meaning of Christianity: An Interpretation* (Baton Rouge: Louisiana State University Press, 1989).

In the relationship among the Father and the Son in the Spirit is freedom to be the free God and the free person.[107] The *homoousion* does not negate this. Without this freedom there would not be the mutual love between the persons of the Trinity. This includes every act of the Son as an act that is done out of love for the Father, and therefore, the world, with no thought of conditions.[108] This relationship between the Father and the Son in the Spirit is a relationship of grace.

Christian freedom, therefore, is not unaware of undulation, the series of troughs and peaks that God uses as we wait upon, for they are meant to make us into "little replicas of himself," where freedom and obedience cohabit. God uses his freedom not to ravish, but to woo.[109] The freedom of God along with the freedom of Job provides a prototype of what is to come in the incarnation.[110] Faith is staring with the freedom of Jesus into the abyss of the cross and still trusting in the love of the Father. Here is where prayer becomes most pleasing to God.[111] The Father already experiences that pleasure in the Son.

The God Jesus Knows Is Love

The Beloved Son Loves God

Jayber Crow's love for Mattie is perhaps unwise, even unethical. Maybe he is fooling himself, he ponders.[112] Why waste his life on a love that is not returned? Does he really know Mattie? Would they really have a happy life together? Jayber is a man who has doubted so he is well aware of the human propensity for self-deception, particularly seeing what we want to

[107] Barth, *CD,* IV/3, first half, 381.

[108] Ibid., 382: "His [the Son's] offering is His free act in the sense that He makes it only in knowledge of God Himself, in fear of Him, in delight in Him, for His own sake, and because He cannot let go of Him . . ."

[109] C. S. Lewis, *The Screwtape Letters,* 37–38. So *theosis* is developed through personhood, not abstract energies; see again Papanikolaou, "Divine Energies or Divine Personhood: Vladimir Lossky and John Zizioulas on Conceiving the Transcendent and Immanent God," *Modern Theology* 19, no. 3 (July, 2003), 355.

[110] Barth, *CD,* IV/3, first half, 432–34.

[111] C. S. Lewis, *The Screwtape Letters,* 39.

[112] Berry, *Jayber Crow,* 247.

see: in a vocation, in the world, in a loved one, in God. His only answer is the answer of love: "I do love her all her life, and still, and always."[113] What good did he get out of his secret love? "I got to have love in my heart," Jayber responds.[114] Ray Anderson suggests that love is not afraid of doubt, in fact includes doubt as the first principle of faith, even when "unreasonable circumstances" provoke doubt.[115] Why can love do this? Because it does not spring from reason but from reality. Jayber's love is not a necessarily "reasonable" love. The Crucified One's love of the Father is not reasonable either. Our love for God is not reasonable (but perhaps genuinely rational).[116] But all are founded on and maintained by a reality of relationship, of genuine encounter, and the fruit of love. Jayber's limitation is that he can only know of Mattie what Mattie reveals to him. The Son's knowledge of the Father, however, is the knowledge of the only-begotten from the Father. The Son has a faith that Jayber can never possess. Yet Jayber is quite aware of the fruit of his love for Mattie: his ability now to be thankful for the world: for Port William in particular. He can now pray again "unreasonably, foolishly, hopelessly, that everybody in Port William might be blessed and happy—the ones I love and the ones I did not. I prayed my gratitude."[117]

How much more does Jesus pray his gratitude: "I thank you, Father, Lord of heaven and earth, because you have hidden these things from the wise and the intelligent and have revealed them to infants" (Matt 11:25). His gratitude is that the gospel message is not based on intellectual reckoning, rationalistic apologetics or even a comprehensive, superior Christian "worldview." Jesus thanks the Father for us. Jesus loves God for us, so that we may be able to love God, and love God again and again. Jesus trusts and loves the Father far beyond Jayber's capacities for trust

[113] Ibid., 248.

[114] Ibid., 247.

[115] Anderson, *Soulprints,* 72.

[116] Genuine rationality is respecting the unique nature of the object. See T. F. Torrance, *God and Rationality; The Ground and Grammar of Theology; Theological Science;* Ray S. Anderson, "Theology as Rationality," *Christian Scholar's Review* 4, no. 2 (1974), 120–33; Barth, "Faith as Knowledge," *Dogmatics in Outline,* 22–27; "A result of the uniqueness of this object of knowledge might well be that the concept of its knowledge cannot be definitively measured by the concept of the knowledge of other objects or by a general concept of knowledge but that it can be defined at all only in terms of its own object." *CD,* I/1, 190.

[117] Berry, *Jayber Crow,* 252.

and love. Love is based on reality, not reason, and, first of all, the reality of Jesus' love for God. Who can deny that the least we can say is that Jesus loved God? The love that Jesus had for the Father confronts our doubts.

Jesus loves the Father based on the *perichoresis,* the mutual indwelling of the three persons of the Trinity in which one person does not exist without the other. Personhood is relationship in the Trinity, not self-subsisting entities. "The relations between the divine Persons belong to what they are as Persons."[118] There is no God we can doubt behind the One whom the Son makes known.

The New Testament epistles are a continual meditation on the active Subject of Jesus in the Gospels: he "emptied" and "humbled" himself (Phil 2:7-8), he "gave" himself (Gal 1:4; 1 Tim 2:6); he "offered" himself (Gal 2:20; Eph 5:2); he "sacrificed" himself (Heb 7:27; 9:14).[119] Jesus does these actions for us in obedience to the Father. Such an obedience is undertaken freely, for God is not coercive in his love. Jayber Crow considers obeying the call to be a preacher as a way to "pay back" his school. But in doing so there is an inflexibility to "the call": it is final, you cannot argue with it.[120] The love at Pidgeonville is conditional, and therefore without freedom. Jesus, in contrast, freely obeys the Father who loves him without conditions. So Jesus' love is also without conditions.[121] Grace is not grace if it is conditional. The vicarious repentance of Christ interrupts even our attempts to provide our repentance as a condition for God's forgiveness.[122] So also the vicarious offering of Christ is a judgment on our attempts to complete God's grace by presenting the offering ourselves, whether in liturgical or social action busyness. This is based on an unfortunate neglect of the humanity of Christ for the sake of his deity.[123]

[118] T. F. Torrance, *The Christian Doctrine of God,* 157.

[119] Barth, *CD,* II/2, 106.

[120] Berry, *Jayber Crow,* 43.

[121] Barth, *CD,* IV/3, first half, 381–82.

[122] Contra John Hick, "Is the Doctrine of the Atonement a Mistake?" in *Reason and the Christian Religion,* ed. Alan G. Padgett (Oxford: Clarendon Press, 1999), 256–57. Cf. Kettler, "Vicarious Humanity as Soteriological Reality: The Vicarious Repentance of Christ" in *The Vicarious Humanity of Christ and the Reality of Salvation,* 187–204 and "The Vicarious Repentance of Christ in the Theology of John McLeod Campbell and R. C. Moberly," *SJT* 38 (1986), 529–43.

[123] According to Richard Swinburne, because Christ is God he cannot offer the sacrifice to himself, therefore we must present the offering. We cannot gain the benefit of

Does the Father "need" to love the Son? Does the Son "need" to love the Father? If the grace of love is unconditional, how could this be so? Yes, mutual love is not averse to receiving from each other. Mutual love (cf. the *perichoresis)* will not say, "I can do everything for you but you can do nothing for me."[124] Yet it is another thing to say that there is a *necessity* in God to love. If so, he would not be the free God. The erotic in the sense of *desire* is fulfilled in agape love.[125] Agape creates a harmony between itself and eros. However, as particularly reflected in the Trinity, this eros is desire, not need.[126]

The love of Jesus takes the form of free obedience, portraying the faithfulness of God to us in the midst of our unfaithfulness (Gal 1:4; 2:20; 3:13-14; 4:4-7).[127] We should not be afraid that this obedience is a genuine human obedience, even to the point where the Scripture says that Jesus "learned obedience" (Heb 5:8). Such an obedience is in living relation to the Father and not a "static perfection."[128] Jesus is in harmony

---

forgiveness "until we associate ourselves with it." He disagrees with the Reformers who emphasize that God forgives people before they seek him for then God would not be taken seriously. "He would be saying, 'Forget it!' Rather, the sinner has to use Christ's death to get forgiveness." *Responsibility and Atonement* (Oxford: Clarendon Press, 1989), 153. Such thinking is unfortunate in that it reveals a tendency towards a docetic Christology and a view of grace that is conditional, which, as James Torrance comments often, is not grace at all. Such a view of conditional grace, yet in terms more of a separation between the Father and the Son, is seen in Philip Quinn's suggestion that God is "persuaded" by Christ's life and death to be lenient on human beings. "Swinburne on Guilt, Atonement, and Christian Redemption," in *Reason and the Christian Religion,* ed. Padgett, 299–300.

[124] Fiddes, *Participation in God,* 212.

[125] Jüngel, *God as the Mystery of the World,* 338. See also Fiddes, *Participation in God,* 212.

[126] Contra Vincent Brümmer, *The Model of Love* (Cambridge: Cambridge University Press, 1993), 236; Fiddes, *Participation in God,* 213, and Thomas Traherne: "He is from all Eternity full of Want [i.e. need]: or else He would not be full of Treasure . . . had there been no Need He would not have created the World . . . Infinit Wants satisfied Produce infinit Joys." Fiddes does not help his case by arguing that "God freely chooses to be in need." *Participation in God,* 214. Speaking of God "willing, deciding, and choosing" is much more akin to desire than need.

[127] Richard B. Hays, "PISTIS and Pauline Christology: What Is at Stake?," in *Society of Biblical Literature 1991 Seminar Papers,* ed. Eugene H. Lovering, Jr. (Atlanta: Scholars Press, 1991), 715.

[128] Susan Buckles, "Life in the Spirit and the Spirit of Life," in *On Being Christian . . . and Human,* ed. Speidell, 132.

with the penitent criminal on the cross (Luke 23:39-43). Both accept their lot from God and do not make God "the defendant."[129] Jesus loves God, even on the cross, for he knows that doubt is not the path of the love of God. The faith of Jesus is founded on the love for the Father that will withstand the cross. We cannot understand this, so we assume that the two cries from the cross, "My God, my God, why have you forsaken me?" (Matt 27:46) and "Father, into your hands I commend my spirit" (Luke 23: 46) are mutually contradictory. There is no explanation, no rationalization from Jesus how these could both be true; only faith and love for the Father makes it possible. There is still a struggle in Jesus ("learning obedience"?), but it is a struggle that is victorious, one that we do not win, but one that has been won for us.

"Faith's eternal happiness," claims Kierkegaard, ". . . is that God is love."[130] Jesus possesses the faith to love God because he knows that he is loved by God; he is "my Son, the Beloved" (Matt 3:17). This is known by revelation, a voice from heaven, not by understanding (cf. Matt 16:16). But people hear voices all the time. How can Jesus be sure this one is from God? How can we? David Koresh and the Branch Davidians made claims about God with just as much certainty as Billy Graham does.

Our focus, however, is on Jesus' certainty. His certainty will be the certainty of paradox, because he knows he is going to the cross. After his baptism Jesus avoids the temptations of the devil to doubt the certainty of the paradox for a demonstrable certainty: commanding the stones to turn into bread; throwing yourself down from the temple's pinnacle in order for the angels to rescue you; and receiving all the kingdoms of the world if he will worship the devil (Matt 4:1-11). Doubt wants "to force itself" onto God and "demonstrate that God is love."[131] Unlike the penitent

---

[129] Kierkegaard, *Upbuilding Discourses in Various Spirits,* 272–73. See also 273: "What does doubt about God's love want? It wants to reverse the relation, wants to sit quiet and safe, judging, and to deliberate upon whether God is indeed love; it wants to make God the defendant, to make him the one from whom something is required. But along this road God's love will never be found; doubt's striving toward God will be banished from God because it begins with presumptuousness. Faith's eternal happiness, on the one hand, is that God is love. This does not mean that faith understands how God's rule over a person is love. Right here is faith's struggle: to believe without being able to understand."

[130] Kierkegaard, *Upbuilding Discourses in Various Spirits,* 273.

[131] Ibid., 279.

robber, doubt is all about making excuses and refusing to admit its guilt before God. The agnostic Bertrand Russell is said to have remarked that if he appears before God after death and is asked why he didn't believe, he will respond, "There wasn't enough evidence." That is doubt working hard at an excuse. Can there ever be enough evidence? What kind of evidence would prove that there is a God? Beginning with doubt means that "God is lost long before the end."[132]

Jesus is not only an active Subject; he is also a passive Object. He is the object of the love of the Father; he is the beloved Son (Matt 3:17). As such, the Son defines the Father, for we are defined by that which we love. Isn't that true of God as well? The sonship of Christ is a manifestation, not just of the Son, but also of God the Father (John 14:9).[133] So knowledge of God does not derive from speculation nor deep feelings but from the object of God's love, the Son. He in turn loves God because he knows that he is loved. We would like to think that of ourselves and God, but we often lose the nerve. We are not sure. Here is where we need the faith of Jesus: faith that God even loves us (particularly when it comes to experiencing suffering or evil; see the next chapter). So the cry of abandonment is both a real abandonment and a real expression of faith, for the cry also reveals the trust of the Son in the Father. The Son cries to the Father because he knows the heart of the Father: One only asks, "Why have you forsaken me?" if one is in conflict. As John McLeod Campbell reminds us, the cry of the child reveals the mother's heart.[134] The Father will respond: the Son will be raised from the dead; but not without that cry, not without the cross and the burial. The Son is able to love God when we are unable. Jayber's initial doubts were based on his realization that Jesus' prayer was refused: the cup was not taken from him; he had to go to the cross. Why should we even begin praying then if every prayer ends with, "Thy will be done"?[135] Who

---

[132] Ibid.

[133] Campbell, *The Nature of the Atonement*, 60, 177.

[134] Ibid, 177: "It is the cry of the child that reveals the mother's heart. It is the cry of sonship in humanity bearing the burdens of humanity, confessing its sin, asking for it the good of which the capacity still remained to it, which being responded to by the Father has revealed the Father's heart. Without taking the form of that cry the mind that was in Christ would have failed by all its other outgoings to declare the Father's name."

[135] Berry, *Jayber Crow*, 50–51.

would ever have the strength to pray, "Thy will be done"? Jayber's questioning continues until it is embraced by the love for Mattie, then love for the world, and then love for God. The reality of a concrete, particular love interrupts yet does not obliterate Jayber's doubts. Then he is able to pray.

Love means vulnerability: the beloved has the potential of devastation like the California forest fires that consumed land the size of the state of Rhode Island.[136] But this is only because we take love seriously: it is at the core of our being. Are we to spare God from the depth of that kind of love? There is tremendous pain between the Father and the Son on the cross: it is a real, not just felt, abandonment. Yet, it is bearable when there is love in return. How much more terrible might be the unrequited love that God feels when he loves us (in both creation and redemption) and we turn away and ignore him! This is nonetheless genuine love, as God proves in his unrelenting love for Israel: "When Israel was a child, I loved him . . . The more I called them, the more they went from me" (Hos. 11:1-2). Here again is the first work of love: patience.[137] In the meantime, who are we to say that such a rejection does not affect God, as it would any lover? The *perichoretic* relationship between the Father and the Son speaks of their own vicarious acts within the Godhead: standing in place of each other, in order to feel empathy, for the Father to feel what it means to be the Son on the cross.[138] The vicarious humanity of Christ, therefore, is not just a function of the economic Trinity, but is founded upon an eternal, immanent subsistence in God himself: God in his very being, dare we say it, eternally acts vicariously!

The Father and the Son love each other with the love that is the Spirit of God ("the bond of love" according to Augustine).[139] There can be no greater love. The problem from a human perspective arises that the greater the love, the more difficult it is to give freedom to the beloved.[140] The father is tortured by allowing new freedom for his teenage daughter, whether it is a first date or a first car. That is why Paul wisely begins his list

[136] Harned, *Patience,* 123.

[137] Ibid., 153.

[138] Fiddes, *Participation in God,* 208.

[139] Augustine, *On the Trinity,* VI.7, NPNF, first series, Vol. 3, 100. See also Alasdair I. C. Heron, *The Holy Spirit* (Philadelphia: Westminster, 1983), 88–89.

[140] Harned, *Patience,* 153.

of the characteristics of love by stating, "Love is patient" (1 Cor 13:8). The Son, in his humanity, is patient with the Father with a patience that we desire to have but so rarely possess. In light of the darkness of the cross and the abyss of the burial, the Son experiences what appears to be the antithesis of love. So Jayber experiences times "when I lived in a desert and felt no joy and saw no hope and could not remember my old feelings. Then I lived by faith alone, faith without hope."[141] What good does he get out this? "I got to have love in my heart."

The Son lives by faith alone: He is the first one justified by faith alone. As a German Catholic bishop said, "At the moment of death, we are all Lutherans!" In other words, when it comes down to it we all depend on the mercy of God, not any amount or quality of works we have ever done in our lives. Depending on the mercy of God is not hoping we will be saved but knowing that we are saved by grace through faith. As a result, Jesus knows that he is loved by the Father, so he can love the Father, on our behalf and in our place. Like Jayber, all Jesus knows is the reality of love in his heart.

Such a love does not make doubt any less real for Jayber, or Jesus. The love in Jayber's heart, he claims, does not answer any doubt, but simply turns away. "It answers all arguments, merely by turning away, leaving them to find what rest they can."[142] But Jayber is changed. He enters upon "the way of love." He begins to pray again. Yet his doubts do not cease; in fact they intensify. Now he reads Bible passages about the two in the field and only one is taken and his heart goes out to the one left behind. He reads of the sheep and the goats and he has compassion for the goats.

Jesus receives no answer on the cross to his cry. Yet his entire life is motivated by love for the Father. The cross is only its culmination, just as the atonement begins with the birth of Jesus and only culminates on the cross. The beloved Son has no ministry of his own but that which is the agenda of the Father.[143] To be a "success" (in contrast to contemporary business and education) is not in his vocabulary. Rather, Jesus is "the perfect Eucharistic Being" (Schmemann), the one who truly gives thanks to the

141 Berry, *Jayber Crow,* 247.

142 Ibid., 248–50.

143 Anderson, "Clergy Burnout as A Symptom of Theological Anemia" in *The Shape of Practical Theology,* 287.

Father, whose faith is not just the end result of frustrations and anxieties, a kind of resignation, but "comes out of fullness, love, and joy."[144] Our problem is that we lack that fullness, love, and joy. We need the fullness, love, and joy of Jesus, not just to drum it up within ourselves, even "enabled" by God's grace. No, a more radical surgery is needed. We can now give thanks because Jesus gives thanks and as Jesus gives thanks. "Here at last is a man who loves the Lord his God with all his heart and soul and mind and strength and his neighbour including his enemy as himself."[145]

God So **Loves** *the World . . .*

How do we dare say that God loves the world? Jayber's love for Mattie creates in Jayber a love for the world, for the ordinary people of Port William. This love leads him to the love of God for the world: "If God loves the world, might that not be proved in my own love for it?"[146] This sounds strange since we assume things work the other way around. The Johannine epistles make it clear: "We know love by this, that he laid down his life for us—and we ought to lay down our lives for one another" (1 John 3:16). Because we know the love of God, then we should be motivated to love the world. "In this is love, not that we loved God but that he loved us and sent his Son to be the atoning sacrifice for our sins" (1 John 4:10). Would we really love God otherwise?[147] Again, this is the motivation for

---

[144] Schmemann, *For the Life of the World,* 38.

[145] Smail, "Can One Man Die for the People?" in *Atonement Today,* ed. Goldingay, 87.

[146] Berry, *Jayber Crow,* 253.

[147] Paul Molnar claims that Karl Rahner contrasts with Karl Barth by equating the love of neighbor with the love of God. "Love of God and Love of Neighbor in the Theology of Karl Rahner and Karl Barth," *Modern Theology* 20, no. 4 (October, 2004), 567–99. According to Rahner, when one loves the neighbor, one is loving God. Molnar suggests that this reveals Rahner's identification of the immanent with the economic Trinity in contrast to Barth's teaching that the two are in relationship but still distinct. Molnar is right to warn against an identification between the love of God and the love of neighbor but one questions if he has allowed for the particular power of concrete love, the person in whom one encounters Jesus Christ in the needs of the world (Matt 25:40: ". . . just as you did it to one of the least of these who are members of my family, you did it to me") to be a form of Jesus Christ in the world. Jayber's love for Mattie is real, yet it does cry out to Jesus for refuge. Bonhoeffer saw in his day "the persecution of justice, truth,

our love of neighbor: "Beloved, since God loved us so much, we also ought to love one another" (1 John 4:11). How does Jayber's love for Mattie lead to love for God?

God's love is loving vicariously, for us and in our place, for we are unable to love with his kind of perfect love. Yes, we can love . . . Jayber can love Mattie. In fact, Jayber loves Mattie "vicariously," in the place of God! The "vicarious" way of loving is not afraid of doubt because love is based on reality, not reason. Jayber does not argue from reason to God's love for the world, but from the particularity of his love for Mattie and then for the world. So the love of the Son works for us. The Son's love for the Father is particular, concrete, and risky. Such suffering love is like Jayber's, allowing freedom, sorrow, and even failure (the "failure" of the Father at the cross?).[148] But the "failure" of the Father is the triumph of the Son. Easter Saturday, the burial of Jesus, reminds us that the Son "has refused to act divinely, to resist his enemies and ours, but has let the forces of destruction overwhelm him."[149] Jesus is victor even before the resurrection, because of his obedience to the Father for our sake.

Jayber loves Mattie, but Jayber also needs Jesus. He knows that in his love for the world he will fail. He does not know if his love will ever bear fruit, whether Mattie would ever return his love, or their relationship could sustain the thousands of trials that a man and a woman encounter. The Son's love for the Father does not fail. Through the Son's love for the Father, the Father is empowered to love the world. That may sound strange to us, but is it not the reality of how the persons of the Trinity, in their *perichoretic* relationship, must affect one another? How much more is this true if the omnipotence of God is demonstrated by God allowing himself to be empowered by the Son, and then, by us?

---

humanity, and freedom that drove people, to whom these values were precious, under the protection of Jesus Christ and thus under his claim; and this experience caused the church-community of Jesus Christ to discover the breadth of its responsibility" (Bonhoeffer, *Ethics,* 345). Ultimately, Jayber's love for Mattie begs for "the protection of Jesus Christ." Love of neighbor needs the love of God.

148 Alan E. Lewis, *Between Cross and Resurrection,* 54–55.

149 Ibid., 82.

150 Berry, *Jayber Crow,* 254.

"All the good I know," claims Jayber, "is in this, that a man might so love this world that it would break his heart."[150] The broken heart of the Father is seen on the cross of the Son. His broken heart is ultimately, not just for the Son, but for the world, for he knows that the Son is there for the life of the world. The vulnerability of love is not foreign to the triune God. The incarnation and the cross are new events for God, but they are not foreign to him. As manifestations of the sheer love of his eternal being, the life, death, and resurrection of Jesus Christ is simply the overflowing of God's being into our desperate, needy world.[151] Jayber's heart could be, and was, broken by Mattie. How much more is God's heart broken by us?

God loves the world through the faith of Jesus, a faith that faces our doubts squarely not only from the vantage point of the cross but also from the resurrection. The purpose of the incarnation is to lift us up with the Son in the life of the loving communion between the Father, the Son, and the Holy Spirit.[152] In a world of disease and destruction, the Son, loving the Father, is able to acknowledge the love of the Father when we are unable (and sometimes unwilling) to do so, testifying by the blood of his cross.[153] Since the *perichoresis* speaks of the mutual indwelling between the Father and the Son, the faith and obedience of Jesus Christ to the Father signifies a genuine human waiting that is a testimony to God's waiting, to God's faithfulness.[154]

The end result for the love of God is a community that reflects the mutual love in the being of the triune God.[155] What God creates can only

---

[151] T. F. Torrance, *The Christian Doctrine of God,* 164–65: "It is that ground of the unbroken relation in Being and Act between Jesus Christ and the Father, of their knowing and loving of one another, and through the mission of the Spirit of the Father and of the Son to be with us and dwell within us, that the movement of Love eternally hidden in God has been revealed to us and a corresponding movement of love has been generated in us toward the Father through the Son and in the Holy Spirit . . . The Love of God revealed to us in the economic Trinity is identical with the Love of God in the ontological Trinity; but the Love of God revealed to us in the economic manifestation of the Father, the Son and the Holy Spirit in the history of our salvation, tells us that God loves us with the very same love with which he loves himself in the reciprocal love of the three divine Persons for Each Other in the eternal Communion of the Holy Trinity."

[152] James B. Torrance, *Worship, Community, and the Triune God of Grace,* 32.

[153] Ibid., 48–49.

[154] Barth, *The Epistle to the Romans,* 96.

[155] T. F. Torrance, *Trinitarian Perspectives,* 3.

be a community of reciprocity, a *perichoretic* community of mutually indwelling love. If the Church seeks to be anything else it is not the Church of the Holy Trinity. God so loves the world that he creates such a community, yet he does not do so in a coercive way. His love for the world is still largely unrequited! Yet he still loves; He is still patient with us, as the Son is patient with the Father.

This new community is not based on its own ability to love, believe, or to intercede with the Father but on that of the Son's ability. Confessing Jesus as Lord is not simply a confession of deity but also of his lordship over our faith. "He is the only one who does what he does."[156] No amount of mystical piety or Christian righteousness can compare with what he can do.[157] As Lord, he is "the Lord as Servant" (Barth) (Phil 2:5-11).[158] He is the one who first believes, "the pioneer and perfecter of our faith" (Heb 12:2).

Jayber is willing to allow his heart to be broken. That is the risk of love. He begins with Mattie, but then extends this love to the world, and to God. The risk is always there, however, no matter who or what you love. The beloved may not give you the response you want. God experiences that every day, so should we be so different?

Mutuality, however, is the goal of God between God and humanity for it reflects his eternal being of communion among the Father, the Son, and the Holy Spirit. Forgiveness is not based on mutuality, on an agreement of both parties.[159] Reconciliation is based on mutuality; it is the ultimate goal, for the relationship between God and humanity and between human beings and other human beings. However, forgiveness comes first. There is a distinction between forgiveness and reconciliation. Forgiveness should always seek its *telos,* its end, in reconciliation, but also be able to stand by itself. Once the abusing parent has died, there is no longer any opportunity for reconciliation. However, if the abused person does not forgive, a lifetime of captivity to anger can be the result. There is a place for "therapeutic

---

[156] Barth, *CD,* I/2, 382.

[157] Ibid., 383, 392.

[158] Barth, *CD,* IV/1, chapter fourteen, 157–780.

[159] Fiddes, *Participation in God,* 209.

[160] This is classically stated by Lewis B. Smedes, *Forgive and Forget: Healing the Hurts We Don't Deserve* (New York: Pocket Books, 1984) and criticized by L. Gregory Jones, *Embodying Forgiveness: A Theological Analysis* (Grand Rapids: Eerdmans, 1995) 47–52.

forgiveness" (although divine forgiveness is more than this).[160] The mutuality of reconciliation is the greatest good but not the only good.

The risk of love, seeking mutuality, therefore, is not something that is left for us do: simply to grit our teeth, clench our fists, and trudge ahead in the battle. No, the good news is that someone else has taken the risk of love. Jayber is admirable in the risk he takes in his love for Mattie. But we are not Jaybers! God's love for the world is vicarious, on our behalf, and in our place. The Spirit enables us to participate in the journey of the Son, in his faith, obedience, and love, so that we too might believe that God loves the world, including ourselves.[161] "Our deepest feelings are often invested in that which has the capacity to break our hearts," Ray Anderson (and Jayber!) remind us.[162] Faith and love can do that. That is why they are so valuable. Anderson's response is to encourage us to follow his farmer father's example: Do not invest in the harvest but in the planting. The planting, the act of love and faith, is all one can do. The harvest is out of one's control. The farmer can be hurt by a bad crop, yet he will not be devastated in his being if he has planted the seed well. Investing yourself in the planting does not shield you from hurt, but only from destruction. So Paul speaks of being "afflicted in every way, but not crushed; perplexed, but not driven to despair; persecuted, but not forsaken; struck down, but not destroyed; always carrying in the body the death of Jesus, so that the life of Jesus may also be made visible in our bodies" (2 Cor 4:8-10). The Son experiences the struggle for us and in our place, becoming the one who, intending to do the Father's will, "looks round upon a universe from which any trace of Him seems to have vanished, and asks why he has been forsaken, and still obeys."[163] That is a tall order for anyone to be such a spiritual athlete. Jayber is not left by himself. So Jesus, in his genuine humanity, believes and obeys the Father, and leaves the rest to God. We can now participate in that act of faith, that manifestation of love. Through that act, God loves the world.

The *perichoretic* love that God has for the world is different from what one would think is God's right: a possessive love, the love the king rightly has for his kingdom. For in the love of the Son for the Father, and the Father for the Son, in the Spirit, the priority is not possession. At the

---

[161] Fiddes, *Participation in God,* 210.

[162] Anderson, *Unspoken Wisdom,* 53.

[163] C. S. Lewis, *The Screwtape Letters,* 39.

[164] Berry, *Jayber Crow,* 351.

end Jayber Crow realizes that his book is about heaven, a reality that cannot be possessed yet is "the realest thing we know."[164] To think that you can possess another person is to live in unreality, yet that is so often the case in human relationships. Despite the depth of his love for Mattie (or because of!), Jayber does not seek to possess her. "But the earth speaks to us of Heaven, or why would we want to go there?"[165] Jayber would not be too pious to say that Mattie brings him a taste of heaven. So also the greatest reality is the reality that cannot begin to be possessed: heaven. Yes, because we cannot possess it, we can easily doubt it. That is where the vicarious faith of Jesus intervenes. He believes in heaven because he is the beloved Son who loves God in our place and on our behalf. The alternative, as Jayber is well aware, is to write a book about hell, which is a place of *failure:* the failure to love.[166] Here are "the leftovers of life; things I might once have done that are now undoable, old wrongs, responsibilities unmet, ineradicable failures . . ."[167] We fail at love, but Christ does not. Jesus intervenes, or else we might very well write a book about hell not heaven. He needs to love vicariously, in our place, or else hell is our destiny however you imagine it: "where we fail to love another, where we hate and destroy one another for reasons abundantly provided or for righteousness' sake or for pleasure, where we destroy the things we need the most, where we see no hope and have no faith."[168] In trying to possess others we so easily lose the possession of faith. Jesus does not.

There is a distinction between the persons of the Trinity, and the vicarious humanity of Christ will not let us forget that. But there is also the *perichoretic* mutual indwelling so that the love that the Son has for the Father spills over into God's love for the world, despite our inability and unwillingness to see it and acknowledge it. Through the Spirit we participate in that mutual love so that subject and object distinctions are not the last word in God or between God and ourselves.[169] This is like, according to John of the Cross, being "seized by the same delight" between the Father and the Son, and "caught into God's great being; breathing his

[165] Ibid., 354–55.
[166] Ibid., 354.
[167] Ibid., 355.
[168] Ibid., 354.
[169] Fiddes, *Participation in God,* 44–45.
[170] John of the Cross, *Ballad* 4, 61; cited by Fiddes, *Participation in God,* 45.

very air!"[170] Paul's view of justification is not apart from being "in Christ" and that "Christ lives in me" (Gal 2:14-21), through "the faith of the Son of God" (Gal 2:20; alternative translation in NRSV).[171] Throughout the Pauline vocabulary there is this richness of what Deissmann calls "the mystical fellowship with Christ": "the love of Christ" (Rom 8:35; 2 Cor 5:14; Eph 3:19); "the hope of Christ" (1 Thess 1:3); "the peace of Christ" (Col 3:15); "the meekness and gentleness of Christ" (2 Cor 10:1); "the tender mercies of Christ" (Phil 1:8); "the patience of Christ" (2 Thess 3:5); "the obedience of Christ" (2 Cor 11:10); "the sufferings of Christ" (Phil 3:10); and "the afflictions of Christ" (Col 1:24).[172] The love of God for the world is to initiate us into this world, the world of the relationship among the Father, the Son, and the Holy Spirit. This participation is not only through his resurrection, but also through his life and death, including his faithfulness and obedience.[173]

Participation in the love of God is more like joining in my uncle's tour of great hamburger joints in Wichita than mysteriously being absorbed into God in a pantheistic sense. My uncle did enjoy going to the "Kellogg Diner" and "J. R.'s Café" (both no longer in existence) and brought my brother and me along, much to our delight (but too close to dinner time, to my mother's chagrin). We participated in his will. We did not just imitate him; he brought us along with him. He knew where the wonderful land of the Kellogg Diner was, with its old-fashioned, greasy spoon atmosphere, the smell of grilled onions and fresh burgers inviting us to follow him, and we followed him gladly.

There is the genuine will of the Son within the Trinity as well.[174] We are to lean upon the "Amen" of the Son to the Father's purpose, a purpose that otherwise, frankly, seems too abstract, general, and vague. Who are we to say we know God's will? We do not, but the Son does. His is "the perfect human response to the everlasting 'Yes' of God."[175]

---

[171] Frank J. Matera, *Galatians* (Collegeville: Liturgical Press, 1992), 100.

[172] Adolf Deissmann, *Paul,* trans. W. F. Wilson (New York: Harper and Brothers, 1957), 162–64.

[173] M. D. Hooker, "*Pistis Christou,*" *New Testament Studies* 35 (1989), 323.

[174] Fiddes, *Participation in God,* 52–53.

[175] Dom Gregory Dix, *The Shape of the Liturgy* (San Francisco: Harper and Row, 1982), 129–30.

The Son's perfect obedience is nonetheless the obedience of faith not sight. This is appropriate to the love of God that does not usually overwhelm us with his presence. Epiphanies, mystic revelations, and miracles are miracles because they are exceptions. An overwhelming presence would be a love that tries to coerce; a love that does not want a free relationship.[176] Jayber could have tried that with Mattie and it would have been a disaster, as all overzealous lovers know. There is no suffering in an attempt to coerce or in an overwhelming display of power (or affection!).[177] The suffering love of the Crucified One enables us to die to that lie, to a false definition of love. This love comes with a price: Christ's death and, since we participate in his, our death. Jayber prays that he would know in his heart the love of God for the world, but the minute he prays that he realizes "this was my most prideful, foolish, and dangerous prayer. It was my step into the abyss. As soon as I prayed it, I knew that I would die."[178] This is the love that breaks the Father's heart. This is the love that will break our hearts. Yet, it is only through the cross that we know this communion between the Father and the Son through the Spirit. A spirituality of communion reflects the distinctions among the Father, the Son, and the Holy Spirit in a willingness to allow a distance between us and God. The more the inaccessible God reveals of himself the more inaccessible he becomes, as the Fathers frequently remark.[179]

The transcendence, the inaccessibility of God, is now a historical reality because of the incarnation (Anderson).[180] Jayber imagines that love motivated by compassion for humanity would have the power (omnipotence) to become human, walk our walk, and suffer our fate.[181] He stops at that point. The vicarious humanity of Christ picks up the rest, for most of us are not able to have Jayber's faith, obedience, patience, love, and even for Jayber himself. We need someone to take us to the Kellogg Diner.

To be taken to the Kellogg Diner is not to be relieved of doubt. To be loved by my uncle, so much that he would take us with him on his trip

---

176 Clément, *The Roots of Christian Mysticism,* 190–91.

177 Berry, *Jayber Crow,* 254.

178 Ibid., 253–54.

179 Clement, *The Roots of Christian Mysticism,* 191.

180 Anderson, *Historical Transcendence and the Reality of God.*

181 Berry, *Jayber Crow,* 251–52.

182 Ibid., 250.

does not ignore a whole world out there that can potentially be very hostile to an eight-year old! Jayber's awakening to love does not obliterate his doubts, but increases them.[182] He has a new heart for those left out, even in the Gospels, where one is left, and for the goats in the parable of the sheep and the goats (Matt 25:31-46). "I had my list of goats, who seemed hopeless enough to me, and I didn't know what to do about them."[183]

Jayber does not know what to do about them. In like manner, doubt is something we do not know what to do about. But Jayber at least realizes his impotence. He at least knows the biblical verse that "God so loved the world . . ." so that he can love Port William like God does, as it is.[184] The vicarious love of God becomes a reality for Jayber. He learns that God loves "like a father with a wayward child, whom He can't help and can't forget." Jayber does not know what to do about them, yet he cannot forget them, just as he cannot forget Mattie. We do not know what to do about doubt, but we cannot forget the faith and love of Jesus (the faith and love that he possesses and that is a part of who he is). So "belief" becomes secondary to Jayber.[185] What is more important is that he now realizes that he was in the light more than he thought, for the people of Port William stand before him, loved by God, loved vicariously by God. Faith, Jayber realizes, is not a resting place, but a place in the dark.[186] Doubts are not to be excused, but we are not to be surprised by them. A man of faith can pray for whom Jayber calls the Man in the Well: a hunter who has stumbled into a well. There is no way he can be rescued. But the man of faith believes nonetheless.

> His belief is a kind of knowledge beyond any way of knowing.
> He believes that the child in the womb is not lost, nor is the man
> whose work has come to nothing, nor is the old woman forsaken
> in a nursing home in California. He believes that those who make
> their bed in Hell are not lost, or those who dwell in the uttermost
> parts of the sea, or the lame man at Bethesda Pool, or Lazarus
> in the grave, or those who pray,

---

[183] Ibid.
[184] Ibid., 251.
[185] Ibid., 252.
[186] Ibid., 356.
[187] Ibid., 357.

'Eli, Eli, lama sabachthani.'
Have mercy.[187]

Even those who pray, "*Eli, Eli, lama sabachthani,*" "My God, my God, why have you forsaken me?" will no longer be lost. Jayber and Jesus finally meet . . . and they are good friends. Yet such a world is hard to believe in: a world of evil and suffering. Jayber, too, needs the cry of the man on a cross.

Jayber can now pray, "Thy will be done" because he knows that vicarious love for the ordinary people of Port William. He describes this as: "I prayed my gratitude." As Jesus prays his gratitude (Matt 11:25), so we can pray our gratitude with him. And it all starts, Ray Anderson reminds us, because love is based on a reality, not reason.

5

Providence, Evil, Suffering, and the God Who Believes

It is good to be with Jesus and not elsewhere. This is
good because it is there that God Himself is good for us.
—Karl Barth[1]

"O taste and see that the Lord is good," sings the refrain of Psalm 34:8. What an invitation! The sensory nature of "tasting" and "seeing" draws us irresistibly in anticipation of a feast of communion with a God who is *good.* Prominent in the communion hymn of the Orthodox Lenten liturgy of the Pre-Sanctified Gifts, this invitation is to intimate communion with one who is good, and we can know that by sharing in him through the body and the blood of the Eucharist.[2] This speaks of an intimacy all of us long for so much but so rarely experience. Why is this so? One of the reasons may be that we so often doubt that God is good. In a world of horrendous suffering how can we believe that God is good? Doubt questions the goodness and providential care of the God of Jesus. However,

[1] Barth, *CD,* II/2, 570.

[2] Archpriest D. Sokolof, *A Manual of the Orthodox Church's Divine Services* (Jordanville, N.Y.: Holy Trinity Monastery, 2001), 103.

in light of the vicarious faith of Christ, can we speak of a God who is not only all-powerful and good but also *believes* despite a world of horrendous evils? Can Jesus "taste and see that the Lord is good" *for us and in our place*?

How Dare We Discuss the Mystery of Evil?

Do we really need to be persuaded that there is a problem of evil for believers in a good and almighty God? The problem may be greater when we dare to even discuss the mystery of evil. The dilemma is stated famously by Ivan in Dostoevsky's *The Brothers Karamazov.* In his argument with his saintly brother Alyosha, Ivan makes it clear that he is all too aware of the absurdity of believing in the providence of God in a world of *dysteleology,* needless suffering, especially the suffering of children. So in disgust he returns the ticket of "eternal harmony" to God.[3] Even if a kind of "eternal harmony" might result from such suffering, Ivan will still hand back his "ticket" to such a world. It is not worth it. And in that refusal he is refusing the morality if not the existence of a God who would create such a world.[4]

This is our world, too. It is a world of injustice. In Albert Goldbarth's poem, "Even, Equal," he describes the "two schoolgirls" found "under half-receded ice, the bruises frozen, into lustrous broaches at their frozen throats."

> Whoever did it is still out there, is free and maybe
> needing more. The word "injustice" doesn't include
> the choking gall that burns through me[5]

In "Meop" Goldbarth expresses for many what has been lost: the belief that "in some megamatrix substrate (God, or atoms, or Imagination) holds the infinite unalike dots at its body in a parity, and daily life reflects this." Why? One needs to look only at a scenario such as

---

[3] Dostoevsky, *The Brothers Karamazov,* 246–64.
[4] Kenneth Surin, "Theodicy" in *The Turnings of Darkness and Light: Essays in Systematic and Philosophical Theology* (Cambridge: Cambridge University Press, 1989), 82–83.
[5] Goldbarth, "Even, Equal," in *Beyond,* 21.

> . . . only yesterday, a girl,
> eleven, was found with the name of a rival gang, *Lady Satans,*
> carefully cut in her thigh and rubbed with drainpipe acid. Somewhere
> there may be a world where such as these are equally legitimatized, but
> not here in the thick and swirling mists of Planet Albert.[6]

"Planet Albert" is my planet, too. Our planet.

The Christian doctrine of providence proclaims that God cares, that he "oversees" the universe. A theologian like John Leith claims, "Christians all acknowledge that everything that happens is the will of God."[7] Theologians are not alone in their belief in a "meticulous providence." Those who have suffered an incalculable loss often cling to such a providential God. One example is the tragic story of Amy Montgomery, a devout Christian teenager working at a sandwich shop in Wichita, Kansas, who was senselessly slaughtered by a friend of a co-worker attempting to rob the shop. When the murderer was charged with the deed, Amy's mother appeared to the press outside the courthouse, saying that she had forgiven her daughter's slayer. Said Mrs. Montgomery:

> Everything happens the way it's supposed to. We have to
> give thanks for this, for this is the will of God. How else
> could she have ever reached the people she was worried
> about, prayed about, but through something like this?
> This is the master plan.

Mrs. Montgomery must, of course, be respected. She had experienced a kind of loss different from most of the losses you and I will ever face. One could easily psychologize her response as a defense mechanism (what theodicy isn't?). However, her pain and the way she dealt with the pain must not be cheapened. But for some of us, for the Ivans and potential Ivans among us, like myself, a different response is needed.

From David Hume to Annie Dillard, many have spoken cries of anguish against a traditional belief in God and creation. Given such a

---

[6] Goldbarth, "Meop," in *Beyond,* 41.
[7] John Leith, *Basic Christian Doctrine* (Louisville: Westminster John Knox, 1994), 25.

world, Hume concludes, God must be either an infant who does not know better or decrepit and cannot do what needs to be done.[8] "God is an underachiever," cracks Woody Allen. Not as popular as a finite God, perhaps a malevolent God is also likely, a God who sets us up for disappointments by giving blessings along with curses, dreams along with reality. Why does God give us a loved one only to take her away by death or by her rejection? Would Jayber have suffered as much if he had never met Mattie? Could he think that a cruel God was behind placing Mattie in his life? Mark Twain believed that God's invention of a fly carrying the African sleeping sickness is evidence that "There is only one father cruel enough to afflict his child with that horrible disease—only one."[9] Twain still held that God possesses "limitless power."[10] Annie Dillard joins in Twain's protest, echoing Nelly Sachs' exasperation, "Who is like You, O Lord, among the silent, remaining silent through the suffering of His children?"[11]

Even the traditional expressions of God acting seem to have ambiguous results. Rabbi Akiva may say that God rewards the virtuous and punishes the evil but this is for Annie Dillard, like so many theodicies, "harsh all around."[12] Where is the evidence that God's "acts" have made any difference? Dillard again:

> That is touching that Allah, God, and their ilk care
> when one ant dismembers another, or note when a
> sparrow falls, but I strain to see the use of it.[13]

---

[8] David Hume, *Dialogues Concerning Natural Religion,* ed. Nelson Pike (Indianapolis: Bobbs-Merrill, 1970), 169; cited by John Sanders, *The God Who Risks: A Theology of Providence* (Downers Grove, Ill.: InterVarsity, 1998), 266.

[9] Mark Twain, *The Bible According to Mark Twain: Irreverent Writings on Eden, Heaven, and the Flood by America's Master Satirist,* Howard G. Baetzhold and Joseph B. McCullough, eds. (New York: Simon and Schuster Touchstone, 1996), 244; cited by Jennifer Michael Hecht, *Doubt: A History* (San Francisco: HarperSanFrancisco, 2003), 442.

[10] Twain, *The Bible According to Mark Twain*; cited by Hecht, *Doubt: A History,* 443.

[11] Annie Dillard, *For the Time Being* (New York: Vintage Books, 1999), 28.

[12] Ibid., 30.

[13] Ibid., 75.

The preacher prays to God, "All your actions show your wisdom and love." Dillard wants to scream back, "That's a lie!"[14] *Where* has God "cast down the mighty," working "all things for the good of those who love him?" "When was that?" moans Annie Dillard. "I missed it."[15]

Being counseled on behalf of a God who causes everything to happen and controls all can be cold comfort for persons in extreme pain. "Why are they teaching me to hate God?" Harold Kushner asks.[16]

So also the ophthalmologist in Woody Allen's film *Crimes and Misdemeanors* is taught by his pious Jewish father that "the eyes of God are all around us," but finds it easy to murder a blackmailing mistress, getting away with the crime literally as well as psychologically in his disappearing conscience.[17] In addition, the irregularities of God's creation often are bizarre and seem cruel. "WHAT'S with the bird-headed dwarfs?" cries Annie Dillard.[18]

Where is Jesus Christ in such an idea of God? In Christ we can see the God who is close to us, who embraces us and does not leave us.[19] We may even view in Christ the God who suffers with us, showing us the benefit of suffering for others.[20] But we can fall into despair all so quickly and completely when faced with horrendous evils, needless suffering, and even the personal rejections from people and a world in which we do not seem often to fit. Can Christ come to our aid at the point of our doubts with his faith? Can Jesus help us believe in a good and all-powerful God in a world of a devout teenager's life being senselessly ended in a petty hold-up?

---

[14] Ibid., 85.

[15] Ibid., 86.

[16] Harold Kushner, *When Bad Things Happen to Good People* (New York: Avon, 1981), 10.

[17] Todd H. Speidell, "God, Woody Allen, and Job," *Christian Scholars' Review* 29, no. 3 (2000), 554.

[18] Dillard, *For the Time Being,* 53.

[19] John Stackhouse, *Can God Be Trusted? Faith and the Problem of Evil* (Oxford: Oxford University Press, 2000), 104.

[20] James Walsh, ed., *Divine Providence and Human Suffering* (The Message of the Fathers of the Church, vol. 17) (Wilmington, Del.: Michael Glazier, 1985), 163–79.

The Incarnation: The Act of the Vicarious Humanity of Christ in an Evil World

God's Risk of Freedom

"Incarnate Word Spoils Homecoming for BC" reads the sports headline: the Catholic college Incarnate Word has triumphed over Bethel College. What a great name for a college! What is more central to the Christian faith than that God has taken upon flesh *(in-carnis)* for our sake? Beyond being a nifty name for a Catholic college, the reality of the eternal Word of God becoming finite, temporal human being should still shock us. We need a greater "shock and awe" than even Saddam Hussein encountered with the U.S. armed forces. Whatever criticisms one might have of Mel Gibson's film, *The Passion of the Christ,* one must admit that the film reminds us that Jesus' suffering was a shocking, cruel experience, not to be sanitized for majestic stained glass windows. What are we to do with this? What are we to make of God in our flesh? And what does it mean as we live with a world of needless, absurd suffering and evil?

We are back to the freedom of God. The incarnation is the declaration that God is free to become human. God is free to experience something new. In that freedom, however, is the risk, and it is the risk of love. Is God never so close to our human experiences than when he takes the risk of love, the risk of being turned aside, rejected, counted as not worthy, not good enough? "My Best Was Never Good Enough" Bruce Springsteen laments in his song, for us and maybe for God. Freedom is a rough town to play in. Freedom is a tough gig. It is at that point, in God's freedom in the incarnation, that he exerts a power not just over our logic or morality but over the entirety of our lives, including our doubts in this suffering world.[21]

The *impassibility* (the serenity of God, a God who does not suffer) and the *immutability* (that God does not change) of God are doctrines that have been challenged mightily in recent years. What is the incarnation but the proclamation that God indeed is moved with compassion and God does experience something new in acting by becoming human?

[21] T. F. Torrance, *Divine and Contingent Order,* 6.

Does this action of God in the incarnation, however, involve a "risk," a kind of vulnerability in God so that God in effect is conditioned by my responses, as some suggest?[22] I risk a great deal when I love someone else. I do not know if the beloved will return that love. I risk a great deal even when I reach out to someone I consider a friend if that friendship is not returned. If it is not returned the effect on one's soul can be devastating. The feelings of worthlessness can rarely be matched by any other experience in life. Some have suggested that the poignancy in the "Peanuts" comic strip by Charles Schulz is found in the repeated theme of unrequited love: Lucy is always rejected by the piano-playing Schroeder; Charlie Brown is rejected by almost everyone (even the kite-eating tree!). Can God experience such a pain? If he cannot, does that mean a certain inability to love? Is God really "open" to human faith, human trust and willing to pay the consequences of not being loved?

The incarnation, John's Gospel reminds us, is the reality that God is the ultimate unrequited lover: "He was in the world, and the world came into being through him; yet the world did not know him. He came to what was his own, and his own people did not accept him." (John 1: 10-11) Isaiah includes this in his messianic prophecy: "He was despised and rejected by others; a man of suffering and acquainted with infirmity; and as one from whom others hide their faces he was despised, and we held him of no account" (Isa 53: 3).

What are we saying then about God? Can God be hurt, rejected, maimed . . . can God be destroyed? Are we going too far? "Exploration into God," as Ray Anderson puts it, can be a dangerous thing. But perhaps we are too protective of God. Love means putting oneself on the line for another. "No one has greater love than this, to lay down one's life for one's friends" (John 15:13). We at least need to dare to ask these questions because of the needless suffering of Ivan Karamazov's innocent children. Some suggest that we do not know the real will of God. We only know the empirically known, "revealed" will of God but his "secret" will, that is, his ultimate will is unknown.[23] Such a God though is not really known.

[22] The literature by and on this school called "open theism" led in recent years by Clark Pinnock and John Sanders is immense. A good place to start is Clark Pinnock et al., *The Openness of God* (Downers Grove, Ill.: InterVarsity, 1994).

[23] Paul Helm, *The Providence of God* (Downers Grove, Ill.: InterVarsity, 1994), 130, 133. See also Calvin, *Institutes* 1.17.2, citing Rom 11:33-34.

In contrast is the God who reveals himself through the Son in the Spirit as "Father." Here is the true freedom of God: to be Father, not as a "God behind God's back."[24] The Son is the one will of God who reveals the Father.[25] Who can call God Father in a world of horrendous evils? Only Jesus has the right . . . only Jesus dares.[26] Therefore, we can "with boldness," as the Orthodox liturgy proclaims, "dare to call upon thee, the heavenly God, as Father, and to say, 'Our Father . . .'" "Only by entering into the heart of Jesus can the name of 'Father' be truly heard." God is a believer as well as a revealer.

God's Risk of Believing

God may be open to our faith; we may want it, desire it, even yearn for it. But can we deliver? Can we deliver even if we want ("For I do not do what I want, but I do the very thing I hate . . . I can will what is right, but I cannot do it. For I do not do the good I want, but the evil I do not want is what I do" [Rom 7:15, 18-19]). God's openness to our faith is a mighty precarious ledge. The history of Israel's unbelief and disobedience, of course, makes this all too clear. Israel's history is our history, our inability and unwillingness to obey our creator. Why should God try again?

The "good news" is nothing less than this: God has provided the "input" himself! There is a risk, a risk of rejection that God has genuinely taken. The God of the Bible is a God who can *believe*, dare we say it, just as much as he can create and sustain. This is what we find in the vicarious humanity of Christ. My trust is so wavering at times, but Jesus' is not. Even those at the cross exclaimed, albeit mockingly, "He trusts in God!" (Matt 27:43). It is not up to us to try to believe in God in a world of needless suffering and evil. God provides the belief, the faith, the trust, as well as the revelation. This is the message of the incarnation, of a truly Chalcedonian Christology that takes seriously the full humanity as well as the full deity of Christ.

---

[24] T. F. Torrance, *Reality and Scientific Theology,* 201, n. 3: "We cannot know God behind his back, as it were, by stealing knowledge of him, for we may know him only in accordance with the way he has actually taken in revealing himself to us."

[25] Barth, *CD,* III/3, 34.

[26] Boris Bobrinskoy, *The Compassion of the Father,* trans. Anthony P. Gythiel (Crestwood, N.Y.: St. Vladimir's Seminary Press, 2003), 91, 104.

The trust of Jesus, however, is not just an example of how to believe.[27] No, the faith of Jesus is vicarious, on our behalf and in our place. Ivan needs more than just the inspiration of an example. A virtuous model may inspire at first but will ultimately frustrate. The hurts are too deep, the reality is too stark.

We should not leave the freedom of God, however. God has indeed taken upon our flesh, our conditions of life. Like the reporters joining the American troops heading towards Baghdad in the second Gulf War, God has become "embedded" with us. He does not report the war from the cozy confines of Paris cafes. But this does not mean that God has surrendered himself to the flotsam and jetsam of our muddied rivers of life.[28] Apart from the vicarious faith of Christ, however, it is hard not to draw that conclusion if we truly grant God's "embeddedness" in our conditions.

The freedom of God is not identical with our freedom.[29] Our freedom is extremely limited by birth, environment, and circumstances. God's freedom is over space and time (Psalm 139), planning the way of salvation before the foundation of the world (Isa 42:9; 44:7; Eph 1:4), not limited by our ways of thinking (Isa 55:8). This includes his ability to become human, even to believe, to have faith, on our behalf and in our place. God has taken on our condition not just to be our representative, to speak our thoughts, but to be our substitute because we do not know God and cannot fathom the ways of God. We are back to the vicarious *knowledge* of Christ (Matt 11:27; John 14, 17). Not one of the sparrows falls to ground "apart from your Father," so "even the hairs of your head are all counted" (Matt 10:29-30). This is not instruction on meticulous providence; the text does not say that God is causing each sparrow to fall, but a reminder of our ignorance and his care.[30] Only the faith that belongs to Jesus knows God in such a way. What the Son knows is the heart of the Father. So he can pray, "Father, forgive them; for *they do not know* what they are doing" (Luke 23:34). For the Son, faith and knowledge are

[27] As in Sanders, *The God Who Risks,* 105.

[28] This is the tendency in open theism. See Sanders, *The God Who Risks,* 30.

[29] Geoffrey W. Bromiley, "Only God Is Free," *Christianity Today* 46, no. 2 (2002) 72.

[30] W. D. Davies and Dale Allison, *A Critical and Exegetical Commentary on the Gospel According to St. Matthew,* Vol. 1 (Edinburgh: T. & T. Clark, 1988), 209.

intertwined.[31] Dare we say it? . . . Only Jesus can believe in the providence of God in a world such as ours.

The God who believes is under no necessity, therefore, to "persuade" the Father through the ministrations of the Son. Moses' ministry as an intercessor is often cited as an example of how God is influenced through "a forceful presentation by one who is in a special relationship with God."[32] Can the *homoousion* between the Father and the Son (that the Son is of the same substance as the Father) of the Nicene Creed, however, allow this? The Son does not need to plea with the Father because the Son knows the heart of the Father, something so very important in our understanding of the atonement (John McLeod Campbell).[33]

Can we say that God "risks"? Yes, because God's love does demand reciprocation: "You *shall* love the Lord your God with all your heart, and with all your soul, and with all your mind," and "your neighbor as yourself" (Matt 22:37, 39; cf. Mark 12:28-34; Luke 10:25-28). For Kierkegaard, love as a duty is the protection of love against change, its happy independence against despair.[34] But what beloved one wants to think that he is loved out of duty? There is reciprocation with God, however, that has already happened: the love and trust of the Son for the Father in the Spirit.[35] Jayber can be troubled by the possibility that Mattie will not reciprocate his love. God's love has already been reciprocated in the response

---

[31] See the discussion in T. F. Torrance, "The Framework of Belief," *Belief in Science and in Christian Life: The Relevance of Michael Polanyi's Thought for Christian Faith and Life,* ed. T. F. Torrance (Edinburgh: Hansel, 1980), 3.

[32] Sanders, *The God Who Risks,* 64.

[33] Campbell, *The Nature of the Atonement.*

[34] Søren Kierkegaard, *Works of Love,* ed. and trans. Howard V. Hong and Edna H. Hong (Princeton: Princeton University Press, 1995). See the criticism by Barth of this example of "the unlovely, inquisitorial and terribly judicial character which is so distinctive of Kierkegaard in general." Neither in the Bible nor in eternity, Barth contends, does love impress because it provokes. Such a kind of Kantian ethics does not change self-love into love. Rather, love is grounded in the same grace as found in the exodus and fulfilled in the new covenant of Jesus Christ. By the power of the electing, purifying, and creating love of God, we are made free for this action. "By this authority and power human love is truly and solidly grounded as a genuine, spontaneous, natural and therefore sincere action which is necessary in its freedom and free in its necessity. 'I will put my law in their inward parts, and write it in their hearts' (Jer. 31:33)." Barth, *CD,* IV/2, 782.

[35] Sanders, *The God Who Risks,* 37. See also Jürgen Moltmann, *The Crucified God,* trans. R. A. Wilson and John Bowden (New York: Harper and Row, 1973), 149.

of the Son. Otherwise, God's love would be the kind of love that insists on its own way (1 Cor 13:4).[36] What Israel has failed at, "the one true obedient Israelite," Jesus Christ, has succeeded, the one who joyfully acknowledges the lordship of Yahweh, a lordship that is not tyrannical (Matt 11:25).[37]

We not only lack knowledge of God but we also lack faith. This becomes particularly acute when attempting to believe in the care of a good and all-powerful God in the light of horrendous evil. Providence is not self-evident but an article of faith. As faith, however, it is dependent upon the Word of God.[38] Ivan's difficulty is not surprising. For many providence is irrelevant in a world that has marginalized its consideration to only a privatized faith relation.[39] Yes, providence needs to be based on faith, not on an examination of physical or biological laws of nature. Yet, *our* faith will fail us. We cannot see into nature deep enough even with our faith. We need someone else's faith, the faith of the only one who truly has heard the Word of God. In the faith of Jesus there is a unity between the one who believes *(fides qua creditur)* and the content of the faith that is believed *(fides quae creditur).*[40] Christian faith is our genuine participation in the hearing of the Word of God by Christ in his faith, obedience, and prayer *(fides qua . . .).*[41] The content of faith for Jesus *(fides quae . . .)* is not belief in creation but in God.[42]

Believing in God immediately relativizes the trouble of believing in creation. We may find this difficult to do but that is why the vicarious faith of Christ in providence is so essential. How curious is the contrast between the Son who cries from the cross, "My God, my God, why have you forsaken me?" (Matt 27:46) (but nonetheless still cries to God!) and Woody Allen's dogmatic skepticism in such films as *Hannah and Her Sisters.*[43] The long shadow of Cartesian doubt again casts its shape. In

---

[36] Sanders, *The God Who Risks,* 181.

[37] Barth, *CD,* III/3, 103, 180. See also IV/2, 823.

[38] Barth, *CD,* III/3, 15–18.

[39] Langdon Gilkey, "The Concept of Providence in Contemporary Theology," *Journal of Religion* 43 (July, 1963), 184.

[40] Heppe, ed., *Reformed Dogmatics,* 527–28.

[41] Barth, *CD,* III/3, 15–16, 246–53.

[42] Ibid., 18–19.

[43] Speidell, "God, Woody Allen, and Job," *Christian Scholars' Review* 29, no. 3 (2000), 551.

Hannah, the hypochondriac demands absolute certainty in order to believe in God. But Jesus does not. The faith of Jesus is the kind of faith that is able to live with the ambiguities of our world rather than to bow to the outdated gods of modernity that demand certainty without paradox. His faith on the cross is a genuine faith *because* of the cry of abandonment. I am not one to claim, however, that I could ever have such faith, even with the comparatively small amount of suffering I have lived through. We need the faith of Jesus, *fides qua* and *quae.*

There is a distinctively human will in Jesus. Some in the history of the Church, overemphasizing his deity, demand that Christ has only one will (Monothelitism). Gethsemane is a frank answer to this.[44] The obedience of the Son is part and parcel of his faith made particularly graphic in the (implicit?) doubt surrounding the agony in the garden. Jesus' human struggles were genuine; he was not playacting: He was "one who in every respect has been tested as we are" (Heb 4:15), learning "obedience through what he suffered" (Heb 5:8).[45] In contrast with Adam, although he exists in "the form of God," Jesus does not desire to "be like God" but is "obedient to the point of death—even death on a cross (Phil 2:6-8).[46] What is exalted is Christ's humanity, and therefore ours with him (Phil 2:9). Jesus does

---

[44] St. Maximus the Confessor, *On the Cosmic Mystery of Jesus Christ,* trans. and introduction Paul M. Blowers and Robert Louis Wilken (Crestwood, N.Y.: St. Vladimir's Seminary Press, 2003), 173–76.

[45] Richard Rice, "Biblical Support for a New Perspective," in Pinnock, et al., *The Openness of God,* 44.

[46] Wolfhart Pannenberg, *Christian Spirituality* (Philadelphia: Westminster, 1983), 82. See also Barth, *CD,* IV/2, 98–99, 116: "It is not, therefore, itself a divinely powerful and authoritarian essence in which Jesus Christ, very God and very man, the divine Subject existing and acting in the world, makes use of His divine power and authority . . . This work concerns man and the world. It therefore demands a human soul and a human body, human reason and human will, human anxiety and trust, human love for God and the neighbour. And it demands all this in an existence in our own human and created time . . . But what is supremely exalted in this way is none other than the human essence common to us all, and it does not change in this exaltation . . . Where Jesus Christ is really known, there is no place for a monistic thinking which confuses or reverses the divine and the human. Again, there can be only a historical thinking, for which each factor has its own distinctive character. The divine and human work together. But even in their common working they are not interchangeable. The divine is still above and the human below. Their relationship is one of genuine action."

not cease to be human when he is exalted. He still genuinely believes. He believes in a good and all-powerful God.

Gethsemane demonstrates the reality, honesty, and strength of Jesus' belief. He prays, "Abba, Father . . . remove this cup from me" (Matt 26:19; Mark 14:36; Luke 22: 42). Jesus honestly does not want to suffer. His caveat, "yet, not what I want, but what you want" is only made more dramatic and significant because of this desire not to suffer. Jesus is not ignorant of the divine plan (Mark 8:31: "the Son of Man must suffer many things . . ."). But the reality and the honesty of Jesus' human will juxtaposes with the trust he has in the will of the Father. As the King of Israel, he is "both the Planner and the Plan, the Orderer and the Order."[47]

The Accomplished Ministry That Continues to Be Accomplished: Believing as an Act of God

Jesus Already Believes in a Good and All-Powerful God

The faith of Jesus is included in the totality of his ministry. In a sense, his ministry is an accomplished deed. He has taught, healed, wrought miracles, was crucified, dead, buried, and was raised from the dead. This has already happened. "It is finished!" is the cry from the cross (John 19:30). Yet a finished ministry is not one that is at an end. The Holy Spirit makes sure that the accomplished ministry of Jesus continues to be accomplished.[48] Like the perfect tense in the Greek language, the event of Jesus is still alive. "Jesus Christ lives," says Karl Barth, "is at once the simplest and the most difficult Christological statement."[49] His living today, however, is not separate from the accomplishment of his life. A unique decision has been made in humanity through the humanity of Jesus Christ. In the midst of the bondage of our sin, a freedom has been bestowed upon us in the humanity of Jesus Christ.[50]

---

[47] Barth, *CD,* III/3, 188.

[48] Anderson, "A Theology for Ministry," *Theological Foundations for Ministry,* ed. Anderson, 17.

[49] Barth, *CD,* IV/3, first half, 39.

[50] Barth, *CD,* IV/2, 267.

A finished work, however, does not mean an arbitrary work. The one who has accomplished the work is still alive. He still thinks of things today! as Ray Anderson quips.[51] A marriage is not (or *should not)* be the end but the beginning of a life together. The "word event" of marriage has made something that can never be done over. Jesus' life and ministry should not be viewed as a memory of a revered yet long-dead hero. The resurrection of Jesus and the gift of the Holy Spirit will not permit that.

So does not providence guarantee that God's will will be done, his power will never be compromised?[52] Is Jesus' faith an act of divine determinism, finished in the past, rejecting our individual responsibility, another act of the God of determinism, the God of "the master plan," comforting to some but frightening to many?

True enough, through Christ's vicarious faith, obedience, and prayers, we are not left up to ourselves, even our own desires.[53] Our freedom has been revealed to be a false freedom, in reality, bondage (Rom 6:23). Yet this is not a mechanistic declaration. God's freedom is the freedom to love. God's work begins before all of our work with the work of his love.[54] And how deep is that love? Deep enough to push us aside in order to believe for us and in our place, to push aside even our doubts. God has *already* loved us in Jesus Christ. I remember so well Bob Myers, my pastor as a young Christian, preaching on 1 John 3:1: "See what love the Father has given us, that we should be called children of God; *and that is what we are*" (1 John 3:1). Bob's voice dramatically lowered as he spoke those last words, "and that is what we are." Grace has been an obsessive, haunting, and troubling theme in my theology ever since.

Something has already taken place for us: This is the proclamation of the resurrection: "Christ is risen! Indeed he is risen!" shouts the Orthodox liturgy. We do not, however, often feel "resurrected" ourselves . . . Christ may be risen, but we are not! We are still in doubt, despair, rejected by others, ourselves, and maybe by God. How can we say "Jesus is Victor!" in the midst of our doubts? Has the devil really been defeated or has his

---

[51] Anderson, *Dancing with Wolves While Feeding the Sheep,* 35.

[52] Helm, *The Providence of God,* 100–01.

[53] Barth, *CD,* III/3, 91.

[54] Ibid., 119.

power just been curtailed?[55] Given tragedies like the two schoolgirls found murdered under the ice, it is hard to believe that is even the case.

Jesus as victor, however, is at the center of the Christian message. Yet this finished work should not be viewed apart from the solidarity of the Word of God with our flesh (John 1:14), the actual humanity we live in is not just a pristine ideal humanity. God has taken on our "fallen human nature."[56] As such, God actually suffers in the cross. His victory in the resurrection does not obliterate the reality of this suffering. As Bonhoeffer famously puts it, "Only the suffering God can help."[57] Resurrection victory is not antithetical to suffering. In fact, perhaps we can say that the reality of the resurrection only increases the suffering of God! The light of the resurrection of Jesus Christ exposes the horror of suffering and evil even more intensely. Jesus' faith in the Father, so evident throughout his life, only exacerbates the cry of abandonment from the cross, "My God, my God, why have you forsaken me?" (Matt 27:46). The Son knows the love and goodness of the Father so much that the abandonment cuts deeply to the quick. Forsakenness is not a reality unless you have known someone's care. Rejection is even deeper when you are rejected by one who has loved you. Betrayal is even more acute when it is by a close friend (Ps 41:9).

The forsakenness of the Son is in solidarity with our forsakenness, an identification with our suffering, our cries, and with our complaints. The "already" of the faith of Jesus and the victory of his resurrection does not leave our present cries behind. In his cry of abandonment Jesus takes our cries and questions, including our doubts, doubts about a good and loving God or even about his existence, and makes those cries his own.[58] The lament tradition in the Scriptures, such as in Psalm 22, is all too pervasive

---

[55] Barth emphasizes the defeat of the devil whereas Donald Bloesch argues that the devil's power has only been curtailed, *God the Almighty: Power, Wisdom, Holiness, Love* (Downers Grove, Ill.: InterVarsity, 1995), 135.

[56] Argued by the Fathers, Karl Barth, T. F. Torrance, and others; see Harry Johnson, *The Humanity of the Saviour* (London: Epworth, 1962) and James Torrance, *Worship, Community, and the Triune God of Grace,* 53. Oliver Crisp offers a survey of the discussion with a critique based on original sin in "Did Christ Have a Fallen Nature?" *International Journal of Systematic Theology* 6. no. 3 (2004), 270–88.

[57] Bonhoeffer, *Letters and Papers from Prison,* 361.

[58] T. F. Torrance, "Questioning in Christ" in *Theology in Reconstruction,* 122. See also Campbell, *The Nature of the Atonement,* 200–12.

to be simply viewed as immature faith.[59] To complain to God is to acknowledge his love and justice as well as his existence. God is there in our suffering. God is "hanging on the gallows," in Elie Wiesel's famous phrase, interpreted in terms of the cross by his mentor Francois Mauriac.[60] God is along for the ride, as bitter as it may be. We should not say anything less. But should we say something more?

Solidarity is not enough. The presence of God in the ovens of Auschwitz is not enough.[61] By itself solidarity can be a cruel joke. Do we really need such a God? We can complain very well by ourselves, thank you.[62]

Yet complaining is also not enough. All the complaining we can do does not change the situation: inexplicable, undeserved, horrendous evil exists. What we do need is for someone to believe for us and in our place, *in order to complain.* One cannot lament to a God one does not believe in. Why even cry to a God of either limited power or malevolent will? We need the cry of the faithful and obedient One to the Father.

Jesus Continues to Believe in a Good and All-Powerful God

Solidarity is good but it has no staying power. Something is needed more than Christ as my *representative,* in solidarity with my sufferings and needs. We also need Christ as *substitute,* yet not as restricted to just paying the penalty for my sin (penal substitution, popularized by Calvin), but in a *total* sense, in the entirety of our lives, including our ability to believe in the providence of God in a world of pain and suffering.[63]

---

[59] Sanders, *The God Who Risks,* 266.

[60] Elie Wiesel, *Night,* trans. Stella Rodway, introduction by Francois Mauriac (New York: Bantam, 1982), x, pp. 61–62. See also Surin, "The Impassibility of God and the Problem of Evil," in *The Turnings of Darkness and Light,* 66, and Moltmann, *The Crucified God,* 273–74.

[61] W. Stacy Johnson, *The Mystery of God: Karl Barth and the Postmodern Foundation of Theology* (Louisville: Westminster John Knox), 99.

[62] John K. Roth, "A Theodicy of Protest," in Stephen Davis, ed., *Encountering Evil: Live Options in Theodicy, A New Edition* (Louisville: Westminster John Knox, 2001), 15.

[63] For the penal substitutionary theory, see J. I. Packer, "What Did the Cross Achieve? The Logic of Penal Substitution," *Tyndale Bulletin* 25 (1974), 3–45. Penalty may be a part of substitution, but one should not say that it is the "key" as Packer does on page 36. Rather, it is a part of the wider vicarious humanity of Christ.

A substitute is hard to swallow in an age that is obsessed with individual "rights." Human rights are essential, yet like the penal aspect of substitutionary atonement, they are not the whole story. Human relationships need a stronger foundation than just jockeying for rights. Otherwise, as so often happens in marriages today, a relationship can degenerate into just a political power play, focused only on guaranteeing "equal rights."[64] A different foundation is needed.

In comes One who reveals to us that we have forfeited our rights as well as our lives.[65] We did not know it, or want to admit it, but we had already lost our rights. "I have been crucified with Christ; and it is no longer I who live, but it is Christ who lives in me" (Gal. 2:20). But he can also immediately add, "And the life I now live in the flesh I live by the faith of the Son of God . . ." (interpreted as a subjective genitive in Greek). I now live a life but it is a life restored by the faith of the Son of God. My rights were not worth defending in the first place, especially my "rights" to believe. My time is no longer my time, having been replaced by God's time.[66] The sad irony is that in the modern world we have a perverse view of the atonement in which we have substituted ourselves for God rather than confessing that God has substituted himself for us![67] Here is the only reality, the reality that gives us direction, in order to believe in the goodness of God.[68] Christ's substitutionary work includes giving us his wisdom (1 Cor 1:30), wisdom we need to embrace the goodness of God, to become, in Karl Barth's self-description, "the joyful partisan of the good God."

Substitutionary atonement is not foreign to the providence of God. The atonement prefigured in the lamb in the thicket in Genesis 22 for Abraham and Isaac is God's providence, his care, as Abraham saw in his trust in God: "God himself will provide the lamb for a burnt offering, my son" (Gen 22:8).[69] The providence of God is in God taking our place in our puzzlement, despair, rebellion, and unbelief in a world that does not make sense. No one is worthy, the Apocalypse reminds us, to open the

---

[64] Ray S. Anderson, *Everything That Makes Me Happy I Learned When I Grew Up* (Downers Grove, Ill.: InterVarsity, 1995), 135–37.

[65] Barth, *CD,* IV/1, 772–73.

[66] Barth, *CD,* I/2, 55.

[67] Pannenberg, *Christian Spirituality,* 74.

[68] Barth, *CD,* IV/2, 362.

[69] Barth, *CD,* III/3, 35.

seals of the book until the Lion of Judah appears, the Lion who becomes a Lamb (Rev 5:1-14).[70]

The Lion becomes the Lamb! As such, God "provides" in an unexpected way. Our cries, our questions, our anguish are answered through an unanticipated means. So salvation is not effected (as even the friends of the Book of Revelation and apocalyptic literature might think) primarily through a dramatic display of raw power, the supreme pyrotechnic display on Independence Day. So a theology that leans toward determinism can suggest. Nor is an "answer" to the problem of evil given. The book of Job readily reminds us of that. No, Christ is instead made "to be sin" for us, taking our place in judgment, exchanging his life for ours (2 Cor 5:21), "the sweet exchange" of his riches for our poverty (2 Cor 8:9).[71]

The Lion becoming the Lamb means that God has relieved us of our problems, including the problem of evil.[72] The burden is now on Jesus. Christ as our substitute means that our contradictions, our puzzles, our problems are now his. The faith of Jesus is now confronted with the problem of evil. Even our doubt is no longer our own. Jesus has to face it because he *has* faced it. What else does it mean for the eternal Son to "descend into hell"? All the torment of all creation has become his.[73] The difference is that he has been raised from the bowels of hell.

The death of Christ signifies as well the "impossibility" of unbelief.[74] Unbelief, with all other contradiction, disorder, chaos, and enmity, has been "nailed" to the cross (Col 2:14-15). What is most difficult to die, of course, is doubt based on the problem of evil. The faith of Jesus interrupts our ideas of faith as simply a possibility that has to be carefully reasoned out and nuanced in harmony with the darkness of horrendous evil. Because of the faith of Jesus, faith is not just a possibility but an actuality whose "joyful certainty" cannot be compared to modern confidences we so easily take stock in.[75]

---

[70] Sanders, *The God Who Risks,* 115.

[71] T. F. Torrance, *The Christian Doctrine of God,* 226, 251.

[72] Barth, *CD,* III/1, 381.

[73] Barth, *CD,* II/2, 496. "Jesus Christ is *the* Rejected of God, for God makes Himself rejected in Him, and has Himself alone tasted to the depths all that rejection means and necessarily involves."

[74] Barth, *CD,* IV/1, 746.

[75] Ibid., 747.

We not only share in the death of Christ but also in his life (Rom 6:8). Christ has taken our place, in unbelief, doubt, and despair. Where we now live is where Jesus lives.[76] Despite all appearances to the contrary, we have been exalted with Christ (Phil 2:5-11).[77] "We live as Jesus lives. We are not somewhere alone. We are in Him. And in Him we are not what suits ourselves, or what we think necessary or desirable."[78] As Jesus lives he lives to continue believing for us. The burden is no longer on us to try hard to believe despite the contradictions that surround us, foremost being the problem of evil. "He who puts his life into his faith in God can lose his faith," remarks Simone Weil. "But he who puts his life in God himself will never lose it."[79] No, one has already believed for us and he continues to believe as he pours out his Spirit upon us. The Spirit of Jesus enables us to participate in the same faith that once said, "Father, into your hands I commend my spirit" (Luke 23:46) even in the midst of the abandonment of an intimate relationship. Only then can we believe that a victory has been won in which the wicked will be punished and the righteous rewarded (Matt 18:23-35). Faith needs length as well as breadth and depth. Jesus believes in the future judgment of evil for us. Otherwise, it is only the most starry-eyed, naïve romanticist that can hope for such an end.[80]

---

[76] Barth, *CD,* IV/2, 363.

[77] Ibid.: "In Him we are no longer below but above; no longer in the far country but home again; no longer servants of God but sons; or no longer lazy and unprofitable, because disobedient, but obedient and profitable servants. The Holy Spirit does not create the ghost of a man standing in decision, but the reality of the man concerning whom decision has already been made in the existence of the man Jesus."

[78] Ibid.

[79] Simone Weil, *Gravity and Grace* (Lincoln: University of Nebraska Press, 1997), 162–63, in the section entitled, "He Whom We Must Love is Absent."

[80] Allison, *Jesus of Nazareth: Millenarian Prophet,* 135.

The Providence of God: God's Intercession in the Vicarious Humanity of Christ

Does God Care? "Everything That Happens is the Will of God" or Fortune and Chance?

Jayber Crow is an intelligent, thoughtful man. He obviously could have been successful in a number of respected professions (including becoming a great writer!). He is well-liked; that would have served him well in furthering a pathway of success in life. Jayber is pleasant to be around, with a deep spirituality that is unobtrusive. Given a different background, Jayber could have been a success, a prominent man. But Jayber is content, content with being a barber. How come? The providence of God becomes a reality for Jayber despite his life of confusion and setbacks with all the cards stacked against him. In fact, he concludes, all his real opportunities have come from simply being a barber.[81] Jayber sees now that he has been led, following a path laid out for him.

The providence of God! What a heady concept. Jayber now believes that a path was laid out for him What does this mean, however? Does providence mean that "everything that happens is the will of God"?[82] According to Zwingli, "the hairs of our head" as numbered in Matt 10:29-30 means "that even the things we call fortuitous or accidental are not fortuitous or random happenings, but are all affected by the order and regulation of the Deity."[83] However, how is this any different from blind acceptance of fate? Is such a view really more Christian than a belief in "fortune" or "chance"? And how does it reckon with the presence of horrendous evils?

Creation does seem to be independent at times, if not full of fortune, chance, and randomness. At best, is providence perhaps only a broad design of God but not an involvement in the parts?[84] Is this a just allowance for the randomness of horrendous evils then?

---

[81] Berry, *Jayber Crow,* 66.

[82] Leith, *Basic Christian Doctrine* (Louisville: Westminster John Knox, 1994), 25. See also Helm, *The Providence of God,* 122; Calvin, *Institutes,* 1.16.3, 7.

[83] Ulrich Zwingli, "On the Providence of God," in *On Providence and Other Essays,* eds. S. M. Jackson and W. J. Hinke (Durham, N.C.: Labyrinth, 1987), 136.

[84] Gordon Kaufman, *God the Problem* (Cambridge: Harvard University Press, 1972), 119–47.

What would, *what does,* Jesus think of all of this?

God Does Care: The Faith of Jesus as Evidence

God cares. We know this because we have rejected him. The Christian message concerns "the God who Himself became a creature."[85] As such, he took the risk of rejection, a rejection that actually happened (John 1:11).[86] Why are we to think that rejection means less to God than to us, unless we have adopted *a priori* a philosophical definition of God as *apatheia?* "The God who Himself became a creature" has already broken apart any philosophical presuppositions we have about God. The eternal Son became a free, responsive human being, possessing a free will, even to the point of being able to say to the Father, "not what I want but what you want" (Matt 26:39). As such, the Son is the proclamation that God does not will to suppress the creature.[87] God has no desire to manipulate, coerce, or control human beings. Our doctrine of providence is already radically qualified by the incarnation.

The implications of providence and the incarnation for our understanding of creation as a whole are profound. Not only has God created a creature *dependent* on him but also the same creature has been granted an *independence.* This, according to T. F. Torrance, is the genuine *contingent,* relationship between God and his creation, as opposed to either a necessary or random relationship. A rationality has been granted creation, a rationality that can especially be explored by human beings, the priests of creation. Here is the grand basis for modern science, Torrance argues.[88]

In the incarnate life of the eternal Son we see a demonstration of what it truly means to be human: to be free *and* obedient to the Father, a contingency *away from* as well as *towards* God. The Gospel narratives portray an encounter between Jesus and the devil that becomes a question about the providence of God: Will God provide for, care for, Jesus, if he would cast himself down from the pinnacle of the temple (Matt 4:1-11;

[85] Barth, *CD,* III/3, 130.
[86] Barth, *CD,* II/2, 165. See also Fiddes, *Participation in God,* 169.
[87] Barth, *CD,* III/3, 130.
[88] T. F. Torrance, *Divine and Contingent Order,* 71–72.

Luke 4:1-13)? "Do you really believe in the providence of God?" challenges the devil. The devil is right to see that the faith of Jesus is the central issue. He is wrong in that he defines providence based on his own logic, like so many have done in the history of theology, e.g., providence can only mean that everything that happens is the will of God, "meticulous" providence. Instead, Jesus himself defines what the providence of God is. Providence is more than Jesus as an example for us in how to trust God, so that any arbitrary or nonsensical act, such as throwing yourself off a building, is seen as its test. No, Jesus demonstrates the care of God in trusting in God when we are unable to, in the midst of our doubts. This is the story of his entire life. He takes our place. In a world of Ted Bundys and schoolgirls drowned under the ice by twisted ghouls, we see one who believes in God even when we have no reason to believe. C. S. Lewis's demonic Screwtape views the greatest danger to the devil is when a human being "looks round upon a universe from which every trace of him seems to have vanished, and asks why he has been forsaken, and still obeys."[89]

Who among us, however, is able to stand in such a pit of despair? The good news is that Jesus, and his faith, stands in our place, believing in the providence of God against all odds. Actual broken, sinful human nature is the stage in which Jesus performs in order to be transformed into his likeness.[90] The brokenness is the result of our lies about our free will. We have been given an independence, but it is a *contingent* independence, not apart from the contingency *toward* God (T. F. Torrance). Communion with God is our goal, but we are often like a lover that refuses to receive anything from one's beloved.[91] In refusing that love we remain in bondage, our free will of no effect. Our ability to believe is decimated.

Only Jesus is able to live "even if there were no God" *(etsi Deus non daretur)*, in Bonhoeffer's famous quotation of Grotius on the foundations of law.[92] Seeing photos of the hapless American engineers hanging lifeless from the bridge in Iraq can only help bring about those thoughts. One must say this along with Bonhoeffer's other cryptic statements about "religionless Christianity," yet doing so "before God!"[93]

---

[89] C. S. Lewis, *The Screwtape Letters,* 39.

[90] Colyer, *How to Read T. F. Torrance,* 93.

[91] Fiddes, *Participation in God,* 211.

[92] Bonhoeffer, *Letters and Papers from Prison,* 359.

[93] Ibid., 360.

Bonhoeffer

> The God who is with us is the God who forsakes us (Mark 15:34). The God who lets us live in the world without the working hypothesis of God is the God before whom we stand continually. Before God and with God we live without God. God lets himself be pushed out of the world on to the cross.[94]

We must say this because of horrendous evil. We must not say this, however, easily or haphazardly. A dualism between the "natural" and the "supernatural" must not be allowed to exist.[95] But how can we avoid it without someone intervening for us? All of the talk of the self-evident "sacramental" nature of creation falls upon the deaf ears of the victims of horrendous evil. Someone needs to intervene. One has, the one who responded to the devil, "Man shall not live by bread alone . . ." (Matt 4:4), challenging the devil's view of providence. This one subsists on the Word of God. Yet we cannot in all good conscience trust ourselves to do the same. We are too needy, too weak, too fickle. We need to follow behind the one whom whether "hungry or satisfied . . . lived as man in the power of the divine providence directed to him through the Word of God."[96]

We are ill. We cannot lift ourselves up to the pool in order to be healed (John 5:2-9). God does not merely give us help (John Cassian) nor does he do it for us apart from our humanity (Augustine), but the help he gives is his act in our humanity so that we might participate in his.[97] Jesus does the act that we are unable to do: believing in a good and all-powerful God in the midst of a world of horrendous evil, and therefore in the midst of our doubts. In doing so, he has given us our freedom, a freedom, however, that does not exist apart from him (our union with the vicarious humanity of Christ).[98]

---

[94] Ibid.

[95] Schmemann, *For the Life of the World,* 129.

[96] Barth, *CD,* III/2, 67–68.

[97] See Owen Chadwick, introduction to John Cassian, *Conferences,* trans. Colin Luibheid (New York: Paulist, 1985), 26–27, who summarizes Augustine's view of God's place in salvation ("Rest in me and I *will* do it") with Cassian's ("Rest in me, and I will help you, so that we shall do it together").

[98] Barth, *CD,* IV/2, 493.

"It is good to be with Jesus and not elsewhere," says Barth.[99] The "elsewhere" may be in bondage to unbelief and doubt; it most probably could be. The answer is to be somewhere else: with Jesus, in his kind of independence. We may live now in a world of fortune and chance, but we do not live in it apart from Jesus. His independence has taken the place of our twisted independence, promising that one day his independence will fully be ours. This kind of independence is neither a slave to our short-sighted agendas, nor is it determined by the indifference of nature, but by the resurrection from the dead. "This Jesus God raised up," Peter proclaimed (Acts 2:32), the one who "was raised for our justification" (Rom 4:25). God will have the last word. Jesus was no fool. He knew what would happen to the sparrows. But the nature of faith is not sight (2 Cor 5:7). His faith in the Father said that "not one of them will fall to the ground apart from your Father" (Matt 10:29). The Father will have the last word, just as he has had the last word concerning Jesus. The Father knows best.

So also God will have the last word concerning us. What God has done in Christ was not done by us, so there is nothing we can do to reverse these acts.[100] Even in our misery of doubt, Jesus lives for us, Jesus believes for us. "It is good to be with Jesus and not elsewhere." We wrestle

---

[99] Barth, *CD,* II/2, 570.

[100] Barth, *CD,* IV/2, 484. Despite the length, the rhapsody and conviction of Barth's thoughts begs to be repeated: "Let us say at once in concrete terms that the descent of the Son of God to our misery and the ascent of the Son of God to God's glory, the existence of the man Jesus within our slothful humanity, His victory in the crucifixion as our Lord and Head and Representative, the revelation of this victory in His resurrection, the issue of His direction, the outpouring of the Holy Spirit on all flesh—all these are facts. As man has not brought them about, he cannot reverse them by anything he does. They are facts even in face and at the very heart of his misery. Even in his turning to nothingness, and under the overwhelming threat of it, he himself has not become nothing. Even in his misery he belongs, not to the devil or to himself, but to God. The Yes of divine grace is terribly concealed in the No of divine judgment, but it is spoken to him too: even to unhappy Nabal; even to the people of Northern Israel; even to David with his petty sin; even to the murmurers in the wilderness. Jesus lives as very man, and therefore as the very God who humbled Himself to man, and who came to him in his misery, who took his misery to Himself. Thus even in his misery man lives as the man for whom Jesus lives. To omit this qualification of man's misery is necessarily to deny Jesus Christ as the Lord who became a servant and the servant who became the Lord, and therefore to blaspheme God."

with the goodness of God in what seems to be a less than good world. So it is very good to be with Jesus in the midst of our misery, rejection, and doubt. "This is good because it is there that God Himself is good for us," continues Barth.[101] Here we find the care, the providence, of God; here is where we find that good which is good for us.

God cares for us by sending Jesus. In his freedom God is free to care by becoming lowly and share in our misery.[102] Only a free God can create a free creature. This is why panentheism (God is neither transcendent nor identical, yet is a part of creation) is so cruel: God loses his freedom when he is not free to become human.[103] "The Lord our God is one Lord" is the first commandment (Deut 6:4; Mark 12:29). His lordship means that he is able to do what no one else can do, a vicarious act.[104] His freedom is found in taking upon our shame and curse, in interceding for us. Providence, therefore, has a unique nature: "His control is a unique control." His lordship is not expressed by merely ruling and commanding but rather, "it is all gift and offer and promise." Herein is a lordship more powerful than a pure *fiat:* the power to take the place of humanity, taking the matter out of our hands and making our business his business.[105] As such, this is a testimony of the uniqueness of this Lord in a pluralistic world of competing "lords." He takes the problem of evil out of our hands. How does he do this? By the freedom of the Son.

If God is free then the Son is free as well, free to be genuinely human in trusting and obeying. In Barth's words, "He was human asking," the One who has already "hallowed" the Father's name, the One who "is already heard and answered."[106] Our place has been taken in "asking" and being "heard" and "answered," but only that it might be reestablished, yet not apart from the Son. A christological analogy is apt at this point. Christ is fully God and fully human. Human logic cannot neatly fit these together, as the centuries of christological controversy remind us. Yet the wisdom

---

[101] Barth, *CD,* II/2, 570.

[102] Barth, *CD,* III/1, 383.

[103] As reflected in Cynthia Rigby, "Free to Be Human: Limits, Possibilities and the Sovereignty of God," *Theology Today* 53, no. 1 (1996), 58: "God cannot choose to become human."

[104] Barth, *CD,* I/2, 382.

[105] Ibid., 383.

[106] Barth, *CD,* III/3, 274–75.

of Nicaea and Chalcedon have stood the test of time. The biblical testimony compels us to confess that Jesus Christ is fully divine and fully human. So also salvation is completely the work of God and completely the work of the human.[107] The very nature of the incarnation, being both the act of God and the act of man, testifies that "all of grace" does not mean "nothing of man."[108] All of grace means all of man! Paul can say, "and *it is no longer I* who live, but it is Christ who lives in me" and immediately add, "And *the life I now live* in the flesh *I* live by the faith of the Son of God" (Gal 2:20). Here we have covenant, not contract, a covenant upheld on both sides by God. *Mystery,* so important to be maintained in theology and the Christian life must be maintained here, and neither dissolved into a determinism of a sovereign God nor a contractual relationship between humans and God.[109]

Our attempts at seeking a logical connection between God's grace and our response practically flounder especially when it comes to prayer. Jayber finally begins to pray again, even "the terrible prayer: 'Thy will be done.'"[110] He prays for strength and forgiveness. That seems reasonable enough. But then he also prays "unreasonably, foolishly, hopelessly, that everybody in Port William might be blessed and happy—the ones I loved and the ones I did not. I prayed my gratitude." His conclusion is that perhaps all the good in the world comes from prayer.[111] How unreasonable is it to pray for enemies, yes, to love our enemies! So also with God's love for us, for "while we were enemies, we were reconciled to God . . ." (Rom 5:10). We do not know this logically. God's providence is seen in the gift of the Son's human asking. This is not known by our logic but by Christ and our experience of faith in Christ. *Sola fide* does not mean that we are left to believe alone.

---

[107] Colyer, *How to Read T. F. Torrance,* 119–20.

[108] T. F. Torrance, *The Mediation of Christ,* xii.

[109] T. F. Torrance, *Christian Theology and Scientific Culture,* 130: In contrast to Calvin's view of Christ as "the mirror of election," Calvinism read back "into God temporal, causal, and logical relations from our experience in this world." So also various forms of synergism read back our experiences of human contractual relations into divine reconciliation, side stepping the divine-human Christ. Our experience of Christ needs to maintain the two natures in Christ. See also Elmer Colyer's pastoral admonition not to mutually exclude grace and free will in *How to Read T. F. Torrance,* 122.

[110] Berry, *Jayber Crow,* 253.

[111] Ibid.

Christ Contra Evil: Believing in a Good God in a Less Than Good World

Does a "Greater Good" Let God Off the Hook?

Doubt holds God responsible. God is responsible for horrendous evil says doubt, such as in the voice of Ivan Karamazov. So I have perfectly good reasons to suspend or even reject belief in God . . . the innocent, suffering children of the world demand this, Ivan says. And so our doubting hearts whisper at times.

Despite some contemporary pleadings, can we really withhold God from responsibility for horrendous evil (beyond that which is clearly a result of the misuse of human free will)?[112] Even if God has to allow evil for the sake of loving relationships or free will, is it not ultimately God's responsibility for creating such a world? Some, however, would claim that God is not guilty morally because it is possible that he created such a world for the sake of a "greater good" unknown to us.[113]

True, life teaches us that wisdom can come from adversity, "the awful paradox," as Reynolds Price remarks.[114] What saint has never encountered the depth of spiritual growth in the depths of greatest despair? Clinging to God is so much more necessary in the midst of crisis. The Protestant Reformation was built on such an experience: Luther's tortured soul. The very nature of human beings seems to speak of the inevitability as well as the great benefit of what C. S. Lewis calls "undulation," the ebbs and flows, troughs and peaks, of life.[115] This even appears to be ontologically grounded: human beings are "amphibians," both soul and body, creatures on the boundary, subject to the pull of both heaven and earth.[116] Our suffering reminds us of our finitude. Recognition of it can result in increased humility.[117]

---

[112] Helm, *The Providence of God,* 177.

[113] Ibid., 184.

[114] Reynolds Price, *Letters to a Man in the Fire: Does God Exist and Does He Care?* (New York: Scribner's, 1999), 64.

[115] C. S. Lewis, *The Screwtape Letters,* 36–39.

[116] Barth, *Dogmatics in Outline,* 59.

[117] Diogenes Allen, "Natural Evil and the Love of God," in Marilyn McCord Adams and Robert M. Adams, eds., *The Problem of Evil* (Oxford: Oxford University Press, 1990), 190–97.

Is not the biblical perspective that the present suffering is "not worthy compared to the glory about to be revealed to us" (Rom 8:18)? Some claim that present suffering will be viewed in the eschaton as inconsequential as a junior high school embarrassment is for an adult.[118] Suffering in this life includes horrendous evils such as a father's vehicle accidentally running over a son. Yet some argue that good can be brought out of those events in the balance of an entire life.[119]

God seems to greatly use the valleys more so than the highs for spiritual growth so that genuine spiritual life is a faith that stands even when everything around it seems to say, "No!", like the faith of the One who cried in abandonment on the cross. As death had to come before resurrection for Christ, so also we need to die before our resurrection (Rom 6). The epigraph for Dostoevsky's *The Brothers Karamazov* is John 12:24: "Very truly, I tell you, unless a grain of wheat falls into the earth and dies, it remains just a single grain; but if it dies, it bears much fruit." For Dostoevsky, good and evil, the skeptic Ivan and the saintly Alyosha, must both exist in order for humanity to possess free will and make a choice of one or the other.[120] The murder of Fyodor Karamazov is the central event in the novel. But only with this evil is there redemption. A frightening thought, perhaps, but does not life bear this out? Does not the "greater good" live?

Why not then celebrate evil and suffering as some of the Fathers rejoiced in the Fall as the *felix culpa,* the "happy fault"? For through the Fall Christ came to give us the fullness of redemption. Often neglected is the significance of the Second Day: the day of Christ's burial. For in that day there is nothing but darkness, a darkness, however, that God participates in. There is an illumination in the darkness that God is not foreign to our deepest despairs, and even doubts.[121]

---

[118] Stephen T. Davis, "Free Will and Evil," in Davis, ed., *Encountering Evil,* 83–85.

[119] Marilyn McCord Adams, *Horrendous Evils and the Goodness of God* (Ithaca, N.Y.: Cornell University Press, 1999), 149, 167; "Afterword," in Davis, ed., *Encountering Evil,* 197.

[120] Geir Kjetsaa, *Fyodor Dostoevsky: A Writer's Life,* trans. Siri Hustvedt and David McDuff (New York: Viking, 1987), 349.

[121] Alan E. Lewis, *Between Cross and Resurrection,* 78: "For it is the grace of the second day which makes that original story what it is—a tale of contrast and reversal; of darkness, night, and finally, light; of death and nothing, and only then of life. But once we know about the light and the life, the grace becomes the point not of antithesis only but also of

The objections to a "greater good" theodicy, however, are biting. What glory can make the ovens of Auschwitz burning with innocent children insignificant?[122] Ivan Karamazov does not question that some benefit may come from suffering. (We are now more sensitive to anti-Semitism than before the Holocaust.) His point would be that such educative value is not *worth* the suffering of the innocents.[123] Granted that some suffering might be beneficial to us, this is not true for an incredible amount of the total suffering: human, animal, and ecological. In addition, such horrendous evil as caused by the event of 9/11 can inversely create more doubts about the goodness and power of God and certainly be detrimental to "soul-making."[124] Worst of all, such a theodicy seems to regard evil as tolerable, and even respectable.[125]

The cross of Christ, however, may be the most powerful argument for a "greater good" theodicy. Is not the cross the defeat of evil, and therefore, despite the fact that Jesus was betrayed, tortured, and put to death, the necessary precursor to the resurrection?[126] Because the cross has a purpose, therefore every evil has a purpose, it is argued. In such a view, there is no such thing as gratuitous evil.[127]

Yet Christ's suffering is unique. Only he has suffered for the whole world. Only his atonement is efficacious for all. He is not just a paradigm for our suffering. Only he is the Lamb of God that takes all the sin of the world (John 1:29, 36). No one else can do this.

Still, the one who follows Jesus is like any servant who imitates the master; that one will suffer the same fate. "A disciple is not above the

---

unity, not of contradiction alone but of identity; an identity-in-contradiction. For by uniting the first day and the third is a single event, the second suggests that the darkness is itself illuminating, the defeat victorious, and death both the opposite and the source of life."

[122] John K. Roth, "Rejoinder," in Davis, ed., *Encountering Evil,* 33.

[123] Surin, *The Turning of Darkness and Light,* 64–65.

[124] See the classic "soul-making" theodicy of John Hick, *Evil and the God of Love,* revised edition (San Francisco: Harper and Row, 1977), 253–71.

[125] James McClendon, *Doctrine: Systematic Theology,* Vol. 2 (Nashville: Abingdon, 1994), 172. See also Weber, *Foundations of Dogmatics,* Vol. 1, 507; Roth, "A Theodicy of Protest," in David, ed., *Encountering Evil,* 17; and Terrence W. Tilley, *The Evils of Theodicy* (Washington, D.C.: Georgetown University Press, 1990).

[126] Adams, *Horrendous Evils and the Goodness of God,* 127.

[127] Helm, *The Providence of God,* 223.

teacher, nor a slave above the master; it is enough for the disciple to be like the teacher and the slave like the master" (Matt 10:24-25). As the world treated Jesus, so the world will treat his disciples. The Church will be in solidarity with the world, yet simultaneously be rejected by the world. It will bear sins, shame, and be driven like a scapegoat out of the city, but only as it is in solidarity with the world.[128] In doing so, however, the Church is constantly being "borne up by Christ."[129] It is not left alone. The faith of Jesus still undergirds the Church. Suffering is not good in itself, argues C. S. Lewis. The good of any sufferer is submission to the will of God.[130]

Once again, then, we are confronted with our *inability* to obey the will of God, not to mention our sheer unwillingness! Can we see the darkness that is illumination (Alan E. Lewis)? For most of us that is very difficult, especially when we ourselves are suffering.

The Faith of Christ vs. Our Faith in "Good Reasons"

> The mind that comes to rest is tended
> In ways that it cannot intend:
> Is borne, preserved, and comprehended
> By what it cannot comprehend.
> —Wendell Berry[131]

> We've all got to go through enough to kill us.
> —Burley Coulter in *Jayber Crow*[132]

Yes, suffering may bring some "good," but only *de facto,* by the facts of life, by our encounter with the undulations of life, but not *de jure,* by law,

---

[128] Bonhoeffer, *Discipleship,* trans. Barbara Green and Reinhold Krauss (Minneapolis: Fortress Press, 2001), 90–91.
[129] Ibid., 90.
[130] Armand M. Nicholi, Jr., *The Question of God: C. S. Lewis and Sigmund Freud Debate God, Love, Sex, and the Meaning of Life* (New York: Free, 2002), 203; C. S. Lewis, *The Problem of Pain* (London: Centenary, 1940).
[131] Wendell Berry, *A Timbered Choir: The Sabbath Poems, 1979–1997* (New York: Counterpoint, 1998), 7.
[132] Berry, *Jayber Crow,* 356.

for the law of God's purpose for humanity is found in Jesus Christ. Christ's faith, obedience, and prayers present us the true order by which evil is confronted and defeated. *Christus Victor.* Jesus is victor![133] In contrast to a theology of victory that overemphasizes the deity of Christ, the vicarious humanity of Christ reminds us that the victory of Jesus is also in the faithful obedience of his humanity.[134] The whole of Christ's life, death, and resurrection is a testimony against and victory over evil and suffering.[135] Evil and suffering are absurd and opposed to God, and therefore something we are to fight against. Ivan is right to look with suspicion on an argument that seeks to harmonize a cosmic order on the backs of the sufferings of innocents. The providence of God in such a world is difficult, if not impossible, to believe. It is not enough to claim that we have "a basic Godward bias" that will inevitably bring us to faith and God.[136] Such romanticism does not give much hope, it seems to me. "We've all got to go through enough to kill us," comments Burley Coulter, a character in *Jayber Crow.*[137] True enough. We need help. We need intervention. We need someone to believe for us.

Still, we cling to a hope that God has "good reasons" for such a world. This does sound rather pious. Is not trust in God trust that there is a purpose and reason for everything? Advocates of "meticulous providence" are particularly fond of this. Would God be God otherwise?

Christ's faith, obedience, and prayers interrupt, however, our search for harmony, order, and "good reasons," all of which may become golden calves. Jesus' faith is trust that God is good and all-powerful and can work his purpose not because of but *in spite of* the absurdity of evil and suffering.[138] This is not belief in a "harmony" but belief in a loving Father.

---

[133] Barth, *CD,* IV/3, first half, 168–71. Notice Barth's story of the deliverance of the "possessed" woman by J. C. Blumhardt uttering the words, "Jesus is victor!"

[134] This is a criticism of the classic work on atonement by Gustav Aulén, *Christus Victor: An Historical Study of the Three Main Types of the Idea of Atonement,* trans. A. G. Hebert (New York: Macmillan, 1969). See Kettler, *The Vicarious Humanity of Christ and the Reality of Salvation,* 125.

[135] T. F. Torrance, *Divine and Contingent Order,* 114–25. See also T. F. Torrance, *The Christian Frame of Mind,* 19–24.

[136] John Hick, "An Irenaean Theodicy," in Davis, ed., *Encountering Evil,* 52.

[137] Berry, *Jayber Crow,* 356.

[138] Barth, *Dogmatics in Outline,* 15: "Christian faith is the gift of the meeting in which men become free to hear the word of grace which God has spoken in Jesus Christ in such a way that, *in spite of all* that contradicts it, they may once for all, exclusively and entirely, hold to His promise and guidance" (emphasis mine).

Our logic does not create such a harmony, as much as it desires it. The goal of Jesus' faith, the faith of the One who cried the cry of abandonment on the cross, does not seek for things to "make sense."[139]

The question remains, however, *how* can we believe in a loving Father in such a world? Jesus will not let us forsake the world, the real world in which we live in, nor will he let us abandon the love and power of God. These are held together by him.[140] It is understandable that we would seek those "good reasons" if we were left with only our own faith. If our faith is based, however, on the vicarious faith of Christ, then our resting is not on those "good reasons," but on the faith of the Son. The "rest" for our mind is not found in what we can comprehend but that which apprehends us: the inexhaustible essence of God, only known by the Son. The recent centuries of skepticism about God, it has been suggested, have been aided by theologians that wanted to tame the mystery of God, through both the culture Protestantism (Ritschl) and the doctrinal orthodoxy (Hodge) of the nineteenth century.[141] The protest of the transcendent God of Kierkegaard and the early Barth, on the one hand, and the liturgical resolve of mystery in Eastern Orthodoxy, on the other, have stood as witnesses against this trend. Awareness of the incomprehensibility of God is knowledge of his essence, a knowledge we can only have through faith (Basil the Great).[142] Such a faith is not entrusting ourselves to our own faith. That faith can fail. Faith in God is something different, and difficult.[143]

The alternative is the faith of the One who is unique. "He is the only one who does what He does."[144] Herein Jesus demonstrates his lordship, a

---

[139] In contrast to Adams, *Horrendous Evil and the Goodness of God,* 82, 203.

[140] Ray S. Anderson, "Reading T. F. Torrance as a Practical Theologian," in Colyer, ed., *The Promise of Trinitarian Theology,* 174.

[141] See James Turner, *Without God, Without Creed: The Origins of Unbelief in America* (Baltimore: The Johns Hopkins University Press, 1985), 202, 267.

[142] Basil, *Letters,* no. 234, NPNF, second series, Vol. 8, 274.

[143] Weil, *Gravity and Grace,* 162–63: In the section entitled, "He Whom We Must Love is Absent": "Evil is the innocence of God. We have to place God at an infinite distance in order to conceive of him as innocent of evil; reciprocally, evil implies that we have to place God at an infinite distance. He who puts his life into his faith in God can lose his faith. But he who puts his life in God himself will never lose it. To put our life into that which we cannot touch in any way. It is impossible. It is a death. That is what is required."

[144] Barth, *CD,* I/2, 382.

demonstration found in his exaltation, the exaltation in which we now share (Phil 2:9-11). This has already happened. We are already in him, sharing in that which is foreign to our fallen state, fellowship with God.[145] Integral to that fellowship is our participation in the obedience of the Son, an obedient movement we have not been able to make. Our existence has been "anticipated and virtually accomplished in His."[146] He has dug deeply into our humanity (he "emptied himself, taking the form of a slave, being born in human likeness . . ." [Phil 2:7]). Because of this solidarity, in our sufferings we can lean upon those of the Son, God suffering not only "with" us but "as" and "in" us.[147] "It is good to be with Jesus and not elsewhere. This is good because it is there that God Himself is good for us" (Barth).[148] Can the providence of God really be found anywhere else?

Here is the impossibility of faith but the reality of Jesus. Faith is impossible because it is like being put into a little boat on a wide river in the dark.[149] There is enough danger there to kill us, a danger we have already seen in Wendell Berry's tale of "The Man in the Well." This is a man who has fallen into the well, far from any help. He cannot save himself. Who would give any hope for this man? Faith, Berry contends, believes that the Man in the Well is not lost. The person of faith believes in the providence of God in a world of rampant doubt. This one's faith is not just a feeling nor a wish but a knowledge beyond any way of knowledge. Berry has to end with the cry of abandonment by Jesus. He knows our inability to be the man of faith, to believe that the Man in the Well can be saved.

The Jesus it is good to be with is the Jesus who confronts and confronted evil, most of all, by becoming a living prayer (Boris Bobrinskoy).[150] He was the "human asking" of the Father. We have boldness to call upon God as Father only because of his boldness.[151] He is the one who, as Bonhoeffer reminds us, prays the Psalms.[152] Therefore, he is the

[145] Barth, *CD,* IV/2, 270.
[146] Ibid.
[147] Fiddes, *Participation in God,* 184.
[148] Barth, *CD,* II/2, 570
[149] Berry, *Jayber Crow,* 356.
[150] Bobrinskoy, *The Compassion of the Father,* 90.
[151] Ibid., 104.
[152] Dietrich Bonhoeffer, *Psalms: The Prayer Book of the Bible,* trans. James H. Burtness (Minneapolis: Augsburg, 1970), 21.

one who is singing the psalm over and over again in the gentle, haunting refrain of the Orthodox liturgy of the Pre-sanctified Gifts: "Taste and see that the Lord is good . . . Taste and see that the Lord is good."

The world is still in a mess. "What we will be has not yet been revealed" (1 John 3:2). There is no explanation for the world but there is the revelation of the Son. It is understandable that Ivan Karamazov would return his "ticket" to a world of eternal harmony fashioned with the suffering of the innocents. But Jesus is able to take that ticket back, for us. He makes a pathway for our faith. He is "the pioneer and perfecter of our faith" (Heb 12:2). Faith deserves and needs nothing less. Flannery O'Connor calls faith "more valuable, more mysterious, altogether more immense than anything you can learn or decide upon in college."[153] She counsels her college friend to cultivate "Christian skepticism." This "will keep you free—not free to do anything you please, but free to be formed by something larger than your own intellect or the intellects of those around you." Here is the "healthy doubt" that is faith seeking understanding. Skeptical doubt, doubting God's Word is something different. We think that that kind of doubt is important, influential, huge, immense in the modern and postmodern world. But faith is larger. Faith is so large that God needs to take it upon himself first. He needs to believe so that we might believe.

---

[153] O'Connor, *Collected Works,* 1165. See also Ralph C. Wood, *Contending for the Faith: The Church's Engagement with Culture* (Waco: Baylor University Press, 2003), 124.

6
The Vicarious Humanity of Christ and the Doubting Self

Our summary goes back to the beginning: the doubting self, Jayber Crow's "lost traveler." What does the vicarious faith of Jesus have to say to the person doubting today and the person doubting tomorrow? Doubt seems to be real for the Son on the cross, yet also real for us, having been judged and consoled by the triumph of his faith. The Son of God reveals that his faith is in the living Father in heaven, not in our projections of needs alone. As such, he becomes the sole source for belief in a world that questions the knowledge of faith and its relevance for facing the challenges of vocation and calling, evil and suffering, and pluralism and postmodernism. But we seem to be left by ourselves as individuals, a point where the methodological doubt of Descartes and the existential faith of Kierkegaard converge. Where is Jesus when I doubt?

Our Doubting Self: Its Present and Future

Living in the Abyss of Helplessness and Lostness

In a pluralistic and postmodern world one is tempted to admit the loss of Christendom, the heritage of a Christian society in the West, and admit the triumph of skepticism. At the end of his study on five Catholic intellectuals of the twentieth century, Walker Percy, Dorothy Day, Thomas Merton, and Flannery O'Connor, Paul Elie proclaims, "We are all skeptics now, believer and unbeliever alike."[1] A "true faith" does not exist, having been "made crooked by our experience" and "complicated by our lives." No longer able to rest on the bedrock of Christendom such as provided by the Catholic Church, even the four Catholic thinkers Elie reviews have been forced to take the burden of belief upon themselves, "where it belongs." Is he right?

Our helplessness and lostness seem so obvious to all except the most triumphalistic believer. Helplessness is not necessarily a character defect. It may be a sign of the one who like Socrates "knows that he does not know," a mark of intellectual humility. "Every man who thinks and lives by thought must have his own skepticism," remarks T. S. Eliot.[2] The postmodern concern for tolerance is not foreign to the healthy kind of doubt that lacks intimidation by the opinions of others. This might be the case because of an epistemological relativism or agnosticism or by the conviction that the truth is much larger than one's subjectivity. This does not necessarily have to mean that one's convictions should be tossed to and fro, but only an openness that allows for the truth to be perceived by another.[3] Humility need not be relativism but the beginning of genuine knowledge. Barth hastens to add that we are always our "own worst enemy." Unfortunately, as Chesterton remarks, in the modern world humility has become misplaced. One used to be doubtful about oneself but not about the truth. The modern world makes one doubtful about the truth but not about oneself.[4]

I remember the dear seminary professor who, obsessed with rationalistic apologetics to defend with reason his fundamentalist father's faith, determined that the only rationale for the truth of Christianity was the supernatural reality of the apostle Paul's conversion! If one could present a naturalistic explanation, the professor contended, he would no longer remain a Christian!

---

[1] Paul Elie, *The Life You Save May Be Your Own: An American Pilgrimage* (New York: Farrar, Strauss and Giroux, 2003), 471–72.

[2] Eliot, "Introduction" in *Pascal's Pensées,* xv.

[3] Barth, *The Epistle to the Romans,* 506.

[4] Chesterton, *Orthodoxy,* 31. See also Guinness, *In Two Minds,* 126.

Hearing that, I winced as I remembered my own rationalistic past in search for the "evidence that demands a verdict." This only betrays the weakness of our Christianity and the feebleness of our faith, it seems to me. We are helpless. We are lost. We can always be vulnerable to another *attack* on Christianity. Who is to say a new one may not arise? Who might be the Voltaire of the twenty-first century? And so does this mean that we have to live in perpetual anxiety of that potential devastating argument that will bring down Christianity like a house of cards? What a tenuous faith.

Our creaturely state, which we know through the Christian doctrine of creation, reminds us of both our exaltation and our helplessness. Listen to Pascal: "Let us then take our compass; we are something, and we are not everything. The nature of our existence hides from us the knowledge of first beginnings which are born of the Nothing; and the littleness of our being conceals from us the sight of the Infinite."[5] The significance of the human being, though, should not hide us from the helplessness of our condition:

Pascal

> This is our true state; this is what makes us incapable of certain knowledge and of absolute ignorance. We sail within a vast sphere, ever drifting in uncertainty, driven from end to end. When we think to attach ourselves to any point and to listen to it, it wavers and leaves us; and if we follow it, it eludes our grasp, slips past us, and vanishes forever. Nothing stays for us. This is our natural condition, and yet most contrary to our inclination; we burn with desire to find solid ground and an ultimate foundation whereon to build a tower reaching to the Infinite. But our whole groundwork cracks, and the earth opens to abyss.[6]

"Our whole groundwork cracks, and the earth opens to abyss"! Can it be said any better? Here we are. "Nothing stays for us." Our problem is that we know that. Our problem is not only the *attack* against our faith by potential arguments, but also what we *lack*: we lack the ability to cope

[5] Pascal, *Pascal's Pensées,* 19.

[6] Ibid., 19–20.

with the mystery of our world and our existence. We lack what we feel belongs to us because of entitlement: a healthy, successful, even easy life with a minimum of disappointments (and certainly no big ones!). Both *attack* and *lack* contribute mightily to our helplessness.

The presence of God, furthermore, is a cause of our helplessness. The Word who is God convicts of us the sheer irrationality of a creature without a home, a creature without a destination. Our very knowledge of God in Christ declares our lostness, the damage and disorder upon our being, including our minds. As much as he will not let us go, he simultaneously convinces us of our helplessness.[7] The eastern Christian tradition is often contrasted with the West's emphasis on the moral and spiritual helplessness of humanity.[8] Whereas the Christian East may be praised for the emphasis on incarnation, resurrection, and the senses, the brute honesty of an Augustine or a Pascal is refreshing in a world with the false self-confidence of the fundamentalist, the modernist, and the postmodernist. Human beings are still plagued by what Flannery O'Connor calls, "a swollen faith in themselves."[9] Faith and unbelief can come and go. C. S. Lewis speaks of "undulation" in the Christian life as "a series of troughs and peaks."[10] The flesh and the Spirit possess opposite desires (Gal 5:17). We are not very reliable. Hazel Motes is the cynical preacher of the Church of Jesus Christ Without Christ in O'Connor's grim novel, *Wise Blood.* "I don't have to run from anything because I don't believe in anything," he proudly proclaims.[11] "If Jesus existed, I wouldn't be clean," he declares.[12] Haze is confident that there is no *attack* or *lack* if one simply withholds belief in God. Then Haze proceeds to have doubts about what he does not believe![13] In a world of grace doubt is sometimes difficult to believe. Even the doubter is helpless and lost. Paul makes it very clear that we are all dead people, incapable of a response (Romans 6; Eph 2:1). Anything else is a delusion.

---

[7] T. F. Torrance, *Theological Science,* v. See also Anderson, "Reading T. F. Torrance as a Practical Theologian" in Colyer, ed., *The Promise of Trinitarian Theology,* 172–73.

[8] Ellen T. Charry, "Editorial: East Meets West," *Theology Today* 61 (April, 2004), 1–6.

[9] Flannery O'Connor, *The Habit of Being* (New York: Farrar, Strauss and Giroux, 1979), 452.

[10] C. S. Lewis, *The Screwtape Letters,* 36–39.

[11] Flannery O'Connor, *Wise Blood* (New York: Farrar, Strauss and Giroux, 1962), 76.

[12] Ibid., 91.

[13] Elie, *The Life You Save May Be Your Own,* 208.

We only really know our need for forgiveness in the midst of God's presence, especially as Christianity lives in the context of a world of religions.[14] We cannot ignore the genuine concerns of a pluralistic culture. It is only because of Jesus' faith that we have forgiveness. Is the Church content simply to be recipients of grace, helpless before the eyes of God, or are we proud and all too ready to proclaim our rightness and superiority at a moment's notice? If not, do we end up surrendering to the pluralist who claims that all religions are saying the same thing? We simply share in the unbelief of all religions rather than the firm foundation of the faith of Jesus of Nazareth. As Karl Barth reminds us, at this point the Christian religion "is in a position of greater danger and defenselessness and impotence than any other religion."[15] Like those who follow the false prophets in 2 Peter, "the last state has become worse for them than the first" (2 Pet 2:20). We are *more* lost, *more* helpless than others for we can only depend on the name of Jesus Christ.

The young Jayber's dilemma is a striking example of our helplessness. Jesus' prayer for the cup to be taken from him was not granted. But he did pray "Thy will be done." Why even pray that then if God's will is to be done anyway? Where does one get the strength to pray, "Thy will be done"?[16] The doubting self is troubled by the fact that one's will may not be the same as God's will. Joy and pain again become joined. How do I even know what God's will is even if I have the strength to submit to it?[17] Jayber is changing into the lost traveler who asks, Where is God's help in our helplessness?

Nothing really appears as divine. Our bodies rapidly decay, a ready host for a traumatic disease or accident at any time. Our earthly desires, as strong as they may be, are constantly thwarted and frustrated. Life appears to promise more than it can deliver.

Enter faith. Faith is the conviction of things not seen, the opposite of sight (Heb 11:1). How seriously do we take this? How serious is our eschatology? Do we really long to be delivered from our helplessness or lostness or are we really quite comfortable (and therefore deluded) as we sit in our recliners? Is there truly a "secret despair of faith" in those who

---

[14] Barth, *CD*, I/2, 355–56.

[15] Ibid., 356.

[16] Berry, *Jayber Crow*, 51.

[17] Ibid., 52.

seek to deny their helplessness or lostness and instead "take refuge in reason or culture or humanity or race" in order to cling to a certainty?[18] Here is the true "secularization" of the Church: when it does not admit its helplessness.

Our faith is placed in question, not just by our doubts, but by Christ himself.[19] The cry of abandonment, "My God, my God, why have you forsaken me?" is not just a question of Jesus' doubt but of our faith. Our faith has been judged even as Jesus utters this cry. The law comes before the gospel, the penultimate before the ultimate (Bonhoeffer), the death of our faith before it can be given back to us.[20] "We must not only believe *in* the risen Christ. We must believe *with* the risen Christ . . ."[21] The "sweet exchange" is based on the reality of our lostness.

The Gospels present the bittersweet scenario of the disciples of the imprisoned John the Baptist sent to Jesus because of John's doubts (Matt 11:2-3; Luke 7:18-19). The one who had baptized Jesus, who had enough confidence in Jesus' holiness that he tried to prevent the baptism (Matt 3:13), whom the Fourth Gospel has proclaim, "Here is the Lamb of God who takes away the sin of the world!" (John 1:29), is now despairing enough in prison to ask the question, "Are you one who is to come, or are we to wait for another?" (Matt 11:3). Had the baptism of Jesus become the source for John's doubts?[22] Being baptized like any other sinner did not fit John's vision of the one who will baptize "with the Holy Spirit and fire," whose "winnowing fork is in his hand," to burn the chaff "with unquenchable fire" (Matt 11:11-12). The tension of the kingdom of God at hand, the kingdom that John had proclaimed (Matt 3:2) had become unbearable for John, for the kingdom had become embodied in the faith of Jesus.

A faith has already taken place; a hearing has already occurred: the faith and hearing of Jesus Christ. The search for God itself can be a denial of God.[23] The vicarious faith of Christ interrupts our search and calls us

---

[18] Barth, *CD*, I/2, 357.

[19] Barth, *CD*, II/1, 253.

[20] Bonhoeffer, *Ethics*, 151–70.

[21] Barth, *CD*, II/1, 253.

[22] Barth, *CD*, IV/4, 63.

[23] Stringfellow, *Count It All Joy*, 50.

to confess our helplessness. To "welcome with meekness the implanted word that has the power to save your souls" (Jas 1:21) is the alternative to being the doubting, "double-minded" person "driven and tossed by the wind" (Jas 1:6-7), the person of "skeptical" doubt. The implanted word is that which proceeds from outside our existence yet embraces our existence, the Word of God.[24] The doubting self can now become something else: the one who is a doer of the Word (Jas 1:22-26). Denying this is to forget what you look like in a mirror, forgetting that the implanted word had come to you. Being and act are indivisible for James, yet it is not simply based on our strength of faith or obedience but the reality of the implanted word from outside. Jesus' answer to John's doubt is only to point to the indivisibility of Jesus' being and his act: "Go and tell John what you hear and see: the blind receive their sight, the lame walk, the lepers are cleansed, the deaf hear, the dead are raised, and the poor have the good news brought to them" (Matt 11:5). These are signs of the kingdom (Luke 11:20), yet John is still in prison, soon to be worse off than that. John is tormented by the tension of the kingdom because Jesus is a doer of the Word.[25] Things are going to get worse before they get better.

This question, of course, is: Do we seek first the kingdom of God, the kingdom of which we pray, "Thy kingdom come"? Are we honest enough for the faith of Jesus? Are we really desperate enough for the faith of Jesus? If John the Baptist had difficulty believing in Jesus, how much more should we?

Helplessness, however, can also mean paralysis. Why try to lift a finger, let alone "press on to maturity" (Heb 6:1, NASB)? Dare we speak of a "self-confidence" and simply look to ourselves, as Paul Elie suggests?[26] Yet faith is not without self-confidence, the kind of confidence that the Son had in the Father through the Spirit. Is there hope in his confidence?

---

[24] Ibid., 73.
[25] Barth, *CD,* IV/4, 76.
[26] See also Barth, *CD,* I/2, 357.

Loving without Fear and with Doubt

> Love dares to include doubt as the first principle of faith . . .
> But love does not fear doubt, for it springs not from
> reason but from reality.[27]
> —Ray Anderson

The doubting self finds oneself not only in helplessness but also in love. What do we do with that? To love and/or to be loved is not just the end result of faith but its first principle. Therefore, Anderson dares to say that love can *include* doubt; it does not have to flee from it or be afraid of it. This is not the same as embracing doubt, as Paul Tillich wants to do. But it does mean that one begins with the reality of love and not just the mechanizations of reason. Love does not come from reason but reality, Anderson suggests. So Jayber Crow learns in his concrete love of Mattie. So the disciples learn when Jesus calls them and the sinners and publicans learn when Jesus sits at table (Eucharist?) with them. So we learn when we are befriended by someone who shares with us the good news. There is a truth to pragmatism and the pragmatic bent of postmodern life.[28] Jesus presented the pragmatic evidence of his healings to John the Baptist's doubts. Love is the pragmatic reality that hits us when we are not looking, much like grace. Like being run over by a truck, we cannot ignore it. "Falling" in love is indeed a vertical drop. Doubt may arise because of lack or attack, as we have seen, but love says, "doubt love if you dare!"[29] A pastor may try to change his people by what he says, but what really changes them is *who* he is.[30] For what is more real to us than the act of love; of our love for another or another's love for us? It may not be a reasonable act; as Jayber found out; yet it is the most real act, the most real place for us. It is a holy place that does not fear doubt.

Yet our love can disappoint; it can even fail. Who will uphold our love when we fail, when others fail us, when life gives us the "twisted face"?

---

[27] Anderson, *Soulprints,* 72.

[28] See the discussion of Richard Rorty, Thomas Kuhn, and John Dewey in Grenz, *A Primer on Postmodernism,* 151–59.

[29] Anderson, *Soulprints,* 72.

[30] Ibid., 82.

Still, we love. Jayber tries to be honest with himself: "Was I fooling myself? . . . Why should I assume that I would have loved her all her life?"[31] His only answer is that he did love, and does love her.[32] This is not an answer to an argument but a "turning away" from all arguments. An argument for love is not worthy of love. Is this a cop-out, then? No, Jayber is simply being honest with the reality of love. To be less than honest with love would be to dissect it, parse it, or deconstruct it to the point that it is no longer living; carved upon until it is unrecognizable like a decimated frog in a high school biology class. But as a living reality, love cannot be ignored . . . even by doubt. For love just "turns away" from doubt and goes about its business. The doubting self, then, is not alone.

Such a concrete love for Jayber became the means by which Jayber then loved God, and then the world. The *idea* of love can be powerful but ultimately frustrating, a fantasy never to be fulfilled. An abstraction, the idea of love seeks to be fitted on someone or something else, but always is two sizes too small. A *concrete, particular* love, in contrast, like Jayber's love for Mattie, opens up the possibility of actually loving the world, that world in which Mattie dwells, a world lovingly created by God and therefore possibly forgiven by God.[33] One can conceive that such a love motivated God to take upon our humanity, walk among us, and suffer our fate for us and in our place. Here is a suffering love, suffering with and for us, in order to demonstrate and change the human condition not by coercion (as Jayber did not try to coerce Mattie's love) but by an invitation to join the God who loves the world even though it is the kind of love that can break your heart (cf. 1 John 4:7-12). God's heart is broken; that is the call to faith and repentance, a love that doubt cannot ignore.

Faith can never be far behind love. However emotional or giddy the relationship is between man and woman or mystic and the divine, one eventually has to trust: faith eventually has to come. For Jayber's heart of love for Mattie, and the world, breaks forth into a life of faith not in what can be seen but like being put out "on a wide river in a little boat, in the fog, in the dark."[34] We are still helpless, still lost. Burley Coulter's saying is

---

[31] Berry, *Jayber Crow,* 247.

[32] Ibid., 248.

[33] Ibid., 252–54.

[34] Ibid., 356.

true: we've all got to go through enough to kill us. How can we love our enemies?[35] How can Jayber love Mattie's jerk husband Troy, who cheats on her, who is a racist and bigot? We need help.

In the midst of "the distressing invisibility of God" love can only believe.[36] But love does "endure all things" as well as "believes all things" (1 Cor 13:7). Love cannot be ignored, but neither can the faith that accompanies it. The doubting self has even more company!

Community: Crutch, Curse, or Co-Humanity?

As we experience love (more or less), we also experience community (more or less). But can it be simply a crutch in which we gullibly accept the beliefs of our peers or ethnic group? Can community be a curse when (like love) it can inevitably fail, betray us, let us down? Was not Jesus betrayed by his "small group"?

However meager or profound our experiences of community have been, they are a part of the stuff of the doubting self's life. Our community includes the earth as well as people. *Jayber Crow* is a novel about relationships: not only with God and others, but also with the land. Jayber realizes that his connection with the earth leads him to heaven. Rather than being polar opposites, Jayber sees our desire for heaven in our experience of the earth.[37] Both are creations of God. The difference is that the earth is "conceivable" and heaven is "inconceivable."[38] But they are both creations of God. Why wouldn't heaven be much like the best of this earth, just fuller and richer?[39] Therefore, the earth, including earthly community, can give us a taste of heaven.

Yet the Church often represents community as both crutch and curse. As Israel so often forgot Yahweh, so the Church can so easily practically forget Jesus Christ for the sake of its "specifically Christian righteousness, holiness and vitality."[40] Here again is the "secularization" of the Church, a

---

[35] Ibid., 50.
[36] Barth, *CD,* IV/2, 835.
[37] Berry, *Jayber Crow,* pp. 354–55.
[38] Barth, *Dogmatics in Outline,* 59.
[39] See C. S. Lewis on creation in *The Magician's Nephew* (New York: HarperTrophy, 1994) and the new creation, in *The Last Battle* (New York: HarperTrophy, 1994).
[40] Barth, *CD,* I/2, 383.

community which only loves itself, is only able to love itself. What is considered by some the angriest entry in Thomas Merton's journals involves his comments about an ex-monk who admitted that he had placed his faith in Merton's faith, not God (a "bizarro" vicarious humanity!).[41] Facing that fact, his faith collapsed. Yet Merton saw this realization as the first step towards truly believing.

In contrast to community as crutch and curse is community as *co-humanity.*[42] Adam only knew he was an individual when he met Eve. The lonely, Cartesian individual ego of the hermit or scholar does not exist. We are bound up with each other whether we like it or not. The doubting self, today and tomorrow, is really a fiction. No one really doubts by oneself. Community, therefore, is essential to our healing, spiritually, emotionally, and physically. In Michael Polanyi's classic words, "Our believing is conditioned at its source by our belonging."[43] The ancient theologian John Cassian, in counseling concerning dejection (depression), warns the monk not to flee from the community. For the source of our problems is not in others but within ourselves.[44] The doubting self is not the retreat to oneself alone. The soul's health is achieved rather by "his living the ascetic life in the company of holy men."

In times of despair, anxiety, grief, and doubt, another person, the community, can be there for us. For the Christian, this is the vicarious humanity of Christ living through the Church, "the community of the Last Adam" (1 Corinthians 15), a Body that is constantly judged by its Head.[45] Here the Christian brother or sister can say to the one in doubt, "Because Jesus believes when we cannot believe, *let me believe for you right now.*" As daring as this sounds, should we do less if the Church is truly the

---

[41] Elie, *The Life You Save May Be Your Own,* 467.

[42] Anderson, *On Being Human,* 44–50.

[43] Polanyi, *Personal Knowledge,* 322. See also Anderson, *Historical Transcendence and the Reality of God,* 206 and Daniel J. Price, "Community in the Life and Theology of Ray Anderson" in Speidell, ed., *On Being Christian . . . and Human,* 19.

[44] John Cassian, "On the Eight Vices" in *The Philokalia,* Vol. 1, compiled by St. Nikodemos of the Holy Mountain and St. Makarios of Corinth; trans. and ed. G. E. H. Palmer, Philip Sherrard, Kallistos Ware (London: Faber and Faber, 1979), 87.

[45] See "Humanity Restored: Christ as the Last Adam and the Church as the Body of Christ" for further implications of the vicarious humanity of Christ living today in the Church in Kettler, *The Vicarious Humanity of Christ and the Reality of Salvation,* 263–88. See also Taylor, *The Myth of Certainty,* 111, 130.

body of Christ and Christ is continuing his vicarious life and ministry through the Church?

Yet can the problem of the monk's falsely placed faith in Merton and not in God be avoided? Only if it is clear that Christ is present, in our midst and we are participating in his continuing ministry, not a ministry of our own. This leads to viewing the present and future life of the doubting self as the reality of *praxis,* not just practice.

4. *Life as Praxis, not Practice*

As the cliché goes, life happens in the midst of living it. The realities of helplessness and lostness, love and community, are not just theories but experiences learned in the living. This is the place where the doubting self lives, today and tomorrow. However, we are very prone to theorize, idealize, and abstract our perceptions of reality so that our doubt cannot be faced honestly. What is true, whether it is belief or unbelief, will be found in the midst of life, not just applying a theory to practice. Rather, to find truth in the midst of life is Ray Anderson's definition of *praxis.*[46]

Jayber Crow's experience of praxis comes in the midst of his doubts. He does not merely theorize about them but experiences them, and in the midst of that he writes, "I was being changed by them."[47] The change is not pleasant; his prayers dwindle away, he loses his sense of calling, he becomes the "lost traveler." He continues to doubt when he encounters Mattie and falls in love. "Was I fooling myself?" he asks.[48] How could he assume the integrity of this love? Yet in the midst of those doubts, this praxis, Jayber discovers that there is no argument to love. All he can do is confess that love in the midst of all of his doubts and ambiguities. He simply "turns away," as he puts it, from the arguments for or against love.

We cannot ignore the praxis, for praxis is genuine pragmatism, William James' "will to believe," whose consequences are so profound because they

---

[46] Ray S. Anderson, "Christopraxis" in *Ministry on the Fireline* (Downers Grove, Ill.: InterVarsity, 1993), 19–98; "Practical Theology as Christopraxis: Hermeneutical Implications" and "The Praxis of Practical Theology," in *The Shape of Practical Theology,* 47–60, 77–188.

[47] Berry, *Jayber Crow,* 52.

[48] Ibid., 247–48.

have been discovered in the midst of life. Bonhoeffer reminds us that God is in the midst of life, not at the boundaries as we so often think (only birth and death and maybe marriage!).[49] Christianity is not defined by its pragmatic character, because it "works," according to our own criteria. But the gospel is not without its pragmatic character. For it is in the midst of his ministry of healing and forgiving that Jesus revealed himself as the Messiah: In the midst of John the Baptist (of all people!) and his doubts about the messiahship of Jesus, Jesus simply recounts what he had been doing. Jesus' messiahship becomes known in its action. Jayber had realized that as much as "the world had so beaten me about the head" it had also "favored me with good and beautiful things."[50] In this process he is able to see that God, too, loves this world, the way it is.

The answers for Jayber's doubts Dr. Ardmire, the wise professor, suggests, will not come easily.[51] It will not be a matter of simply clarifying the problem (theory) and then providing the rational, logical solution (practice).[52] No, Dr. Ardmire suggests, the answers will be revealed in the midst of living life, in the midst of praxis. The praxis will give the meaning, he is saying. Even his sense of vocation, his calling, will be discovered in the midst of life; not something to be theorized about. You have been called, says Dr. Ardmire to Jayber, "But not to what you thought." You will have to be surprised by grace, he is saying. And this will take a long time, maybe all your life, Jayber, or even longer.

So Jayber reflects that "all my real opportunities" have come from becoming a humble barber in a small, rural town.[53] He is able then to look back at those early years when he seemed to be adrift, a "lost traveler" and see instead a guiding hand laying out a path for him. But he can only see that in reflection. The path is uncovered in the walking on it. So the doubting self will never deal with doubt apart from the actual walking of the path. And in doing so, he might discover that Someone was already believing when we were unable to believe.

---

[49] Bonhoeffer, *Letters and Papers from Prison,* 282, 369–70.

[50] Berry, *Jayber Crow,* 250–51.

[51] Ibid., 54.

[52] See also Barth, *CD,* IV/3, first half, 47: In the life of Christ "there is no place for the well-known dualism of word and act, for the nervous tension between theory and practice."

[53] Berry, *Jayber Crow,* 65–66.

Jesus in Our Present and Future

Jesus is the one who discovers in the midst of living that "all things work together for good" (Rom 8:28).[54] He is the one who tastes and sees "that the Lord is good" (Ps 34:8). His faith and vocation were discerned in the praxis of life, a life that confronts evil and suffering (the problems of faith, vocation, and evil and suffering in chapter one). He, too, is confronted by "the divine invisibility" as he loves the Father with the love we need to love God as well. He is the only man who does this.[55] Jesus is still the "Pilgrim and Warrior," a stranger in a strange land, the one true Israelite, the one good Samaritan (Luke 10:25-26) who does not ignore the beaten ones on the path, the one who is the neighbor to us, the beaten, beaten in our doubts and despairs.[56] Only then can there be others that will follow in his path and continue with him down the path to help more beaten victims of life.[57] In the midst of a pluralistic and postmodern culture, we can only join with the disciples in their pragmatic, rhetorical question, "Lord to whom can we go? You have words of eternal life" (John 6:68). Sometimes that is all we can or need to say. What is the witness of this Jesus who stands with the doubting self in one's present and future?

Believing Because Jesus Believes

In the pluralistic, postmodern context we can easily be intimidated by the opinions of others. Isn't faith just a subjective mood, a feeling, a preference for chocolate over vanilla ice cream? So tolerance must be viewed as the most important virtue. Thus the postmodern mantra speaks. The presence of Jesus, and particularly his faith, however, interrupts such critiques of

---

[54] Barth, *CD*, IV/2, 794.

[55] Ibid., 822–24.

[56] Barth, *CD*, IV/3, first half, 331.

[57] Ibid., 330: "Since He precedes us, and it is His good will to act as He does, the only possible thing for the world, the community and ourselves, and indeed the only right thing, is to follow Him, to accompany Him on the way to His goal, in His movement from here to there, from the first to the final form of His coming again, in His still incompleted conflict, concerning the issue of which there is no doubt, but in which He still wills to engage."

faith. Should we even take our faith that seriously? Is not that our problem? Much more important is the faith of Jesus that meets the doubting self, embracing one's doubt, but ultimately relieving it of its power to destroy. We may and will encounter people with opinions differing from our own, but we should not be moved by them or even pay them much attention.[58] We should just "turn away" from them, as Jayber's love does with arguments for or against love.

We should remember, however, that our opinions are to be relativized as much as the other. Christ has taken our place so our certainty is in him, not in ourselves and our opinions.

Christ comes upon us. That is the central truth of the incarnation, the epiphany. He comes with his own certainty. Indeed it is the certainty of paradox for he is the one who cries, "My God, my God, why have you forsaken me?" We do, too. Ultimately only he is able to do this from the standpoint of faith. His incarnate presence continues today through the Holy Spirit and impresses upon us his own rationality that challenges our irrationality.[59] Such an impression has led some even to question doubt!

> I've never had any doubts. Why should I?
> To me, the living God is the most real thing there is.
> Knowledge of God is the most natural, most intuitive
> thing of all, especially for me. I was raised in a
> Christian home. My mother was a wonderfully pious
> woman, one who was, in her own way, an excellent
> theologian. Belief in God simply pervaded everything.
> To me, it has always seemed so natural.[60]

This testimony by T. F. Torrance may be startling, even off-putting to some. Those of us who have struggled with doubts may find it difficult to embrace. Yet based on Torrance's theology of the vicarious humanity of Christ it may be easier to understand. There is a presence of Christ for Torrance and his family that was there from the beginning, a praxis of

---

[58] Barth, *The Epistle to the Romans,* 506.

[59] T. F. Torrance, *Theological Science,* v.

[60] T. F. Torrance in Michael Baumann, *Roundtable: Conversations with European Theologians* (Grand Rapids: Eerdmans, 1990), 111.

love and community in the midst of a lost world. Doubt is a reality for many of us, but the faith of Christ reminds us that we are not born to doubt. We might be "born to run" like Bruce Springsteen but we are not "born to doubt"!

As Christ comes to us, he comes grounded in his own certainty. We cannot achieve certainty about God by first establishing the certainty of our own logic or emotional state.[61] Knowing God can only be a gift given from God. There is a "clear distinction" between our self-awareness, our consciousness of an idea of God and the mind of God.[62] The disciples did not at first recognize the resurrected Jesus on the road to Emmaus. But when he broke bread with them (Eucharist!), "then their eyes were opened, and they recognized him" (Luke 24:30-31). He will vanish and then appear again, startling them because they think he is a ghost (v. 37). "Why are you frightened," Jesus asks them, "and why do doubts arise in your hearts?" (v. 38). Invited to examine his real physicality, they still "disbelieved for joy" (v. 41, RSV). Yet the process from doubt to recognition was already in place, by God's own initiative. T. F. Torrance grew up in an environment in which there was already an objectivity of faith, a Christian family, a community of love and integrity, a reality in our world, in which recognition of Christ was second nature and doubt, therefore, not a consideration. Of course, this is simply a gift of God not given to all, yet the goal of "recognizing" Christ, not doubting, is the real stuff of Christian existence in word and sacrament. The goal is "the basic end of all doubt."[63]

Christ comes to the doubting self providing the "sweet exchange." Taking our place, our standards for God are not just filled out or improved upon but replaced.[64] The substitutionary reality of Christ is total: no part of our humanity is left untouched, including our religious attempts. Our restored faith consists only in admitting that something was done for us once and for all. Someone has believed for us once and for all. A genuine exchange (*katallage*—reconciliation) has taken place (2 Cor 5:19), including our faith for his faith.

---

[61] Barth, *CD*, I/2, 196. See also Alan Torrance, *Persons in Communion*, 27, and Chesterton, *Orthodoxy*, 31.

[62] Barth, *CD*, III/1, 364.

[63] Ibid., 365.

[64] Barth, *CD*, I/2, 308.

"Jesus Christ lives . . . is at once the simplest and the most difficult christological statement."[65] The living presence of Christ is not just the hopeful end result of revelation (and theological thinking) but is its substance, ground, and reality at every point, including in the encounter with the doubting self. The Christian has no other option than to say this to the doubting person (oneself or another): "Jesus Christ lives." Unpacking that reality is where one finds that the living Jesus Christ speaks for himself, acts for himself, even providing the Yes to God's Yes of us.[66] An objectivity exists which is nothing less than the living person of Jesus Christ. As "the Word of life" (1 John 1:1) and "the light of life" he is his own objectivity. This is why the story of Jesus is so important. It is the story that we have fallen into; "Like it or not, we come to life in the middle of stories that are not ours," observes Paul Elie.[67] This is not always a bad thing. The objectivity of faith for the world of the doubting self is found in our swimming in the pool with Jesus, in participating in his story, his story becoming intertwined with ours.[68] This story is nothing less than the "self-witness" of Jesus, the story that he tells about himself: the vicarious humanity of Christ.[69]

The Yes of God is no less than a critique of our temptation to give equal value to light and darkness.[70] The knowledge of faith is not involved in a perilous dialectic between belief and unbelief. If that is the case, then our goal is to live by doubt not by faith (justification by doubt?). No, if we are reconciled by God then we have a revelation of God.[71] As Flannery O'Connor exhorted her friend who had lost her faith, speaking of the divinity of Christ: "It is worthless if it is not true."[72] It may be repugnant to the intellect and the culture yet still be true, a true intimacy for which we all search. Knowledge of God in the Bible is not neutral information but intimacy.[73] Within this intimacy with the Triune God is our hope.

---

[65] Barth, *CD,* IV/3, first half, 39.
[66] Ibid., 47.
[67] Elie, *The Life You Save May Be Your Own,* 472.
[68] A christological approach to narrative theology is stressed by Hans Frei, *The Identity of Jesus Christ* (Philadelphia: Fortress Press, 1975).
[69] Barth, *CD,* IV/3, first half, 274.
[70] Ibid., 172.
[71] Ibid., 182.
[72] O'Connor, *The Habit of Being,* p. 452. See also Elie, *For the Life You Save May Be Your Own,* 471.
[73] Barth, *CD,* IV/3, first half, 183–84.

Darkness does not merit our astonishment as light does. "The light of life" in Jesus Christ supremely shines in the resurrection. Resurrection and astonishment need to always go hand in hand.[74] Astonishment is "healthy" doubt . . . faith seeking understanding. "We must have seen and heard the angels at the open and empty tomb if we are to be sure of our ground . . ." (Barth).[75] Jesus maintains that astonishment for us.

Our helplessness further reminds us of how unfitted we are to ask questions of Jesus.[76] Jesus' faith stands regardless of whether or not we acknowledge it, ignore it, or spit upon it. Where is our light, our love, our community that can criticize him? He graciously silences us even in the middle of our questions.

Jesus Our Advocate

Christ comes to the life of the doubting self as our advocate as well. He does not come merely to condemn Thomas but to embrace his doubt so that it can be transformed into faith (John 20:24-29). Jesus utters the cry of abandonment so that our doubt would be embraced by his faith. Job knows that God is his advocate in a dynamic way that his pious friends do not.[77] Jayber may be in torture when he considers why he loves Mattie with an impossible love, yet by refusing the arguments and just "turning away, leaving them to find what rest they can," he turns the love over to Someone beyond himself.[78]

The great commandment is, "You shall love the Lord your God with all your heart, and with all your soul, and with all your mind" (Matt 22:37). Who has not felt the intolerable burden of this commandment? Was not Jayber's love for Mattie a constant temptation to ignore this commandment? Who is able to love God? Christ is our advocate when it comes to what is of supreme importance. Here is the key that has to be unlocked by Christ alone. The Son knows that he is beloved by the Father, so he responds with love himself. This is our hope. This is how we love

[74] Ibid., 286–89.

[75] Ibid., 287.

[76] Ibid., 73.

[77] Speidell, *Confessions of a Lapsed Skeptic,* 45.

[78] Berry, *Jayber Crow,* 116.

God truly, through the Son our advocate.[79] Our love can only grow "in Jesus Christ Himself." This intercession brings us to repentance.[80]

As we have seen, Jesus knows the inexhaustible God whom we know in his essence, yet not exhaustively. The reality of the transcendence of God as reflected in the incarnation ("historical transcendence" in Ray Anderson's language) does not only speak of separation but also of belonging to God.[81] Jesus is our advocate before the incomprehensible God in order to give us true freedom in contrast to the freedom that we foolishly equate with autonomy. To "transfer" us "into the kingdom of his beloved Son" is to transfer us gloriously into his humanity, not just his deity (Col 1:13). He is the Son whose humanity graciously takes our place in order for us to know the inexhaustible riches of God. Such an advocacy is a genuine human advocacy in the vicarious faith of Christ, keeping the faith we did not keep.

Jesus our advocate, therefore, is not only a critic of our ideas of God but also of our ideas of spirituality. If he keeps the faith that we cannot keep, then this casts a question over a spirituality that centers in "striving" to become spiritual "athletes."[82] Jesus is not just a coach who instructs us how to train for spiritual fitness. A true vicarious mysticism of Christ begins with Jesus' spirituality, neither our piety nor our mystical strivings. Often our spirituality is presented as our word that is the response to God's word. Even the traditional liturgy separating "the Ministry of the Word" from "the Ministry of the Faithful" can communicate this unless it includes the all important middle term of the vicarious response of Christ. Worship is being caught up in *his* response! Otherwise worship and spirituality simply reflect "polarity and tension," in Barth's words.[83] Here is the source for either a kind of nervousness or anxiety on the one hand or a kind of triumphalism and false certainty on the other hand. Both create a distortion of worship and spirituality. Who can ever be freed from doubt if one's spirituality is defined by striving? "Christians are found

Critique our spirituality

[79] Barth, *CD*, I/2, 384.

[80] Ibid., 390: "Love to God takes place in the self-knowledge of repentance in which we learn about ourselves by the mirror of the Word of God which acquits and blesses us, which is itself the love of God to us."

[81] Ibid., 391.

[82] Barth, *CD*, I/1, 392.

[83] Barth, *CD*, I/2, 790–91.

only in Christ, not independently."[84] Will there be struggle, striving, even discipline in the Christian life? Of course, yet never apart from the Son's own striving, the Son's own mysticism, the Son's own spiritual discipline. Our new humanity "no longer has any particularity of its own, but belongs only to Him."[85] This is good news!

Here is true spirituality: casting ourselves upon Jesus our advocate, a Jesus who is truly human and who truly acts vicariously, on our behalf and in our place.[86] Our spirituality is to allow God "to do what we cannot do and go where we need not go."[87] Is a "pilgrimage" metaphor then really that apt for the spiritual life? Are we really competent to embark on a spiritual pilgrimage? Do we even know the right questions? If we do, does that not assume that we lack an experience of Christ as the light of life, the very Word of God, but approach him as a criminal investigator or inquisitorial judge?[88] As our advocate, Jesus is forced to silence our questions yet not without compassion for our doubting selves. Despite the admitted limitations of the judicial metaphor for theories of the atonement, at this point perhaps we need to reintroduce the legal world in the context of the Advocate, the defense attorney is on our side no matter what. Our role is simply to listen to our attorney, to do what he tells us. We know nothing, comparatively, of the law. If we try to be our own attorneys, we quickly get into trouble. So also with the spiritual life.

The point at which the legal metaphor breaks down, of course, is the incarnation. The attorney never "becomes" the client. But God does in Jesus Christ (John 1:14). "For the love of us, God has made the problem of existence His own."[89] "Spirituality" is a problem for us, but not for God. The goodness of creaturely being has been made manifest in God taking that being upon himself. The free God is able to become one of us in order for us to regain our freedom. The freedom of the Son, as we have seen, is this reality.

God makes the problem of our existence his own by believing for us, becoming our advocate in the midst of our paltry faith. Jesus has the faith

---

[84] Ibid., 791.

[85] Barth, *CD,* I/1, 391.

[86] Alan E. Lewis, *Between Cross and Resurrection,* 430–31.

[87] Ibid., 431.

[88] Barth, *CD,* IV/3, first half, 73.

[89] Barth, *CD,* III/1, 382.

that can move mountains; we do not (Matt 17:20; 21:21-22; Mark 11:22-23; Luke 17:5-6).[90] Thomas Aquinas famously protests that Christ did not have faith because he was God.[91] Furthermore, although it is a virtue, faith is based on assuming a "defect," which Christ could not have. But who is to assume that faith is only important for the sinful human state? Does not Christ by his life of complete faithfulness to the Father (especially see the cry of abandonment) demonstrate what it truly means to be human? In doing so, he sees us as his neighbor, assuming solidarity with us in our tears.

Jesus as Present . . . Jesus as Absent

The doubting self today finds oneself in the presence of Jesus. "Jesus Christ lives . . . is at once the simplest and most difficult christological statement" (Barth).[92] While it cannot be proven by any criteria outside its own reality, "Jesus Christ lives" meets the doubting self in a doubting world. "The Word of life" (1 John 1:1) cannot be authenticated by logic or proof beyond itself without ceasing to be the Word of life, the origin and goal of all that is, who speaks life into being.[93] Yet the Word is still verbal; he still speaks, even to the doubting self. "Grace would not be grace if it were to remain mute and obscure . . . As such, it is indeed eloquent and radiant."[94] Grace is God speaking love to us; speaking and acting in the prophetic life of Jesus Christ, a presence among our doubting.

But in that presence is also absence. Where is God in a world of horrendous evils, in a world so prime in anticipation yet so often ripe with disappointment, a life that seems to promise so much and deliver so little, in a world in which the promise of the good in life so often remains a dream? We are back to the question of providence. Bringing in Jesus does not simply resolve the issue. In fact, the presence of Christ may even exacerbate the absence of God we often feel. We know the love of God in

[90] Wallis, *The Faith of Jesus Christ in Early Christian Traditions,* 12–13.
[91] Thomas Aquinas, *Summa Theologica,* 3a.7.3, Vol. 4, trans. the Fathers of the English American Province (Westminster, Md.: Christian Classics, 1981), 2061.
[92] Barth, *CD,* IV/3, first half, 39.
[93] Ibid., 47.
[94] Ibid., 81.

Christ, but how do we reconcile that with the kind of world God has created, the kind of fates we seem destined to live (Job!)?[95] Jesus is our advocate, yes, in the midst of our present doubts, taking them seriously although not permitting us to wallow in them.

Faith is not a resting place, Jayber Crow reminds us, but like sitting in a boat in the dark. We will face enough in our brief life span to kill us, literally and metaphorically.[96] Disappointments will mount more with each passing year. Advancing age seems to only create more opportunities for disappointment. Dreams will be dashed, emaciated, trampled upon. These are our lives, the lives of doubting selves. Yet they are lives in which walks the presence of Jesus; a presence-in-absence, yes, but still a presence, even with an absence.[97] Desperately we cling to the faith of Jesus as we float about in the dark.

Jayber's dreams of being a pastor, having a wife and coming home with her from the grocery store late in the afternoon are never realized.[98] Did life's dreams promise too much for Jayber? Why should he not become bitter? Is this too much to ask? Could not God give at least this gift to a "lonely, ignorant boy"? The absence of God seems most powerful in the absence of the most simple and virtuous desires. So also Jesus' prayer to have the cup taken from him is refused.[99] To then say, "Thy will be done" is to speak what may be the most startling theological confession outside of the Nicene Creed: Your will and God's will may not be the same. Like double predestination for Calvin, this is for Jayber the "horrible decree," true yet terrible to admit to yourself. What you most fervently desire may not be granted. In refusing you God turns his back on you (or so it seems): the absence of God in the presence of God.

Yet, as Dr. Ardmire later points out to Jayber, you may be called to something different than what you thought.[100] And this can only be discovered through living it out, through *praxis.* Our helplessness is joined

---

95 Speidell, *Confessions of a Lapsed Skeptic,* 45–47.

96 Berry, *Jayber Crow,* 356.

97 John D. Zizioulas, "Human Capacity and Human Incapacity: a Theological Exploration of Personhood," *SJT* 28, no. 5 (1975), 401–47. See also Anderson, *Historical Transcendence and the Reality of God,* 240, n. 29.

98 Berry, *Jayber Crow,* 45.

99 Ibid., 50.

100 Ibid., 54.

together with God's loving purpose as it is propelled and maintained by the faith of Jesus. This faith, however, has stood the test of hell: its darkness, sitting in the boat in the dark is the darkness of hell, Holy Saturday, the burial of Jesus, and since it held together by both the cross and the resurrection "the darkness is itself illuminating," an "identity in contradiction" (Alan E. Lewis).[101] The goal is not certainty but embracing both faith and reason, doubt and belief: "I believe, help me in my unbelief" (Mark 9:24).[102]

The resurrection of Jesus itself is not only a victory but also a creation of the absence of God. Since we know the victory has already been won by the resurrection we become acutely aware that the consummation of all things has yet to occur. The kingdom of God has not yet come in its fullness, so we cry, "Thy kingdom come!"[103] We feel profoundly the "lack," the tension of the kingdom felt by John the Baptist. Barth's words ring true: "What other time or season can or will the Church ever have but that of Advent?"[104]

Where is God in this? God is in the suffering, in the absence! This is the truly christological doctrine of God the Church always desperately needs.[105] The crucified Messiah has always been that "stumbling block" and "foolishness" in many different ways (1 Cor 1:23). The God revealed here is a different kind of God: "a servant Lord, a guilty judge, a wounded healer." God is not afraid of perishability, not afraid of being absent. We cannot say that about God ourselves; only Jesus can.

God's absence may even be an indication that he is in places we do not know.[106] Who are we to say? Without dogmatically identifying a presence of God apart from Jesus Christ (the problem of a natural theology) one might still have an openness to God working among non-Christians

[101] Alan E. Lewis, *Between Cross and Resurrection,* 78.

[102] Miguel de Unamuno, *Tragic Sense of Life* (New York: Dover, 1954), pp. 118–19. See especially 119: "For my part, I do not wish to make peace between my heart and my head, between my faith and my reason—I wish rather that there should be war between them!"

[103] Barth, *CD,* IV/3, first half, 320–22.

[104] Ibid., 322. Here is evidence that the futurized aspect of eschatology is not wholly absent from Barth's well-known realized eschatology.

[105] Alan E. Lewis, *Between Cross and Resurrection,* 91.

[106] Barth, *CD,* IV/3, first half, 365.

in a way we do not expect. The freedom of God is at stake here, is it not? For the Church, what appears to be another example of the absence of God is a manifestation of presence-in-absence.

Jesus himself, in his vicarious humanity, is still "a Pilgrim and Warrior," making the pilgrimage we cannot make, struggling in the war we cannot fight, and thus living the presence of God in absence.[107] Our eschatological waiting for the day of the Lord is a genuine sense of the absence of God, yet an absence we know because we have known his presence. The entire "strange new world within the Bible," to use Barth's famous phase, testifies to this.[108]

This is not to say that presence and absence should be viewed as a necessary dialectic, eternal principles of "light" and "darkness" that cannot exist without each other.[109] The faith of Jesus will not permit this. There is not darkness in his faith. The darkness he possesses (the cross) is our darkness that he voluntarily takes upon himself. He embraces our doubt with his faith. The resurrection of Jesus may create doubt as well as faith, but its final outcome is the consummation of all things, the final return of Jesus Christ in which the victory that is hidden now will be made manifest in all of its fullness. The Church's attempt at times to "replace" Christ through triumphalism only exacerbates the absence.[110] "The Vicarious Humanity of the Church" is a bad theology to live by and a good recipe to encourage doubt. But here is where the opposite makes all the difference: Christ "replacing" the Church, the vicarious humanity of Christ, the fact that "He alone is the perfect Christian," displaces us in order that we might find our freedom and identity only in him.[111]

Jesus Still Believes . . . Today

The vicarious faith of Jesus stands with the doubting self, even today. "Doubt love if it dare!" is its cry to us.[112] The vicarious faith of Jesus stands in stark

---

[107] Ibid., 331.

[108] Karl Barth, *The Word of God and the Word of Man,* trans. Douglas Horton (n.p.: The Pilgrim Press, 1928), 28–50. See also Barth, *CD,* IV/3, first half, 366.

[109] Barth, *CD,* IV/3, first half, 172.

[110] Ibid., 349.

[111] Ibid., 342.

[112] Anderson, *Soulprints,* 72.

contrast to Paul Elie's characterization of the twentieth-century Christian intellectuals as looking to themselves and their own faith. No, the vicarious faith of Jesus brings a love that points us to the faithfulness of God when we cannot see, experience, or feel that faithfulness. Instead of looking to ourselves we should be looking *away* from ourselves to the faith of Christ.[113] Healthy doubt (faith seeking understanding) always looks away from itself. Skeptical doubt maintains the individual Cartesian mind as the sole criterion of truth. Jayber's ability to love another is a sign that the answer is beyond ourselves. His own death, he reflects, became "the least important thing in my life."[114] In contrast to him are those who, losing their faith in God, substitute "a swollen faith in themselves."[115] Our faith comes and goes . . . so also can unbelief. In contrast, Jayber is ready for the vicarious faith of Christ. He believes the Man in the Well is not lost though all the circumstances would give him no hope.[116] So it is true with many if not most in the history of the human species. God goes where we cannot go. Thomas is not commended for his lack of faith; the blessing is for those who believe and have not seen (John 20:29). Yet Jesus still allows him to place his hand in his side. Christ is gentle with our doubts, aware of our frailties. Here is the ministry of the Church to the doubter today. How wrong it is to seek desperately for death bed conversions, thinking that one's eternal fate is based on saying "the magical word," like in a bad 1950s quiz show.[117] What a terrible burden for all. Jesus believes that the Man in the Well is not lost, and we should believe that too. "Be merciful to those who doubt," Jude beseeches (v. 22), yet he is aware of the danger of doubt as well: "snatch others from the fire and save them; to others show mercy, mixed with fear . . ." (v. 23). "Maybe I'm runnin' on faith . . . What else can a poor boy do?" sings Eric Clapton. The good news is that we do not have to run on our own faith.

The man in the Gospels whose son lives a life of terrible convulsions, "an unclean spirit," desperately yearns for his son to be healed. (Mark 9:14-29). He brings his child to Jesus with the plea to "have pity on us and help us," for this has been their life since his childhood. "But if you are able to do anything . . ." he pleads to Jesus. Jesus immediately picks up

[113] Barth, *CD,* I/2, 357.
[114] Berry, *Jayber Crow,* 120.
[115] O'Connor, *The Habit of Being,* 452.
[116] Berry, *Jayber Crow,* 357.
[117] Alan E. Lewis, *Between Cross and Resurrection,* 110.

on the words, "if you are able": "If you are able!—All things can be done for the one who believes." The father of the child does not trust in his own ability or his own faith but that of Jesus, who casts out the spirit even though the disciples could not because, as Jesus explains, "This kind can come out only through prayer" (9:29).[118] Whose prayer? There is no evidence of the father praying; in fact his response is the classic ambiguity of the doubter: "I believe; help my unbelief!" (9:24). Jesus is "able" when the father of the child finds it difficult to believe. Could prayer be a part of Jesus' ability to cast out the spirit? Does healthy doubt mean an openness to God working? He is beginning to believe. He wants to overcome this ambiguity; yet in that moment his life will never again be the same.[119]

As much as faith may be a gift, it is also a matter of the will, yet the will freed from its bondage to sin.[120] We need to recognize our lostness and bondage. We need to realize the strangeness of the Word, a Word strange and new even in a world reconciled to him.[121] The man in the Gospels has admitted his helplessness and yet the power of Jesus, "the Yes of his tiny but honest faith." He is not far from the kingdom. This is not unbelief on his part, but the tortuous no-man's land of doubt. This is where Jesus' faith continues to intervene for us even today. Whether faith is the end of the struggle (Simone Weil) or faith is the beginning that introduces us into the struggle (Flannery O'Connor), our faith is relativized by the faith of Christ.[122] In contrast to much popular theology, our faith is not the equivalent "Yes" to God's "Yes."[123] The Son has his own "Yes" to the Father, for us and in our place. His faith has the last word.

---

[118] Ralph P. Martin, *Mark: Evangelist and Theologian* (Grand Rapids: Zondervan, 1973), 109.

[119] Barth, IV/4, 42–43. See also John Calvin, *Calvin's New Testament Commentaries,* eds. David W. Torrance and Thomas F. Torrance, Matthew, Mark, and Luke, Vol. 2, trans. T. H. L. Parker (Grand Rapids: Eerdmans, 1972), 209: "Nowhere is there a perfect faith, and therefore it follows that we are partly unbelievers. Yet in His kindness, God pardons us and reckons us as believers on account of our small portion of faith. Meanwhile it is for us to shake off carefully the remnants of unbelief that remain within us, and fight against them and ask the Lord to correct them; and so often as we toil in this struggle we must flee to Him for success."

[120] O'Connor, *The Habit of Being,* 452.

[121] Barth, *CD,* IV/3, first half, 366.

[122] Elie, *The Life You Save May Be Your Own,* 271.

[123] Paul Evdokimov, *In the World, for the Church,* Michael Plekon, ed., Alexis Vinogradov, trans. (Crestwood, N.Y.: St. Vladimir's Seminary Press, 2001), 189: "Faith is the reciprocity of the two *fiats,* the two yeses, the encounter of love descending from God and our love ascending to him." The vicarious faith of Christ is unfortunately missing here.

In effect, the apostle Paul was well aware that Christ still believes, particularly in the midst of the chaos of his church at Corinth: "He is the source of your life in Christ Jesus, who became for us wisdom from God, and righteousness and sanctification and redemption . . ." (1 Cor 1:3). Even "sanctification," usually reserved for our human actions, has its source in Christ. Paul assumes the whole life of Christ as the essence of our Christian life: ". . . and it is no longer I who live, but it is Christ who lives in me. And the life I now live in the flesh I live by the faith of the Son of God (subjective genitive) who loved me and gave himself for me" (Gal 2:20). "So if anyone is in Christ, there is a new creation: everything old has passed away; see, everything has become new!" "Jesus Christ *is* our human response to God," T. F. Torrance dares to say.[124] To reply that this leaves no place for a human response refuses to take seriously the seriousness and desperation of our situation. We are helpless and lost, unloved or at least loved only conditionally in a hostile world of which we contribute through our own selfishness and desire to be God. Yes, we are called to faith and repentance, but never apart from the one response to God in the humanity of Jesus Christ. The true Son of God is "the prototype of all doxology," the true worshipper of the Father.[125] His worship precedes our worship; his self-witness precedes our self-witness.[126] He is our human response to God especially in times of doubt and despair.

The faith of Jesus Christ is not just in "cloud-cuckooland," a platonic or idealistic wish, but concretely enacted in the Church, the body of Christ.[127] Christ replaces the Church of our making with his body. His faith is ontologically connected with us, his body, so that again we should not speak of our response to God apart from that of Christ the High Priest, the obedient Son to the Father in the power of the Spirit. One must be careful, however, not to speak of the Church as identical with Christ. Christ exists as community but the community is not Christ (Bonhoeffer). Christ always remains "the primary acting Subject," not "a mere vehicle" of our Christian existence, the Head who is always head over the body.[128] It should not be surprising, therefore, that Thomas' doubt

[124] T. F. Torrance, *The Mediation of Christ,* 80.
[125] Barth, *CD,* IV/3, first half, 48.
[126] Ibid., 73.
[127] T. F. Torrance, *The Trinitarian Faith,* 267.
[128] Barth, *CD,* IV/3, first half, 214.

is resolved into the high point of christological confession in the New Testament; "My Lord and my God!" (John 20:28).[129] Christ takes upon our doubt in order that we might come to faith. Thomas represents the genuine self-confidence of the Church when it looks away from itself.[130] Any kind of triumphalism ignores the vicarious faith of Christ and paves the way for uncertainty. What is the triumphant pride of the "truth" or "rightness" of the Church or taking refuge in human logic or the *Zeitgeist* but a manifestation of a deep-seated insecurity, "a despair of faith"?

Our experience is tricky. We should not place our faith in our faith. "He who puts his life into his faith in God can lose his faith" (Simone Weil).[131] The complexity and crookedness of our experiences give every reason for Paul Elie to pronounce us "all skeptics now, believer and unbeliever alike."[132] But skeptical doubt is not the only alternative. Flannery O'Connor's call to "Christian skepticism" is what I would call healthy doubt as opposed to skeptical doubt. What we can do is place our faith in the faith of Jesus. "He who puts his life in God himself will never lose it," Weil continues.[133] Jesus has done this and continues to do this. The "swollen faith" we have in ourselves is hardly justified. We are helpless and lost. Jesus is not.

People are not just full of "swollen faith" in themselves. They are also tragic or at the least misled. The lives of broken dreams are of greater plenty than any stereotype of "happiness." Science fiction and comic book fandom are filled with those "geeks" and "nerds" that never quite fit in with successful and beautiful of society (although they can number over eighty thousand at the annual "Comicon International" in San Diego!). Who can easily condemn the pious Muslim who has never known a genuine presentation of Jesus Christ (as represented by the noble character Emeth in C. S. Lewis' *The Last Battle*)? Emeth ("faithful" in Hebrew) is the dutiful worshipper of Tash, the false god, whose service to Tash is considered by the true ruler, Aslan, as service to himself.[134] Many have

---

129 Raymond E. Brown, *The Gospel According to John,* Vol. 2 (Garden City, N.Y.: Doubleday, 1970), 1032.

130 Barth, *CD,* I/2, 357.

131 Weil, *Gravity and Grace,* 162.

132 Elie, *The Life You Save May Be Your Own,* 472.

133 Weil, *Gravity and Grace,* 163.

134 Paul F. Ford, *Companion to Narnia* (San Francisco: HarperSanFrancisco, 1980), 166.

been dealt a bad deck of cards by life. Their environment might be poisoned with toxic religion. Hazel Motes, the cynic in Flannery O'Connor's *Wise Blood,* is fed up with the hypocrisy of his father the hell-fire evangelist (played deliciously by John Huston in the film version). *Film Noir* movies are filled with down and out characters that seem to be caught in tragic situations, deceived by others and a world that is hostile towards them. Dix, a small time "hooligan" played by Sterling Hayden in John Huston's *The Asphalt Jungle* (1950), desperately yearns to return to the peace of his Kentucky farm yet is connived into a burglary "caper" that ends his dream. Bad decisions continually haunt human experience. Who can ever have confidence in the countless decisions big and small that make up the tapestry (and then sometimes the wicked web) of life? Decisions about vocations and relationships seem to determine our lives forever. So much for modern autonomy that we foolishly call "freedom"!

Others have been held victim by the decisions of others and of nature. Countless lives have been interrupted in the womb by wanton murder. The lives of the family of Amy Montgomery, the teenager coldly murdered in a Wichita sandwich shop, are changed forever. Our physical and emotional makeup may be nothing but the casualties of bad genes: the world may not make sense to us and we may not make sense of the world. A young woman, beautiful, intelligent, and spiritual, works in a home for the mentally retarded including a woman who thinks she is a cat. Who has been dealt the better deck of cards by life? Who will believe for the victims of life? Should they be pressured to memorize the Nicene Creed or recite the Four Spiritual Laws? How much do they have to understand of good evangelical doctrine to be saved? Should they just blindly obey their religious pastor, priest, rabbi, or imam? Or has Someone else believed for all of us in the poverty of our twisted and grim existences? The good news of Jesus Christ says, "Yes, someone has."

Name Index

Subject Index